The Hamiltonian Approach to Dynamic Economics

ECONOMIC THEORY AND MATHEMATICAL ECONOMICS

Consulting Editor: Karl Shell

UNIVERSITY OF PENNSYLVANIA
PHILADELPHIA, PENNSYLVANIA

The Hamiltonian Approach to Dynamic Economics

EDITED BY

DAVID CASS and KARL SHELL

UNIVERSITY OF PENNSYLVANIA
PHILADELPHIA, PENNSYLVANIA

Academic Press   New York   San Francisco   London   1976

A Subsidiary of Harcourt Brace Jovanovich, Publishers

ACADEMIC PRESS, INC.
111 Fifth Avenue, New York, New York 10003

United Kingdom Edition published by
ACADEMIC PRESS, INC. (LONDON) LTD.
24/28 Oval Road, London NW1

Library of Congress Cataloging in Publication Data

Main entry under title:

The Hamiltonian approach to dynamic economics.

    (Economic theory and mathematical economics series)
    "Originally appeared as papers in the Journal of
economic theory, volume 12, number 1 (February
1976)."
    Bibliography: p.
    Includes index.
    1.   Economics, Mathematical.   2.   Statics and
dynamics (Social sciences)   I.   Cass, David.
II.   Shell, Karl.
HB135.H35   330'.01'51   76-28781
ISBN 0–12–163650–X

Contents

v

Acknowledgments

Our eight essays originally appeared as papers in the *Journal of Economic Theory*, Volume 12, Number 1 (February 1976) and are reprinted here with only minor changes. We are grateful to the Mathematical Social Science Board, which supported the two excellent seminars that enabled us to bring this work together in its present form.

David Cass
Karl Shell

About the Authors

William Brock is Professor of Economics at the University of Chicago and Cornell University. He taught at the University of Rochester for two years after receiving his Ph.D. from the University of California, Berkeley, in 1969. He is a Fellow of the Econometric Society and has been awarded National Science Foundation research grants. He has published many articles on dynamic economics. He is associate editor of the *Journal of Economic Theory* and the *International Economic Review*, as well as review writer for *Mathematical Reviews* and *Zentralblatt für Mathematik*. His research interests are intertemporal economics, differential games, stochastic control theory, and asymptotic analysis of differential equations arising from optimal control problems in economics.

David Cass is Professor of Economics at the University of Pennsylvania and was previously on the faculties at Yale University and Carnegie-Mellon University. He holds an A.B. from the University of Oregon and a Ph.D. from Stanford University. Professor Cass has been a coeditor of *The Review of Economic Studies*, the *Journal of Economic Theory*, and the *Journal of Financial Economics*, and an author or coauthor of several scholarly articles. He is a Fellow of the Econometric Society and has been a Guggenheim Fellow. Professor Cass's main research interests have been in the theory of intertemporal allocation.

Robert Gaines is a Professor of Mathematics at Colorado State University. He is the holder of a Ph.D. degree from the University of Colorado and B.S. and M.S. degrees from the University of Illinois. Professor Gaines is coauthor of a monograph entitled *Alternative Problems, Coincidence Degree, and Applications to Differential Equations* as well as several articles on nonlinear differential equations.

Lawrence J. Lau is Associate Professor of Economics at Stanford University. He is the holder of a Ph.D. degree from the University of California, Berkeley and a B.S. degree from Stanford University. Professor Lau is American Editor of the *Review of Economic Studies*. He has authored numerous articles in the scholarly journals. He has been awarded National Science Foundation research grants and a John Simon Guggenheim Memorial Foundation Fellowship. His research interests include the theory of production, the theory of consumer behavior, agricultural economics, and East Asian studies. Currently, Professor Lau is collaborating on a book, *Duality in the Theory of Production*, with Professor Dale W. Jorgenson of Harvard University.

Tyrrell Rockafellar is Professor of Mathematics at the University of Washington, Seattle. He received Ph.D. and A.B. degrees from Harvard University and has taught at Princeton University, the University of Texas, and the University of Grenoble, France, in addition to his present post. Professor Rockafellar is coeditor of the *SIAM Journal on Control and Optimization*. He is the author of *Convex Analysis* and many scholarly articles on the mathematical theory of optimization.

José Alexandre Scheinkman is Assistant Professor of Economics at the University of Chicago. He holds a Ph.D. in Economics from the University of Rochester, an M.S. in Mathematics from the Instituto de Matemática Pura e Aplicada (Brazil) and a B.A. from the Universidade Federal do Rio de Janeiro. Professor Scheinkman has written articles in intertemporal economic theory, dynamic programming, welfare economics, and international trade. He has been awarded a National Science Foundation research grant, and a University of Chicago Post-Doctoral Fellowship in Political Economy. His present research interests include comparative dynamics, intertemporal general equilibrium theory, and the economics of exhaustible resources.

Karl Shell is Professor of Economics and Public Policy Analysis at the University of Pennsylvania. He has also been on the faculties of Stanford and MIT. His doctoral degree is from Stanford; his bachelor's degree is from Princeton. Professor Shell is editor of the *Journal of Economic Theory*, editor of *Essays on Theory of Optimal Economic Growth*, coauthor of *The Economic Theory of Price Indices*, coeditor of *Mathematical Theories of Investment and Finance*, and author of numerous articles in the scholarly journals. He is a Fellow of the Econometric Society, and has been awarded National Science Foundation research grants and a Ford Foundation Faculty Research Fellowship. While continuing his research interests in intertemporal economic theory and the pure theory of price indices, Professor Shell is, in addition, beginning new studies on what he calls "the endogeneous theory of public policy."

ESSAY I

Introduction to Hamiltonian Dynamics in Economics

DAVID CASS AND KARL SHELL

Economics during the fifties and sixties was marked by a substantial resurgence of interest in the theory of capital. While the advances during this period were very impressive, there was also an unevenness in the development of the subject. One-good models were studied in detail, as were many-good models of production–maximal growth and many-good models of consumption–optimal growth for the special case in which there is no social impatience. When treating heterogeneous capital, the literatures on decentralized or descriptive growth and consumption–optimal growth with positive time discounting were dominated by special cases and examples.

Reliance on examples and special cases proved to have some unfortunate consequences. The Battle of the Two Cambridges, ostensibly an argument over approaches to modeling distribution and accumulation, often seemed to focus on the robustness (or lack of robustness) of certain "fundamental" properties of the one-sector model and other worked-out examples when extended to more general heterogeneous-capital models. Furthermore, in large part because growth theory appeared to be an enterprise based only on proliferating special cases, the attention of the young able minds in the profession turned elsewhere, for example, to the— at least seemingly—more evenly-developed general equilibrium tradition.

This is a shame. Intertemporal allocation and its relationship with the wealth of societies is one of the most important problems in our discipline. Growth models are natural vehicles for the study of what is called "temporary equilibrium." Dynamic models of multi-asset accumulation provide the theoretically most satisfactory environment for modeling the macroeconomics of income determination, employment, and inflation.

The papers in this volume can be thought of as attempts at providing some unification of the theory of heterogeneous capital. The major topic, although by no means the only one, which we investigate here is the stability of long-run steady-state equilibrium in models of heterogeneous capital accumulation. However, the basic techniques used in our investigations have wide application to economic dynamics in all its manifestations. This follows from the observation that the economic growth models which we treat each belong to a class of general intertemporal economic models which is essentially representable by what we call a Hamiltonian dynamical system.

The static technology of our growth models can in general be described by an instantaneous technology set, T, with feasible production satisfying

$$(c, z, -k, -l) \in T \subset \{(c, z, -k, -l): (c, k, l) \geqslant 0\},$$

where c denotes the vector of consumption–goods outputs, z the vector of net investment–goods outputs, k the vector of capital–goods inputs, and l the vector of primary–goods inputs. There is an alternative representation of static technological opportunities that is more congenial to dynamic analysis, i.e., the representation of the technology by its Hamiltonian function.

Let p be the vector of consumption–goods prices and q the vector of investment–goods prices. Define the Hamiltonian function,

$$H(p, q, k, l) = \sup_{(c', z')} \{pc' + qz': (c', z', -k, -l) \in T\}.$$

H is typically defined on the nonnegative orthant $\{(p, q, k, l): (p, q, k, l) \geqslant 0\}$, and is precisely interpreted as the maximized value of net national product at output prices (p, q) given input endowments (k, l).

If the set T is closed, convex, and permits free disposal of outputs, then technology is also completely characterized by a (unique) continuous Hamiltonian function which is convex and linear homogeneous in output prices (p, q), and concave in input stocks (k, l). For each such T-representation, there is a unique H-representation of technology and, conversely, for each such H-representation there is a unique T-representation of technology. While we focus on macroeconomic dynamics, the Hamiltonian function is of more general usefulness. Thus, in his paper in this volume, relating properties of the set T to properties of the function $H(p, q, k, l)$, Lau quite properly refers to the Hamiltonian function as the "restricted profit function."

Lau studies the case where technology can be described by production functions. For the case in which the production functions are twice differentiable, Lau develops identities linking the Hessians of the production function with those of the Hamiltonian (or restricted-profit) function. Lau also analyzes some special cases in which increasing returns to scale are allowed. For these cases, the Hamiltonian function may not be concave but is quasiconcave in the input stocks (k, l).

Representation of static technology by the Hamiltonian function allows us to describe all the growth models in this volume as *Hamiltonian dynamical systems*. In continuous time, $t \in [0, \infty)$, the system follows the laws of motion

$$\begin{cases} \dot{k}(t) \in \partial_q H(p(t), q(t), k(t), l(t)), \\ \dot{q}(t) \in -\partial_k H(p(t), q(t), k(t), l(t)) \end{cases} \quad \text{(HDS)}$$

where $\dot{k}(t)$ and $\dot{q}(t)$ are time derivatives of $k(t)$ and $q(t)$, respectively; $\partial_q H$ and $\partial_k H$ are respectively the subdifferentials (or generalized gradients) with respect to q and k. The first correspondence in (HDS) follows from the definition of net investment since it is equivalent to the equation $\dot{k}(t) = z(t)$. The second correspondence in (HDS) is somewhat more subtle and can be rewritten (employing static duality theory) as $\dot{q}(t) + r(t) = 0$, where $r(t)$ is the vector of competitive capital–goods rental rates. Thus, the second line in (HDS) states that the return to asset holders (including rentals and capital gains) are equal across capital goods. If there is (short-run) perfect foresight about price changes, this is the asset-market-clearing equation that follows from a simple arbitrage argument for competitive economies. The existence of prices $(p(t), q(t))$ satisfying (HDS) also follows from the necessary conditions in the optimal and maximal growth problems.

For discrete time, $t = 0, 1,...$, the Hamiltonian dynamical system can be represented by

$$\begin{cases} k_{t+1} \in k_t + \partial_q H(p_t, q_t, k_t, l_t), \\ q_{t+1} \in q_t - \partial_k H(p_{t+1}, q_{t+1}, k_{t+1}, l_{t+1}). \end{cases} \quad \text{(HDS)}'$$

Line one of (HDS)′ follows from the definition of net investment, since it is equivalent to $k_{t+1} = k_t + z_t$. Line two is the (short-run) perfect-foresight, competitive, asset-market-clearing equation, since it is equivalent to $q_{t+1} - q_t + r_{t+1} = 0$, where r_{t+1} is the vector of capital–goods rentals in period $t + 1$. (HDS)′ can also be derived from the discrete-time necessary conditions in optimal and maximal growth problems.

From (HDS) and (HDS)′, we see that the properties of static technology as characterized by the Hamiltonian function will be basic to the dynamic analysis of competitive and optimizing economic dynamical systems. So far, as can be seen in (HDS) or (HDS)′, the development of consumption goods prices, $p(t)$ or p_t, and of primary factors, $l(t)$ or l_t, has been left as exogenous to the model.

The Hamiltonian dynamical system is said to be autonomous if H depends on time solely through q and k. The system would be autonomous if, for example, p and l are constant through time, i.e., $p(t) = \bar{p}$ and $l(t) = \bar{l}$, or $p_t = \bar{p}$ and $l_t = \bar{l}$. Autonomous Hamiltonian dynamical systems have special structure that has been exploited in the mathematics and physics literature. (For references, see [8, 10, 19]).

Let (q^*, k^*) be a rest point to the autonomous version of the Hamiltonian dynamical system so that

$$0 \in \partial_q H(\bar{p}, q^*, k^*, \bar{l}),$$

$$0 \in \partial_k H(\bar{p}, q^*, k^*, \bar{l}).$$

Of course, (q^*, k^*) is a rest point for the autonomous version of (HDS) if and only if it is a rest point for the parallel autonomous version of (HDS)′. Assume further that H is quadratic in (q, k) so that the (HDS) is a system of linear differential equations and (HDS)′ is a system of linear difference equations. In this case, a theorem of Poincaré tells us that if λ is a root to the characteristic equation for the autonomous version of the system (HDS) at (q^*, k^*) then $-\lambda$ is also a root. For the autonomous version of (HDS)′, the analogous theorem tells us that if λ is a characteristic root, so also is $1/\lambda$.

The Poincaré theorem, although extremely simple, is suggestive of deep fundamental results. If, for example, in the continuous-time case we could rule out λ's with zero real parts (Re $\lambda \neq 0$), then we would have established a saddlepoint result for the autonomous version of the linear Hamiltonian dynamical system: In (q, k)-phase space, the dimension of the manifold of (forward) solutions tending to (q^*, k^*) as $t \to +\infty$ is equal to the dimension of the manifold of (backward) solutions tending to (q^*, k^*) as $t \to -\infty$, and each manifold is equal in dimension to half the dimension of the phase space.

Since this "saddlepoint property" and related properties turn out to be of basic interest in dynamic economic analyses, a natural question is: Are there interesting restrictions that can be imposed on the Hamiltonian function (i.e., on technology) such that the general (nonlinear) autonomous Hamiltonian dynamical system will possess the saddlepoint property (or related properties)? Rockafellar [12], in a paper motivated by problems of economic growth (see [18]), established the saddlepoint property of the autonomous version of (HDS) for cases in which H is *strictly* concave in k and *strictly* convex in q. Rockafellar goes on to consider the (HDS) as derived from an intertemporal optimization model which can be interpreted as the problem of consumption–optimal growth with zero discounting. Here $c(t)$ is interpreted as the (scalar) current instantaneous utility at time t. Because of zero-discounting, the (scalar) price of "utility" $p(t)$ must be constant. $l(t)$ is also considered to be a constant scalar.

Global stability is established for the optimal trajectory: Given initial capital stocks $k(0) = k_0$, $\lim_{t \to \infty} k(t) = k^*$. Rockafellar's stability result had been foreshadowed, in one form or other, in the earlier literature on maximal growth and optimal growth. For continuous-time versions, see, e.g., [15, 16]. For discrete-time versions, see, e.g., [3, 9, 11].

Consider next the problem of consumption–optimal growth with positive (constant) rate of time discount, $\rho > 0$. Again, $c(t)$ or c_t must be interpreted as the (scalar) instantaneous utility at time t. Assume, for simplicity, a constant scalar fixed factor, $l(t) = 1$ or $l_t = 1$. Because of discounting, $-\dot{p}(t)/p(t) = \rho$ or $-(p_t - p_{t-1})/p_t = \rho$. In this case, (HDS) and (HDS)′ are no longer autonomous and further analysis is required. (HDS) can now be rewritten as

$$\begin{cases} \dot{k} \in \partial_Q H(Q, k), \\ \dot{Q} \in -\partial_k H(Q, k) + \rho Q \end{cases} \qquad \text{(PHDS)}$$

where $Q \equiv q/p$ is the vector of current capital–goods prices and $H(Q, k) \equiv H(1, q/p, k, 1)$ is the current value Hamiltonian. The above system can be thought of as a perturbation (by the term ρQ) of a Hamiltonian dynamical system. In discrete time, the perturbed Hamiltonian dynamical system is

$$\begin{cases} k_{t+1} \in k_t + \partial_Q H(Q_t, k_t), \\ Q_{t+1} \in Q_t - \partial_k H(Q_{t+1}, k_{t+1}) + \rho Q_t. \end{cases} \qquad \text{(PHDS)}′$$

Let (Q^*, k^*) be a steady state, or rest point to (PHDS) and (PHDS)′. Then

$$0 \in \partial_Q H(Q^*, k^*),$$
$$0 \in -\partial_k H(Q^*, k^*) + \rho Q^*.$$

One can ask the question: Do the properties of models based on (HDS) and (HDS)′, such as the stability of optimal economic growth, carry over to models based on the perturbed systems, (PHDS) and (PHDS)′, for the case of ρ positive? The simple answer is, of course, "no," as Kurz's local analysis [6] shows. Two approaches to modifying this question have been studied: (1) Papers such as that by Samuelson [16] and José Scheinkman's contribution in this volume take technology as fixed and investigate whether or not global stability properties of the optimal growth model are preserved as the discount rate ρ is changed from zero to a small positive number. (2) The approach taken by the contributions in this volume by Cass and Shell, Rockafellar, and Brock and Scheinkman can be thought of as generalizations of the Samuelson–Scheinkman approach. Conditions are sought on the geometry of the Hamiltonian function (i.e., on static technology) that suffice to preserve under (not necessarily small) perturbation the basic properties of the Hamiltonian dynamical system.

Scheinkman's paper treats local and global stability in a discrete-time, optimal growth model with an indirect, current, instantaneous utility function which is discounted at some small rate $\rho > 0$. His model therefore satisfies (PHDS)' although he does not work directly with the Hamiltonian formalism. A critical assumption is that linearization of the Euler equations in the neighborhood of the "optimal steady state" possesses no characteristic roots with $|\lambda| = 1$. Using Radner's bounded-value loss technique, a turnpike property is established for $\rho > 0$ sufficiently small. Scheinkman's proof is in two steps. First, an ingenious argument shows that optimal paths "visit" neighborhoods of the "modified optimal steady state," (Q^*, k^*). Second, local stability follows directly from his assumption about characteristic roots.

The contribution by Cass and Shell treats optimal growth and decentralized or descriptive growth models in both continuous and discrete time as applications of Hamiltonian dynamics. They review the problem of optimal growth with zero discounting and show that a steepness condition on the Hamiltonian function (a condition weaker than Rockafellar's [12] strict convexity–concavity of the Hamiltonian) suffices to insure uniqueness of the steady-state capital vector, k^*. Furthermore, a uniform strengthening of the steepness condition insures global stability of k^* and can be thought of as a generalization of Radner's assumption of bounded value-loss. This approach relies crucially on the property that (q^*, k^*) is a saddlepoint of the Hamiltonian function $H(1, q, k, 1)$.

In the optimal-growth model with discount rate $\rho \neq 0$, the rest point (Q^*, k^*) is not a saddlepoint of $H(Q, k)$. Therefore, the Cass–Shell steepness condition must be modified by a term dependent on ρ. The modified steepness condition establishes the uniqueness of k^*. A uniform strengthening of the steepness condition insures global stability of k^* for the continuous-time, optimal growth model. Because of different effects of "interest compounding," a different steepness condition is required to establish stability in the discrete-time, optimal growth model.

While optimal growth with time-discounting yields a very simple perturbation of a Hamiltonian dynamical system, there are other perturbed Hamiltonian dynamical systems that arise in economic theory. Cass and Shell discuss the general problem of decentralized growth with instantaneously adjusted expectations about price changes. In its general form, the model allows for the interpretation of competitive growth with utility-maximizing agents. However, in such a model the form of the perturbation from Hamiltonian dynamics can be very subtle. The formal analysis in the Cass–Shell paper is thus restricted to the continuous-time version of the model in which demand for consumption is Marxian. It is shown that if in addition to the strengthened steepness assumption from zero-discount optimal growth, the Hamiltonian is such that a "capital-intensity" condition is satisfied, then decentralized growth in the Marxian decentralized model is stable.

In his first contribution to this volume, Rockafellar studies the basic mathematics of the problem which arises in continuous-time, optimal growth with positive discounting. His paper is thus a generalization of his earlier work [12], where his results follow from the strict convexity–concavity of the Hamiltonian function. In the present paper, he relies on a strengthened convexity–concavity: The Hamiltonian function, $H(Q, k)$, is assumed to be α-concave in k and β-convex in Q with $\alpha > 0, \beta > 0$, and $4\alpha\beta > \rho^2$. This convexity–concavity hypothesis is substantially stronger than the related Cass–Shell steepness condition (because Rockafellar's hypothesis ignores cross effects between Q and k), but Rockafellar goes substantially beyond the Cass–Shell paper in the range of results established for this model. In addition to local and global stability results, Rockafellar establishes the existence of solutions to optimizing programs satisfying (PHDS). He shows directly that the saddlepoint property holds when his convexity–concavity hypothesis is satisfied: The dimension of the manifold of solutions to (PHDS) tending to (Q^*, k^*) as $t \to +\infty$ is equal to the dimension of the manifold of solutions to (PHDS) tending to (Q^*, k^*) as $t \to -\infty$. Each manifold has dimension equal to half the dimension of the (Q, k) phase space. Rockafellar goes on to develop deep results on intertemporal duality, which have important bearing on the economic theory of the asymptotic behavior of $(Q(t), k(t))$.

Gaines' paper in this volume is a study of the existence of solutions to the full dynamical system arising in the time-discounted, optimal growth problem. He follows the Cass–Shell formulation and appends to (PHDS) appropriate nonnegativity conditions and boundary conditions, an initial capital-stock endowment condition and a transversality condition. The full system is thus

$$\begin{cases} \dot{k} \in \partial_Q H(Q, k), \\ \dot{Q} \in -\partial_k H(Q, k) + \rho Q, \\ Q(t) \geqslant 0, \\ k(t) \geqslant 0, \\ k(0) = k_0 \geqslant 0, \\ \lim_{t \to +\infty} Q(t) \, e^{-\rho t} k(t) = 0. \end{cases} \qquad \text{(FPHDS)}$$

Gaines assumes only that H is convex in Q and concave in k, a much
weaker assumption than Rockafellar's curvature assumption, but his
methods require exploitation of other structural features of the
Hamiltonian function. In the spirit of the Cass–Shell paper, he assumes
(1) the existence of a stationary point (Q^*, k^*), (2) limitation of feasible
output by primary factors, (3) productivity of technology, (4) bounded
rate of depreciation, and (5) free disposal in allocation. From these
conditions, a priori bounds are developed for solutions to a finite-time
problem associated with (FPHDS). The proof of existence relies on a
continuation principle from the theory of fixed points for multivalued
mappings in infinite-dimensional spaces.

Both the Cass–Shell and Rockafellar papers in this volume make heavy
analytic use of monotonicity properties of the Lyapunov function
$V = (Q - Q^*)(k - k^*)$ in studying optimal growth (as did, for example,
the Samuelson paper [16]). The contribution to this volume by Brock and
Scheinkman also investigates stability of optimal growth in continuous-
time models and develops "local" properties of the Hamiltonian function
that insure monotonicity of V or some alternative Lyapunov function,
and thus insure stability of optimal growth for bounded trajectories.
They assume throughout that the Hamiltonian function is twice-
continuously differentiable. Much of their analysis is based on what they
call the "curvature matrix"

$$C = \begin{bmatrix} H_{QQ} & (\rho/2)I \\ (\rho/2)I & -H_{kk} \end{bmatrix},$$

where H_{QQ} is the matrix of cross partial derivatives with respect to current
prices and H_{kk} is the matrix of cross partial derivatives with respect to
capital stocks.

Brock and Scheinkman show that if the quadratic $(\dot{Q}, \dot{k}) \, C(\dot{Q}, \dot{k})$ is
positive except when $(\dot{Q}, \dot{k}) = 0$, then every bounded trajectory satisfying
(PHDS) converges to a rest point. Their result is obtained by using the
Lyapunov function $\dot{Q}k$. In their paper, it is also shown that if
$(Q - Q^*)\dot{k} + (k - k^*)\dot{Q} = 0 \Rightarrow (Q - Q^*, k - k^*)C(Q - Q^*, k - k^*) > 0$
and if the matrix C evaluated at (Q^*, k^*) is positive definite, then every
bounded trajectory satisfying (PHDS) converges to (Q^*, k^*). The last
conditions imply the Cass–Shell steepness condition, and thus insure that
the Lyapunov function $V = (Q - Q^*)(k - k^*)$ is monotonically increasing for trajectories from (PHDS).

By convexity–concavity of H, the matrices H_{QQ} and $-H_{kk}$ are positive
semidefinite. Let α be the smallest eigenvalue of H_{QQ} and β be the smallest
eigenvalue of $-H_{kk}$. For the special case of twice continuous differentiability, the Rockafellar curvature condition is that $4\alpha\beta > \rho^2$, which

insures the positive definiteness of the matrix C. While the matrix C, when it is calculable, does provide a measure of "curvature" of H, it does not allow for the more general interpretation of Hamiltonian steepness since information about the interaction terms between the Q's and the k's, representable for the differentiable case by the matrix of cross partials H_{Qk}, are ignored in the C matrix.

In his second contribution to this volume (and our final paper), Rockafellar offers an (apparently weaker) alternative to the Cass–Shell steepness condition. With the Rockafellar growth condition, which is very much like the steepness condition, trajectories satisfying (PHDS) and the transversality condition $\lim_{t \to \infty} (Q(t) - Q^*)(k(t) - k^*) = 0$ are shown to converge to (Q^*, k^*).

The present volume has been in planning and preparation for more time than we would like to admit. Extensive (and often intense) communication among the authors was stimulated by two fruitful conferences—one at the Minary Center, Squam Lake, New Hampshire, the other at the University of Pennsylvania, Philadelphia. We are grateful to the Mathematical Social Science Board for its generous and understanding support of these opportunities for scholarly interaction.

While the topics treated here have mostly to do with the theory of economic growth, in particular, with existence and stability of macroeconomic growth, we hope you will be able to read between the lines and appreciate the potential usefulness to economic theory of what we call the Hamiltonian approach to economic dynamics.

ACKNOWLEDGMENT

Research support from National Science Foundation grants SOC 74-03974 and SOC 74-19469, and from the Mathematical Social Science Board is gratefully acknowledged.

REFERENCES

1. W. A. BROCK AND J. A. SCHEINKMAN, Global asymptotic stability of optimal control systems with applications to the theory of economic growth, *J. Econ. Theory* **12** (1976), 164–190. Reprinted as Essay VII in this volume.
2. D. CASS AND K. SHELL, The structure and stability of competitive dynamical systems, *J. Econ. Theory* **12** (1976), 31–70. Reprinted as Essay III in this volume.
3. H. FURUYA AND K.-I. INADA, Balanced growth and intertemporal efficiency in capital accumulation, *Int. Econ. Rev.* **3** (1962), 94–107.
4. R. E. GAINES, Existence of solutions to Hamiltonian dynamical systems of optimal growth, *J. Econ. Theory* **12** (1976), 114–130. Reprinted as Essay V in this volume.

5. F. H. Hahn, On some equilibrium paths, *in* "Models of Economic Growth" (J. A. Mirrlees and N. H. Stern, Eds.), pp. 193–206, Macmillan, London, 1973.

6. M. Kurz, The general instability of a class of competitive growth processes, *Rev. Econ. Studies* **35** (1968), 155–174.

7. L. Lau, A characterization of the normalized restricted profit function, *J. Econ. Theory* **12** (1976), 131–163. Reprinted as Essay VI in this volume.

8. D. Levhari and N. Liviatan, On stability in the saddle-point sense, *J. Econ. Theory* **4** (1972), 88–93.

9. L. W. McKenzie, Accumulation programs of maximum utility and the von Neumann facet, *in* "Value, Capital, and Growth" (J. N. Wolfe, Ed.), pp. 353–383, Edinburgh University Press, Edinburgh, 1968.

10. H. Pollard, "Mathematical Introduction to Celestial Mechanics," Prentice–Hall, Englewood Cliffs, N.J., 1966.

11. R. Radner, Paths of economic growth that are optimal with regard only to final states; a turnpike theorem, *Rev. Econ. Studies* **28** (1961), 98–104.

12. R. T. Rockafellar, Saddlepoints of Hamiltonian systems in convex problems of Lagrange, *J. Optimization Theory Appl.* **12** (1973), 367–390.

13. R. T. Rockafellar, Saddlepoints of Hamiltonian systems in convex Lagrange problems having a nonzero discount rate, *J. Econ. Theory* **12** (1976), 71–113. Reprinted as Essay IV in this volume.

14. R. T. Rockafellar, A growth property in concave–convex Hamiltonian systems, *J. Econ. Theory* **12** (1976), 191–196. Reprinted as Essay VIII in this volume.

15. P. A. Samuelson, Efficient paths of capital accumulation in terms of the calculus of variations, *in* "Mathematical Studies in the Social Sciences" (K. J. Arrow, S. Karlin, and P. Suppes, Eds.), Stanford University Press, Stanford, 1960.

16. P. A. Samuelson, The general saddlepoint property of optimal-control motions, *J. Econ. Theory* **5** (1972), 102–120.

17. J. A. Scheinkman, On optimal steady states of *n*-sector growth models when utility is discounted, *J. Econ. Theory* **12** (1976), 11–30. Reprinted as Essay II in this volume.

18. K. Shell, On competitive dynamical systems, *in* "Differential Games and Related Systems" (H. W. Kuhn and G. P. Szegö, Eds.), pp. 449–476, North Holland, Amsterdam, 1971.

19. K. Shell, The theory of Hamiltonian dynamical systems, and an application to economics, *in* "The Theory and Application of Differential Games" (J. D. Grote, Ed.), pp. 189–199, Reidel, Dordrecht, Boston, 1975.

ESSAY II

On Optimal Steady States of *n*-Sector Growth Models when Utility is Discounted*

JOSÉ ALEXANDRE SCHEINKMAN

This paper contains results on local and global stability of *n*-sector growth models when utility is discounted mostly for small rates of discount. It is well known that when future utility is not discounted one can prove precise results about optimal steady states (OSS's) under fairly general assumptions. In particular, existence, uniqueness, and turnpike properties have been established by several authors. The counter examples presented by Kurz, Sutherland, and Weitzman, however, show that when utility is discounted, additional assumptions are required to obtain turnpike results. In general, it would be interesting to know how the submanifolds of stability change as δ changes. One hopes that certain conditions on the utility function would be sufficient to "classify" the submanifolds of stability and instability. Such a question is apparently very difficult to answer, but we think that the results obtained here will help in this task.

The proof that the turnpike theorem holds for discount factors near one is divided in two parts. First, we prove that optimal paths "visit" neighborhoods of the modified OSS's. Then, we prove that local stability holds for such neighborhoods.

In order to show this fact, we must prove that the local "stable manifold" varies continuously with the discount factor. This roundabout method is necessary since our problem is similar to proving uniform continuity with respect to a parameter of solutions of a differential equation in a noncompact interval of time.

Other problems analyzed here include uniqueness and continuity of OSS's. We also discuss the relation between the saddle-point property and the local stability of infinite horizon optimal growth paths.

* This paper contains results from my Ph.D. dissertation at the University of Rochester (1973). I would like to thank my advisor Professor Lionel W. McKenzie for his guidance and encouragement. Several discussions with my friends William Brock, Getulio Katz, Anjan Mukherjee, and Michael Mussa were also very useful. David Cass, as non-anonymous referee, gave me very useful advice. Support from the Ford Foundation and the Instituto de Matematica Pura e Aplicada (Brazil) is gratefully acknowledged.

11

I. The Visit Lemma, Continuity, and Local Properties of
Optimal Steady States

1. *Introduction*

Part I contains basic results that will later be used in the study of the behavior of paths of optimal growth in n-sector models. We first prove that any optimal path "visits" a neighborhood of the undiscounted optimal steady state (OSS) when the discount factor δ is sufficiently near 1. As a corollary, we obtain the continuity of the OSS correspondence, which associates to each δ a set $K(\delta)$ of OSS's when the rate of discount is δ at $\delta = 1$. Both results are proven for general models such as the ones presented by Gale [3] and McKenzie [11]. We then use those results to prove that uniqueness and the saddle-point property also hold for δ near 1, for a model like the one used by Samuelson and Solow in [17]. We also show how the saddle-point property "implies" uniqueness.

2. *The Visit Lemma and Continuity*

In this section we use the value-loss technique of Radner [12] to prove that given any ϵ-neighborhood of the undiscounted OSS k^*, we can find $\delta(\epsilon) < 1$ such that if the discount factor δ is at least as large as $\delta(\epsilon)$, optimal paths have to visit such ϵ-neighborhoods. The model used is essentially McKenzie's [11] although an assumption similar to Gale's strict concavity of the utility function at the "turnpike" (cf. [3]) is used. For completeness, we repeat here the basic assumptions made in [11].

A.1.   There exists a closed convex set $Y \subset R \times R_+^n \times R_-^n$ of "triples" $(u, k^1, -k)$ where u is the utility achievable with initial capital stocks k and final capital stocks k^1. Also $(u, k^1, -k) \in Y$ implies $(u(1), k^1(1), -k(1)) \in Y$ if $u(1) \leqslant u$, $0 \leqslant k^1(1) \leqslant k^1$, and $k(1) \geqslant k$.

Definition 1.   A sequence $\{k_t\}$ is called a *growth path* if there exists sequence $\{u_t\}$ such that $(u_t, k_t, -k_{t-1}) \in Y$ for all t.

A.2.   There exists $\tilde{k}$ with $(u, k, -\tilde{k}) \in Y$ and $k > \tilde{k}$, i.e., $\tilde{k}$ is *expansible*.

A.3.   (a) For any r, $\exists \eta$ such that $\| k \| < r$ and $(u, k^1, -k) \in Y$ implies $u < \eta$ and $\| k^1 \| < \eta$. (b) There exists R and $\gamma < 1$ such that $\| k \| \geqslant R$ and $(u, k^1, -k) \in Y$ implies $\| k^1 \| < \gamma \| k \|$.

Lemma 1.   *There exists* $(u^*, k^*, -k^*)$ *such that* $u^* \geqslant u$ *for any*

$(u, k^1, -k)$ *with* $k^1 \geqslant k$.

Proof.   McKenzie [11].

A.4. k^* is expansible. From A-4, there exists $k^1 > k^*$ such that $(u, k^1, -k^1) \in Y$, i.e., k^* is not *saturated*.

LEMMA 2. *There exists p^* such that $p^* \geqslant 0$ and for $(u, k^1, -k) \in Y$ we have $u + p^*(k^1 - k) \leqslant u^*$.*

Proof. McKenzie [11].

A.5. There exists a unique "triple" $(u^*, k^*, -k^*)$ that satisfies Lemma 1. Furthermore, $u + p^*(k^1 - k) < u^*$ for any $(u, k^1, -k) \neq (u^*, k^*, -k^*)$. This assumption is similar to Gale's strict concavity of $u(k^1, k)$ at the turnpike (k^*, k^*).

LEMMA 3. *k^0 expansible and k not saturated imply that there exists $T < \infty$ and sequence $(u_t, k_t, -k_{t-1})$, $t = 1,..., T$ with $k_T = k$.*

Proof. McKenzie [11].

LEMMA 4. (*Radner–Atsumi*). *For a fixed M suppose $\| k \| < M$ and $(u, k^1, -k) \in Y$. Then, for any $\epsilon > 0$, there exists $\rho > 0$ such that if $d((u^*, k^*, -k^*), (u, k^1, -k) > \epsilon$ (with $d(x, y) = \| x - y \|$ for any $x \in R^n$, $y \in R^n$), we have $u + p^*(k^1 - k) < u^* - \rho$.*

Proof. If the assertions were false, there would exist a sequence $y(s) = (u(s), k^1(s), -k(s)) \in Y$ with $d((u^*, k^*, -k^*), y(s)) > \epsilon$ and $u(s) + p^*(k^1(s) - k(s)) \to u^*$. However, by assumption A.3(a), since $\| k(s) \| < 2M$, we have $\| k^1(s) \| < M'$, $| u(s) | < M'$ for some $M' > 0$. Hence, $y(s)$ lies in a bounded region for all s. Thus, there is a point of accumulation $\bar{y} = (\bar{u}, \bar{k}^1, -\bar{k})$, and $\bar{u} + p^*(\bar{k}^1 - \bar{k}) = u^*$ although $d(\bar{y}, (u^*, k^*, -k^*)) > \epsilon$.
                                                                Q.E.D.

DEFINITION 2. *$k \in R^n$ is said to be sustainable if there is $u \in R$ such that $(u, k, -k) \in Y$.*

DEFINITION 3. *Given $0 < \delta < 1$ and $k_0 > k$, where k is sustainable, a growth path $\{k_t\}$ is called optimal if there exists $\{u_t\}$ associated with $\{k_t\}$ and $\lim_{N \to \infty} \sum_1^\infty \delta^t u_t \geqslant \sum_1^\infty \delta^t u_t'$ for any other utility sequence $\{u_t'\}$ associated with any growth path k_t' with $k_0' = k_0$. We will also write $k(t, k_0, \delta)$ to indicate the tth element of such an optimal path.*

We use "lim" in Definition 3 instead of "lim sup" because assumption A.3 assures us that for any path, either the limit exists, or the sum converges to $-\infty$. Also, there always exists a path, namely $(u_0, k_0, -k_0)$ for any sustainable k_0, such that $\sum_1^\infty \delta^t u_0 = u_0/(1 - \delta)$. If k_0 is not sustainable, by free disposal, one can consider the path $(u, k, -k)$.

We do not discuss here the problem of existence of an optimal path since this subject is extensively treated elsewhere (cf. [18]).

DEFINITION 4. k^δ is an optimal steady state if $(u^\delta, k^\delta, -k^\delta)$ is an optimal solution to

$$\text{Max} \sum_{t=1}^{\infty} \delta^t u_t$$

$$\text{s.t. } k_0 = k^\delta \qquad (u_t, k_{t+1}, -k_t) \in Y.$$

We will write $K(\delta)$ for the set of all such optimal steady states k^δ.

LEMMA 5 (THE VISIT LEMMA). *Let $\underline{k}$ be expansible. Given any $k_0 \geq \underline{k}$ and given $\epsilon > 0$, there exists $\delta(\epsilon) < 1$ such that if $1 \geq \delta \geq \delta(\epsilon)$, any optimal path $k(t, k_0, \delta)$ with $k(0, k_0, \delta) = k_0$ has the property that there exists a $\bar{t}$ such that $\| k(\bar{t}, k_0, \delta) - k^* \| < \epsilon$.*

Proof. Since k_0 is fixed, write $k(t, k_0, \delta) = k_t(\delta)$ and suppose

$$\| k_t(\delta) - k^* \| > \epsilon \text{ for all } t.$$

First assume that $\| k_0 \| < R$. Then by A.3(a), $\| k_1 \| < M$ for some $M > 0$. Suppose $\| k_t \| < \max(R, M)$. If $\| k_t \| < R$, then $\| k_{t+1} \| < M$. If

$$R \leq \| k_t \| < M,$$

then by A.3(b), $\| k_{t+1} \| < \| k_t \|$. Hence, $\| k_{t+1} \| < \max(R, M)$ for all t. By the Radner–Atsumi lemma, there exists $\rho > 0$ such that

$$\delta^t u_t(\delta) + \delta^t p^*(k_t(\delta) - k_{t-1}(\delta)) < \delta^t u^* - \delta^t \rho \qquad \text{for } t = 1, 2, \dots.$$

Summing, one gets

$$\sum_{1}^{\infty} \delta^t u_t(\delta) + \sum_{1}^{\infty} \delta^t p^*(k_t(\delta) - k_{t-1}(\delta)) < \sum_{1}^{\infty} \delta^t u^* - \sum_{1}^{\infty} \delta^t \rho.$$

Hence,

$$\sum_{1}^{\infty} \delta^t u_t(\delta) + \sum_{1}^{\infty} (\delta^t - \delta^{t+1}) \, p^* k_t(\delta) - p^* k_0 < \sum_{1}^{\infty} \delta^t u^* - \sum_{1}^{\infty} \delta^t \rho,$$

or,

$$\sum_{1}^{\infty} \delta^t u_t(\delta) - p^* k_0 < \sum_{1}^{\infty} \delta^t u^* - \sum_{1}^{\infty} \delta^t \rho, \qquad (1.1)$$

since

$$p^*k_t \geq 0 \quad \text{and} \quad \delta^{t-1} \geq \delta^t. \quad (1.1)$$

By Lemma 3, there exists a path $\underline{k}_t$ with $\underline{k}_0 = \underline{k}$ and $\underline{k}_N = k^*$ for some $N < \infty$. Let $\underline{u}_t$ be the associated utility sequence and $\lambda(\delta) = \sum_1^N \delta^t \underline{u}_t$. Since $\lambda(\delta)$ is a continuous function of δ, there exists $\hat{\lambda}$ such that $\hat{\lambda} \leq \sum_1^N \delta^t \underline{u}_t$ for $0 \leq \delta \leq 1$. By free disposal (A.1), there exists a path $\{k_t\}_1^N$ leading from k_0 to k^*, and such that $\sum_1^N \delta^t \underline{u}_t \geq \hat{\lambda}$, where $\underline{u}_t$ is the associated utility sequence.

Consider the following alternative path.

$$k_t = \underline{k}_t \qquad t = 1,...,N,$$
$$k_t = k^* \qquad t = N, N + 1,....$$

Since $k_t(\delta)$ is optimal, we must have

$$\sum_N^\infty \delta^t u^* + \hat{\lambda} \leq \sum_1^\infty \delta^t u_t(\delta). \quad (1.2)$$

Equations (1.1) and (1.2) imply

$$\sum_N^\infty \delta^t u^* + \hat{\lambda} - p^*k_0 < \sum_1^\infty \delta^t u^* - \sum_1^\infty \delta^t \rho$$

or,

$$-\hat{\lambda} + p^*k_0 + \sum_1^{N-1} \delta^t u^* > \sum_1^\infty \delta^t \rho.$$

Since $\sup_{\|k_0\| < R} p^*k_0 \leq \max_{\|k_0\| \leq R} p^*k_0 = \tilde{\lambda}$, we get by setting $\lambda = \tilde{\lambda} - \hat{\lambda}, \lambda + ((\delta^{N-1} - 1)\delta u^*/(\delta - 1)) + \rho > \rho/(1 - \delta)$. This, of course, is a contradiction for δ close to 1. Also, if $\| k_0 \| \geq R$, then there exists finite $\underline{t}$ such that $\| k_{\underline{t}} \| < R$ (by A.3(b)). Hence, one can apply the previous proof to the path $k(t, k_{\underline{t}}, \delta)$. Since $k(t - \underline{t}, k_{\underline{t}}, \delta) = k(t, k_0, \delta)$ the result follows. Q.E.D.

Before starting our result concerning continuity of OSS's, we need

A.6.   There exists $\delta^* < 1$ such that if $\delta \geq \delta^*$ then $\underline{k} < k^\delta$, where $\underline{k}$ is expansible.

COROLLARY 1.   *For any $\epsilon > 0$ there exists $\delta(\epsilon)$ such that $\| k^\delta - k^* \| < \epsilon$, for $1 \geq \delta \geq \delta(\epsilon)$ for any $k^\delta \in K(\delta)$.*

Proof.   By A.6, $k^\delta \geq \underline{k}$, where $\underline{k}$ is expansible, for $\delta \geq \delta^*$. By the visit lemma, given $\epsilon > 0$, there exists $\delta(\epsilon) < 1$ such that if $1 \geq \delta \geq \delta(\epsilon)$ any optimal path $k(t, k^\delta, \delta)$ with $k(0, k^\delta, \delta) = k^\delta$ has the property that there exists $\bar{\imath}$ such that $\| k(\bar{\imath}, k^\delta, \delta) - k^* \| < \epsilon$. Since $k(t, k^\delta, \delta) \equiv k^\delta$, this means $\| k^\delta - k^* \| < \epsilon$. Hence, for any $\delta \geqslant \bar{\delta}(\epsilon)$, $\| k^\delta - k^* \| < \epsilon$.

COROLLARY 2. *Let $\underline{k}$ be expansible. Given any $k_0 \geqslant \underline{k}$ and given $\epsilon > 0$, there exists $\bar{\delta}(\epsilon) < 1$ such that if $1 \geqslant \delta \geqslant \bar{\delta}(\epsilon)$, any optimal path $k(t, k_0, \delta)$ with $k(0, k_0, \delta) = k_0$ has the property that there exists a $\bar{\imath}$ such that*

$$\| k(\bar{\imath}, k_0, \delta) - k^\delta \| < \epsilon.$$

Proof. By the visit lemma, there exists $\delta^1(\epsilon/2)$ such that if $1 \geqslant \delta \geqslant \delta^1(\epsilon/2)$, there exists $\underline{t}$ such that $\| k(\underline{t}, k_0, \delta) - k^* \| < \epsilon/2$. By Corollary 1, one can find $\delta^2(\epsilon/2)$ such that $\| k^\delta - k^* \| < \epsilon/2$ for $1 \geqslant \delta \geqslant \delta^2(\epsilon/2)$. Hence, if $\bar{\delta}(\epsilon) = \max(\delta^1(\epsilon/2), \delta^2(\epsilon/2))$, we have that there exists $\underline{t}$ such that $\| k(\underline{t}, k_0, \delta) - k^\delta \| < \epsilon$. $\qquad$ Q.E.D.

3. *Local Properties*

We need now to make use of differentiability properties of the utility function. For this purpose we postulate a discrete version of the Samuelson and Solow model (cf. 17, p. 542]). Here one maximizes

$$\sum_{t=1}^{\infty} \delta^t V(k_t, k_{t+1}),$$

where $V : A \subset R_+^{2n} \to R$, A a closed convex set with $(k^*, k^*) \in \mathring{A}$. We will also assume

A.7. (a) V is C^3 (i.e., at least three times continuously differentiable) in $\mathring{A}$ and concave. (b) The matrix

$$\begin{bmatrix} V_{k_t k_t}(k^\delta, k^\delta) & V_{k_t k_{t+1}}(k^\delta, k^\delta) \\ V_{k_{t+1} k_t}(k^\delta, k^\delta) & V_{k_{t+1} k_{t+1}}(k^\delta, k^\delta) \end{bmatrix} \equiv \begin{bmatrix} A^\delta & B^\delta \\ B^{\delta\prime} & C^\delta \end{bmatrix}$$

is negative definite at (k^*, k^*).

A.8. All solutions are interior solutions so that the Euler "difference" equation system

$$\frac{\delta \, \partial V(k_t, k_{t+1})}{\partial k_t} + \frac{\partial V(k_{t-1}, k_t)}{\partial k_t} = 0 \qquad (1.3)$$

is satisfied at any optimal path.

A.7 and A.8 are going to be used only in a fixed neighborhood of (k^*, k^*).

The linearization of Eq (1.3) at an OSS k^δ is given by

$$B^{\delta\prime} X_{t+1} + [\delta A^\delta + C^\delta] X_t + \delta B^\delta X_{t-1} = 0.$$

Hence, the characteristic equation of the Euler difference system becomes

$$| B^{\delta\prime}\lambda^2 + (\delta A^\delta + C^\delta) \lambda + \delta B^\delta | = 0. \tag{1.4}$$

We will assume

A.9. $\lambda = 0$ is not a root for $\delta = 1$.

A.9 is clearly a "generic" assumption. This assumption is equivalent to $\det B = | B | = | B' | \neq 0$ at $\delta = 1$.

The following lemmas are proved in Levhari and Leviatan [8].

LEMMA 6. *If $\lambda \neq 0$ solves (1.4) then $1/\delta\lambda$ is also a solution.*

LEMMA 7. *If $\delta = 1$ and λ solves (1.4), then $\| \lambda \| \neq 1$.*

We can now prove

THEOREM 1. *There exists ϵ such that if $\delta > 1 - \epsilon$, then k^δ possesses the saddle-point[1] property.*

(Samuelson [16] contains a similar result.)

Proof. From Lemmas 6 and 7, there exists a set of n roots for $\delta = 1$, e.g., $\lambda_1^1,..., \lambda_n^1$, where each root is counted with its multiplicity such that $\| \lambda_1^1 \| < 1$. Since (1.4) is a polynomial equation of degree $2n$ with coefficients, say p_i^δ, there exists by Rouché's theorem a μ such that if $\| p_i^\delta - p_i^1 \| < \mu$, then there exists n roots λ_i^δ with $\| \lambda_i^\delta \| < 1$. Since p_i is a continuous function of δ and the elements a_{ij}^δ, b_{ij}^δ, and c_{ij}^δ of A^δ, B^δ, and C^δ, respectively, one can find η such that if $\| \delta - 1 \| < \eta$ and $\| \gamma_{ij}^\delta - \gamma_{ij}^1 \| < \eta$, where $\gamma = a, b, c$, then $\| p_i^\delta - p_i^1 \| < \mu$. Because V is C^2, there exists η' such that if $\| k^\delta - k^* \| < \eta'$, then $\| \gamma_{ij}^\delta - \gamma_{ij}^1 \| < \eta$. But by Corollary 1 of the visit lemma there exists $\eta^{1\prime}$ such that $\| \delta - 1 \| < \eta^{1\prime}$ implies $\| k^\delta - k^* \| < \eta'$. Choosing $\epsilon = \min\{\eta, \eta^{1\prime}\}$ and using Lemma 6, the proof is complete.   Q.E.D.

The saddle-point property established above for δ near 1 makes one expect that uniqueness should also prevail in a neighborhood of $\delta = 1$. We now prove that this is so. Our strategy here consists in formulating an implicit function problem such that if k^δ is an OSS, then k^δ solves our

---

[1] We use here the word saddle point for a fixed point of a difference equation such that half of the roots have absolute value greater than one and half of the roots are nonzero, and with absolute value less than one.

implicit function problem. In the end we indicate how the proofs presented here can be generalized for the Gale model with (twice) differentiable utility function.

Recall that if k^δ is an OSS, then it must solve

$$\delta \frac{\partial V}{\partial x} (k^\delta, k^\delta) + \frac{\partial V}{\partial y} (k^\delta, k^\delta) = 0, \tag{1.5}$$

where $V = V(x, y)$. Let us define $f : \mathring{R}_+ \times B(k^*, \eta) \to R^n$ [2]

$$f(\delta, k) = -\delta \frac{\partial V}{\partial x} (k, k) - \frac{\partial V}{\partial y} (k, k);$$

then if k^δ is an OSS for some $0 < \delta \leqslant 1$, we have $f(\delta, k^\delta) = 0$ with $0 < \delta \leqslant 1$. We can now prove that uniqueness prevails near $\delta = 1$.

THEOREM 2.   *There exists $\epsilon > 0$ such that if $1 - \epsilon < \delta \leqslant 1$, there exists only one OSS k^δ.*

Proof.   Note that $D_k f(\delta, k^\delta) = -B^{\delta'} - \delta A^\delta - C^\delta - \delta B^\delta$. By assumption A.7

$$\begin{bmatrix} A^1 & B^1 \\ B^{1'} & C^1 \end{bmatrix}$$

is negative definite, hence, $-A^1 - B^1 - B^{1'} - C^1$ is positive definite. By the implicit function theorem, there exists neighborhoods V of $(1, k^*)$, and U of 1 such that for each $\delta \in U$, there exists a unique $k(\delta) \in R_+^n$ with $(\delta, k(\delta)) \in V$ and $f(\delta, k(\delta)) = 0$. By Corollary 1 of the visit lemma, we have that k^δ is unique for $1 \geqslant \delta > 1 - \epsilon$ for some $\epsilon > 0$.
                                                                                Q.E.D.

The next lemma is very similar to Brock's Theorem 1 [2, Section 3.1].

LEMMA 8.   *If $| B^{\delta'} - \delta A^\delta - C^\delta - \delta B^\delta | \neq 0$ for $\underline{\delta} \leqslant \delta < 1$, there exists at most one OSS k^δ for $\underline{\delta} \leqslant \delta \leqslant 1$.*

Proof.   The proof of 2, Section 3.1, Theorem 1 applies with the obvious modifications.

COROLLARY.   *If the saddle-point property holds for all OSS corresponding to δ for $\bar{\delta} \geqslant \delta \geqslant 1$, then uniqueness holds.*

---

[2] $B(k^*, \eta) = \{k \in R^n / | k - k^* | < \eta\}$.

Proof. Since there exists no λ with $|\lambda| = 1$ such that

$$| B^\delta \lambda^2 + (\delta A^\delta + C^\delta)\lambda + \delta B^\delta | \neq 0,$$

we have, in particular, $| B^{\delta'} + \delta A^\delta + C^\delta + \delta B^\delta | \neq 0$.

Although we used here the model of Samuelson and Solow, we note that except for the corollary, we actually only used (1.5). In the Gale model, Sutherland has shown than under certain conditions every OSS has the so-called support property, i.e., an OSS (k^δ, k^δ) maximizes

$$\Phi_\delta(k_{t-1}, k_t) = u(k_{t-1}, k_t) - p^\delta k_{t-1} + \delta p^\delta k_t,$$

for an appropriate vector p^δ. If an OSS k^δ is interior, one has

$$\frac{\partial u}{\partial x}(k^\delta, k^\delta) - p^\delta = 0$$

and

$$\frac{\partial u}{\partial y}(k^\delta, k^\delta) + \delta p^\delta = 0,$$

or

$$\delta \frac{\partial u}{\partial x}(k^\delta, k^\delta) + \frac{\partial u}{\partial y}(k^\delta, k^\delta) = 0,$$

i.e., (1.5). There is no need of assuming that all optimal paths do in fact satisfy (1.3).

II. The Continuity of the Stable Manifold

1. *Introduction*

In Part II we establish continuity properties of the local stable manifolds associated with the Euler difference equations generated by optimal growth problems. For this purpose, we start by transforming these second-order difference equations into first-order difference equations around the steady states. We then use the "stable manifold theorem for a point" of Hirsch and Pugh to show that the stable manifold varies continuously with the parameter δ.[3] We also study the relationship between the existence of such local stable manifolds and the convergence of

---

[3] If one is willing to assume that the linearization of the Euler equation at the undiscounted optimal steady state has no multiple eigenvalues, one can furnish a proof of the "continuity" of the stable manifold using only elementary results in linear algebra, and a result on upper-semicontinuous correspondences from Berge [1]. The proof is long, however, and quite messy. It may be found in my paper [13].

optimal paths that start sufficiently close to the optimal steady state, the so-called local turnpike result.

The proof of the local turnpike theorem usually consists in showing that a system of difference equations on the capital stocks variable and some dual variable possesses a saddle point singularity, together with the fact that a convergent path is optimal. This reasoning assumes that the "stable manifold" S is such that there exists $\epsilon > 0$ such that given any capital stock k' with $\| k' - k^* \| < \epsilon$, where k^* is the singularity, one can find a value for the dual variable, say y', such that $(k', y') \in S$. There is no *a priori* reason for that to be true. Suppose, for instance, that $n = 2$ and that $S = \{ (k^1, k^2, y^1, y^2)/k^1 = (k^*)^1, \ y^2 = \Phi(k^2, y^1), \ \| k^2 - (k^*)^2 \| < \epsilon, \ \| y^1 - y^* \| < \epsilon \}$. Then S is a two dimensional manifold but given $\bar{k} = (\bar{k}^1, \bar{k}^2)$ with $\bar{k}^1 \neq (k^*)^1$, there exists no y such that $(\bar{k}, y) \in S$. What needs to be shown is that $(k^*, y^*) \in \mathrm{Int}(\Pi_1(S))$, where $\Pi_1(S)$ is the projection of S on the k subspace. The only author, to our knowledge, who took care of this problem was McKenzie (cf. [10]). There he assumes, essentially, that the projection on the k subspace of the stable manifold S' associated with the linear system that approximates the original system at (k^*, y^*) has a nonempty interior. Since S' and S are tangent, this ensures the result. It turns out, however, that because our $2n$-dimensional system is generated from a second-order n-dimensional system with concavity properties, if all eigenvalues are nonzero, $(k^*, y^*) \in \mathrm{Int}(\Pi_1(S'))$.

2. Reduction to a Standard Form

In this section, we show how one can reduce the Euler "difference" equations that are satisfied by optimal paths to a standard form in a neighborhood of $\delta = 1$ when these equations are given by

$$\delta \frac{\partial V}{\partial k_t} (k_t, k_{t+1}) + \frac{\partial V}{\partial k_t} (k_{t-1}, k_t) = 0. \qquad (*)$$

More precisely, we prove that one can write $(*)$ as $z_{t+1} = F_\delta(z_t)$, where F_δ is a diffeomorphism in a neighborhood of a fixed point z^δ. We will also prove some continuity results that will be needed later.

LEMMA 9. *There exists $\epsilon^* > 0$ such that if $1 \geqslant \delta \geqslant 1 - \epsilon^*$ then, Eq. $(*)$ can be written as $k_{t+1} = g(\delta, k_t, k_{t-1})$ in an ϵ^* neighborhood of $(1, k^*, k^*, k^*)$. Furthermore, g is C^2.*

Proof. Let $f(\delta, k_{t-1}, k_t, k_{t+1}) = \delta(\partial V/\partial k_t)(k_t, k_{t+1}) + (\partial V/\partial k_t)(k_{t-1}, k_t)$. Hence, $| D_{k_{t+1}} f(1, k^*, k^*, k^*)| = | B | \neq 0$, by A.9. By the implicit function theorem [7, Theorem 8, p. 362], there exists function g

such that in a ϵ^* neighborhood of $(1, k^*, k^*, k^*)$, one has $f(\delta, k_{t-1}, k_t, k_{t+1}) = 0$ iff $k_{t+1} = g(\delta, k_{t-1}, k_t)$. Also, since $f \in C^2$, we have $g \in C^2$.

Let us call U the neighborhood obtained in the above lemma. By defining functions $g_\delta : R^{2n} \to R^n$ by $g_\delta(k_{t-1}, k_t) \equiv g(\delta, k_{t-1}, k_t)$, one can rewrite $(*)$ as

$$k_{t+2} = g_\delta(k_t, k_{t+1}). \tag{2.1}$$

We can then define $y_t = k_{t+1}$ and rewrite (2.1) as

$$k_{t+1} = y_t,$$
$$y_{t+1} = g_\delta(k_t, y_t),$$

or

$$z_{t+1} = F_\delta(z_t), \tag{2.2}$$

where $z_t = (k_t, y_t)$ and $F_\delta(z_t) = [\Pi_2(z_t), g_\delta(z_t)]$ where Π_2 is the projection on the y plane. Since Π_2 is C^∞, we have $F_\delta \in C^2$. Alternatively, one can define a function F by $F(\delta, z_t) = F_\delta(z_t)$ and write

$$z_{t+1} = F(\delta, z_t). \tag{2.3}$$

Our theorems here will depend partly on local analysis around the OSS k^δ. Since F is C^2, we may write around any point x that

$$F(\delta, z) = F(\delta, x) + D_z F(\delta, x)(z - x) + r(\delta, z),$$

where given $\alpha > 0$, there exists $\beta = \beta(\alpha, \delta, x)$ such that if $\| z - x \| < \beta$, then $\| r(\delta, z) \| \leqslant \alpha \| z - x \|$.

Since $F \in C^2$, the application

$$D_z = U \subset R^{2n+1} \to M(R^{2n}, R^{2n}),$$
$$(\delta, x) \to D_z F(\delta, x),$$

i.e., the application which gives us the partial derivative matrix with respect to z calculated at (δ, x), is continuous. Here $M(R^{2n}, R^{2n})$ indicates the set of all $2n \times 2n$ matrices with real entries.

By Theorem 2 of Part 1, there exists function $K : [\underline{\delta}, 1] \to R^n$ such that $K(\delta) = k^\delta$ is the (unique) OSS when the rate of discount is δ. Furthermore, $K \in C^2$.

Consider the function $r = R \times R^{2n} \times R^{2n} \to R^{2n}$ defined by $r(\delta, z, x) = F(\delta, z) - F(\delta, x) - D_z F(\delta, x)(z - x)$. Since $F \in C^2$, we have $r \in C^1$. Also $D_z r(\delta, z, x) = D_z F(\delta, z) - D_z F(\delta, x)$. Hence, $\lim_{z \to x} D_z r(\delta, z, x) = 0$. Since $D_z r$ is continuous, it is uniformly continuous in any compact set.

Hence, given ϵ, there exists $\beta(\epsilon)$ such that $\| D_z r(\delta, z, x)\| < \epsilon$, if $\|(\delta, z, x) - (\delta, x, x)\| < \beta(\epsilon)$. Hence, if z^δ is a fixed point of F_δ, we have $\| r(\delta, z, z^\delta) - r(\delta, z', z^\delta)\| \leqslant \sup_{z \in [z, z']} \| D_z(r, z, x^\delta)\| \| z - z' \| \leqslant \epsilon \| z - z' \|$. Let $r^\delta(z - z^\delta) = r(\delta, z, z^\delta)$.

We now summarize in Lemma 10 the results obtained above.

LEMMA 10. *There exists $\bar{\epsilon}$ and $\bar{\bar{\epsilon}}$ such that if $1 \geqslant \delta \geqslant 1 - \bar{\epsilon}$ and $\| z - z^\delta \| < \bar{\bar{\epsilon}}$, where $z^\delta = (k^\delta, k^\delta)$ we have*

(a) *The difference equation $(*)$ is equivalent to $z_{t+1} = F_\delta(z_t)$.*

(b) *Given δ, one has $F_\delta(z) = z^\delta + D_z F_\delta(z^\delta)(z - z^\delta) + r^\delta(z - z^\delta)$ where given $\alpha > 0$; there exists $\beta(\alpha)$ such that if $\| z - z^\delta \| < \beta, \| \tilde{z} - z^\delta \| < \beta$, then $\| r^\delta(z - z^\delta) - r^\delta(\tilde{z} - z^\delta)\| < \alpha \| z - \tilde{z} \|$.*

(c) *The application*

$$\tilde{D}_z : [1 - \bar{\epsilon}, 1] \to M(R^{2n}, R^{2n}),$$

$$\delta \to D_z F_\delta(z^\delta),$$

is continuous.

(d)

$$D_z F_\delta(z) = \left[\begin{array}{c|c} 0 & I \\ \hline M & N \end{array} \right]$$

where all blocks are $n \times n$.

(e)

$$D_z F_1(z^*) = \left[\begin{array}{c|c} 0 & I \\ \hline -B^{-1}B' & -B^{-1}(A + C) \end{array} \right]$$

3. *The Stable Manifold Theorem*

The stable manifold theorem of Hirsh and Pugh [4], stated below, establishes the existence and continuity properties of the stable manifold that are needed to prove our results. Before stating the theorem, we need certain definitions and preliminary results:

DEFINITION 1. A map $f: X \to Y$ between metric spaces is Lipschitz if there exists number l such that $d(f(x), f(y)) \leqslant ld(x, y)$ for all $x, y \in X$. The smallest such l is the Lipschitz constant $L(f)$.

Observation. Every continuously differentiable map $f: U \subset R^m \to R^n$ is Lipschitz in a compact set $K \subset U$.

DEFINITION 2.   Let $T: R^m \to R^m$ be an isomorphism. T is hyperbolic if T has no complex eigenvalue of unit norm.

Observation.   Given any hyperbolic operator T, there exists decomposition of $R^m = E_1 \oplus E_2$ such that $T \mid E_i = E_i$ and all eigenvalues of $T_1 = T \mid E_1$ have absolute value less than one, and of $T_2 = T \mid E_2$ have absolute value greater than one. Hence, for every $x \in R^m$, x can be written uniquely as $x = x_1 + x_2$ with $x_i \in E_i$. Also one can renorm $E_1(E_2)$ such that $T_1(T_2^{-1}$ resp.) is a contraction. We can then choose a norm for R^m as $\| x \|' = \max\{\| x_1 \|', \| x_2 \|'\}$ for $x_1 \in E_1$, $x_2 \in E_2$. The quantity

$$\tau = \max(\| T_1 \|', \| T_2^{-1} \|') < 1$$

is called the skewness of T. In what follows, we consider R^m with the norm $\| \|'$. Let $B(r)$ be the closed ball of radius r about the origin. Let $B_i(r) = B(r) \cap E_i$. Define $f^{-n}(B(r)) = \{x \in B(r)/f(x), ..., f^n(x) \in B(r)\}$, and $W(f) = \bigcap_{n \geqslant 0} f^{-n}(B(r))$.

DEFINITION 3.   The space $C^i(B(r), R^m)$ is the set of all functions $f: B(r) \subset R^m \to R^m$ of class C^i with bounded i-norm $\| f \|_i' = \sup_{x \in B(r)} \mathrm{Max}(\| f(x)\|', \|(Df)(x)\|', ..., \|(D^i f)(x)\|')$.

DEFINITION 4.   For $r > 0$ fixed, a "Lipschitz neighborhood" of $T \mid B(r)$ in $C^i(B(r), R^m)$ is the set $N_\epsilon{}^i(T) = \{f \in C^i(B(r), R^m) \mid L(f - T) < \epsilon, \| f(0)\|' < \epsilon\}$.

DEFINITION 5.   Let $f: B(r) \subset R^m \to R^m$ be such that $f(0) = 0$. The stable manifold of f is the set $S(f) = \{x \in B(r) \mid \lim_{n \to \infty} f^n(x) = 0\}$.
We are now ready to state

LEMMA 11 (THE STABLE MANIFOLD THEOREM FOR A POINT)   *Let $0 < \tau < 1$ and $r > 0$ be given. There exists $\epsilon > 0$ independent of r and $0 < c < \epsilon$ with the following property. If T is a hyperbolic operator in $R^m = E_1 \oplus E_2$ of skewness τ and $f: B(r) \to R^m$ is Lipschitz and satisfies $L(f - T) < \epsilon$, $\| f(0)\|' < c$, then $W^r(f) = W$ is the graph of a unique function $g_f: B_1(r) \to B_2(r)$. Moreover, $L(g_f) \leqslant 1$ and g_f is of class C^i if f is. The assignment $f \to g_f$ is continuous as a map $N_\epsilon{}^i(T) \to C^i(B_1(r), B_2(r))$. The map $f \mid W: W \to W$ contracts W into its interior.*

Proof.   [4, pp. 146–147]. Note that the theorem actually says that $W(f) \subset S(f)$ the stable manifold of f since $f \mid W(f)$ is a contraction.
We will apply Lemma 11 to the diffeomorphisms F_δ defined in Section 2. For this purpose, let $T = DF_1(z^*)$.

LEMMA 12. *T is a hyperbolic operator and, furthermore, T has n non-zero eigenvalues (counting multiplicity) with absolute value less than one, and n eigenvalues with absolute value greater than one.*

Proof. Let λ be an eigenvalue of T. Hence, there exists $x \in \mathbb{C}^{2n}$ [4] such that $Tx = \lambda x$. Write $x = (x_1, x_2)$, $x_i \in \mathbb{C}^n$, $i = 1, 2$. By Lemma 10(e), $Tx = (x_2, -B^{-1}B'x_1 - B^{-1}(A + C) x_2)$. Since $Tx = \lambda x$, we must have $x_2 = \lambda x_1$. Hence, $-B^{-1}B'x_1 - B^{-1}(A + C) \lambda x_1 = \lambda^2 x_1$. By A.9, $|B| \neq 0$, and, hence, $B'x_1 + (A + C) \lambda x_1 + \lambda^2 Bx_1 = 0$, i.e., $|B' + \lambda(A + C) + \lambda^2 B| = 0$. Again using A.9, we have that $\lambda = 0$ is not an eigenvalue of T. Hence, if λ is an eigenvalue of T, $1/\lambda$ solves Eq. (1.4) of Part I, Section 3. The result follows from Lemmas 6 and 7. Q.E.D.

Let us define $G_\delta(x) = F_\delta(z^\delta + x) - z^\delta$. By Lemma 10, there exists $\bar{\epsilon} > 0$ and $\bar{\bar{\epsilon}} > 0$ such that if $1 \geqslant \delta \geqslant 1 - \bar{\epsilon}$ and $\|x\| < \bar{\bar{\epsilon}}$, then G_δ is well defined. Since $\|\;\|'$ is equivalent to any of the standard norms of R^m, there exists η such that $B(0, \eta) \subset \{x \in R^m / \|x\| < \bar{\bar{\epsilon}}\}$, where $B(0, \eta)$ is taken with reference to $\|\;\|'$.

LEMMA 13. *Let $T: R^{2n} \to R^{2n}$ be defined by $Tx = DF_1(z^*) \cdot x$. Then given any $\epsilon > 0$, there exists $\rho(\epsilon)$ and $\delta^1 < 1$ such that if we consider $G_\delta: B(0, \rho) \to R^{2n}$, then $\|G_\delta - T\|_1' < \epsilon$ and $L(G_\delta - T) < \epsilon$.*

Proof. $\|(G_\delta - T)(x) - (G_\delta - T)(y)\|' = \|G_\delta(x) - Tx - G_\delta(y) + Ty\|'$
$= \|DF_\delta(z^\delta)x + r^\delta(x) - Tx - DF_\delta(z^\delta) y - r^\delta(y) + Ty\|' < \|DF_\delta(z^\delta) - T)(x - y)\|' + \|r^\delta(x) - r^\delta(y)\|'$. By Lemma 10, given $\epsilon > 0$, there exists $\rho^1 > 0$ such that if $\|x\|', \|y\|' \leqslant \rho^1$, then $\|r^\delta(x) - r^\delta(y)\|' < \epsilon/2 \|x - y\|'$, for $1 \geqslant \delta \geqslant \delta^2$. Also, by the same lemma, there exists $1 > \delta \geqslant \delta^2$ such that if $1 \geqslant \delta \geqslant \bar{\delta}$, then $\|DF_\delta(z^\delta) - T\|' < \epsilon/2$. Hence, $L(G_\delta - T) < \epsilon$. Also, $\|G_\delta(x) - T(x)\|' = \|G_\delta(x) - Tx - G_\delta(0) - T0\|' < \epsilon/2 \|x\|'$, and $\|DG_\delta(x) - T\|' = \|DF_\delta(z^\delta + x) - T\|' = \|D_zF(\delta, z^\delta + x) - D_zF(1, z^*)\|'$. Since F is C^1 and the function given by $z(\delta) = z^\delta$, $1 \geqslant \delta \geqslant \delta^2$ is continuous, there exists $\rho^2 \geqslant 0$ and $1 > \bar{\bar{\delta}} \geqslant \delta^2$ such that if $x \in B(\rho^2)$ and $\delta > \bar{\bar{\delta}}$, then $\|D_zF(\delta, z^\delta + x) - D_zF(1, z^*)\|' < \epsilon/2$. Let $\rho = \min(\rho^1, \rho^2)$ and $\delta^1 = \max\{\bar{\bar{\delta}}, \bar{\delta}\}$. Then $\|G_\delta - T\|_1' < \epsilon$ and $L(G_\delta - T) < \epsilon$, for $\delta \geqslant \delta^1$.

Lemmas 11, 12, and 13 allow us to construct a local stable manifold around $z^\delta = (k^\delta, k^\delta)$ for δ sufficiently close to one which varies continuously with δ. However, as mentioned in Section 1, we are interested in showing that given any k_0 sufficiently close to k^δ, one can find a k_1 such that (k_0, k_1) belong to the stable manifold. The following lemma is needed to show such result.

---

[4] $C^{2n} = \{(x_1,..., x_n)/x_i \in C\}$ where C is the field of complex numbers.

LEMMA 14. *Let $T: R^{2n} \to R^{2n}$ be defined by $Tx = DF_1(z^*)\, x$. Assume also that T has $2n$ eigenvalues, $\lambda_1, ..., \lambda_{2n}$ with $|\lambda_i| < 1$ for $i = 1, ..., n$, $|\lambda_i| > 1$ for $i = n+1, ..., 2n$. Let $E_1 \oplus E_2$ be a decomposition of R^{2n} such that $T_1 = T \mid E_1$ has eigenvalues λ_i, $i = 1, ..., n$, and $T_2 = T \mid E_2$ has eigenvalues λ_i, $i = n+1, ..., 2n$. Then, there exists $b > 0$ and $\mu > 0$ such that given any $g: B_1(r) \to B_2(r)$ with $g(0) = 0$ and $L(g) < b$, there exists $\tilde{g}$: $B(0, \mu) \subset R^n \to R^n$ such that if $y \in$ graph g and $\| \Pi_1(y)\|' < \mu$, then $\Pi_2(y) = \tilde{g}(\Pi_1(y))$.*[5]

Proof. By the primary decomposition theorem [5, p. 180], there exists a real matrix P such that

$$P^{-1}AP = \begin{bmatrix} L_1 & 0 \\ 0 & L_2 \end{bmatrix} = L,$$

where each L_i is $n \times n$, and the eigenvalues of L_1 are those of A with absolute value less than one, and the ones of L_2 are those of A with absolute value greater than one. Hence, $E_1 = \{v \in R^{2n}/v = Qw, w \in R^n \times \{0\}\}$. Write $v = (v_1, v_2)$. Then if

$$Q = \begin{bmatrix} Q_1 & Q_2 \\ Q_3 & Q_4 \end{bmatrix},$$

where all blocks are $n \times n$, and if Q_1 is invertible, $E_1 = \{v \in R^{2n}/v = (v_1, Q_3 Q_1^{-1} v_1)\}$ for any $v_1 \in R^n$. We will show that this is, in fact, so. For if $\det Q_1 = 0$, then there exists $z \in R^n \times \{0\}, z \neq 0$, such that $Qz = (0, v_2)$ and $v_2 \neq 0$ since Q is invertible. Hence, $(0, v_2) \in E_1$, and, hence,

$$\lim_{t \to \infty} A^t \begin{pmatrix} 0 \\ v_2 \end{pmatrix} = 0.$$

Consider now the problem (P)

$$\text{Max} \sum_{t=0}^{\infty} (z_t, z_{t+1})^T D^2V(k^*, k^*)(z_t, z_{t+1})$$

subject to $z_0 = 0$. It is easy to see that since D^2V is negative definite that $z_t \equiv 0$ is the optimal solution to (P). The Euler equation associated with (P) is exactly $(z_{t+2}, z_{t+1}) = A(z_t, z_{t+1})$. Since

$$\lim_{t \to \infty} A^t \begin{pmatrix} 0 \\ v_2 \end{pmatrix} = 0,$$

there exists solution $\{z_t\}$ of the Euler equation system with $z_0 = 0$ and $z_1 = v_2 \neq 0$ such that $\lim_{t \to \infty} z_t = 0$. This solution must yield a negative

---

[5] If $v \in R^n$, $\| v \|' = \|(v, 0)\|'$.

value for (P) since $(0, v_2)^T D^2 V(k^*, k^*)(0, v_2) < 0$. Let $w(z_t, z_{t+1}) = (z_t, z_{t+1})^T D^2 V(k^*, k^*)(z_t, z_{t+1})$. By concavity of w,

$$\lim_{T \to \infty} \sum_{t=0}^{T} w(z_t, z_{t+1}) = \lim_{T \to \infty} \sum_{t=0}^{T} w(z_t, z_{t+1}) - w(0, 0)$$

$$\geqslant \lim_{T \to \infty} \sum_{t=0}^{T} \frac{\partial w}{\partial y_1}(z_t, z_{t+1}) z_t + \frac{\partial w}{\partial y_2}(z_t, z_{j+1}) z_{t+1}$$

$$= \lim_{T \to \infty} \frac{\partial w}{\partial y_2}(z_T, z_{T+1}) z_{T+1},$$

since $(\partial w/\partial y_2)(z_t, z_{t+1}) z_{t+1} + (\partial w/\partial y_1)(z_{t+1}, z_{t+2}) z_{t+1} = 0$ and $z_0 = 0$. But since $\lim_{t \to \infty} z_t = 0$, we must have

$$\lim_{T \to \infty} \frac{\partial w}{\partial y_2}(z_T, z_{T+1}) z_{T+1} = 0.$$

Hence, $\sum_{t=0}^{\infty} w(z_t, z_{t+1}) = 0$. This is a contradiction. Hence Q_1 must be invertible. Therefore, given any $v_1 \in R^n$, there exists unique $v_2 = Q_3 Q_1^{-1} v_1 \in R^n$ such that $(v_1, v_2) \in E_1$. Since $\| v_2 \|' \leqslant \alpha \| v_1 \|'$ for some $\alpha > 0$, there exists $\bar{r}$ such that if $\| v_1 \|' < \bar{r}$, then $\| v \|' < r$.

Given any $y \in$ graph g, write $y = (y_1, y_2)$. Then, there exists $z \in E_1$ such that $y_1 = g_1(z) + z_1$ where $g_1(z) = \Pi_1(g(z))$, $z_1 = \Pi_1(z)$, etc., $y_2 = g_2(z) + z_2$. Let $\bar{g}_i : B(0, r) \subset R^n \to R^n$ be given by $\bar{g}_i(v_1) = g_i(v_1, Q_3 Q_1^{-1} v_1)$. Then, there exists $b > 0$ such that if $L(g) < b$, $L(\bar{g}_1) < 1$. Hence, $h_1 : B(0, \bar{r}) \to R^n$ defined by $h_1(v_1) = v_1 + \bar{g}_1(v_1)$ is an homeomorphism over $B(0, \mu) \subset R^n$ for some $\mu > 0$. Given $y \in$ graph g with $\| y_1 \|' \leqslant \mu$, we can define $v_1 = h_1^{-1}(y_1)$. Hence,

$$y_1 = v_1 + \bar{g}_1(v_1) = v_1 + g_1(v_1, Q_3 Q_1^{-1} v_1).$$

Let $z = (v_1, Q_3 Q_1^{-1} v_1)$. Then,

$$y_2 = g_2(v_1, Q_3 Q_1^{-1} v_1) + Q_3 Q_1^{-1} v_1 = \bar{g}_2(v_1) + Q_3 Q_1^{-1} v_1$$

$$= \bar{g}_2 \circ h_1^{-1}(y_2) + Q_3 Q_1^{-1} h_1^{-1}(y_1) \equiv \tilde{g}(y_1).$$

Hence, $y_2 = \tilde{g}(y_2)$ for $\| y_1 \|' < \mu$.   Q.E.D.

LEMMA 15. *Under assumptions A.1–A.9, there exists* δ^* *and* $\mu > 0$ *such that if* $\bar{y} \in B(0, \mu) \cap R^n$, *there exists* $\bar{\mu}, \bar{\bar{\mu}} > 0$ *and* $\bar{y} = \bar{y}(\delta, \bar{y}) \in R^n \cap B(0, \bar{\mu})$ *such that* $\tilde{y}_0 = (\bar{y}, \bar{\bar{y}}) \in W^{\bar{\mu}}(G_\delta) \subset S(G_\delta)$ *for any* $1 \geqslant \delta \geqslant \delta^*$. *Furthermore, if* $y_t(\tilde{y}_0)$ *solves* $y_{t+1} = G_\delta(y_t)$ *with* $y_0 = \tilde{y}_0$, *we have* $\| y_t(\tilde{y}_0) \|' < \bar{\mu}$ *and* $\lim_{t \to \infty} y_t(\tilde{y}_0) = 0$.

Proof. Choose $r = \eta/2$ in Lemma 14. Then there exists $\epsilon > 0$ *independent of* r *such that if* $L(f - T) < \epsilon$ *and* $\| f(0) \|' = 0$ *and* $f : B(r) \to R^m$

is Lipschitz, then there exists a unique map $g_f \colon B_1(r) \to B_2(r)$ whose graph is $W^r(f)$. Now choose $\rho = \rho(\epsilon)$ as in Lemma 13 and $\bar{\rho} = \min(r, \rho)$. Then there exists $\bar{g}_f = g_f \mid B_1(\bar{\rho})$ whose graph is $W^{\rho}(f)$. Note that $\bar{g}_f(B_1(\bar{\rho})) \subset B_2(\bar{\rho})$ since g_f is a contraction. Note that $g_T = 0$. Since the assignment $f \to g_f$ is continuous in the C^1 topology, we have $\| Dg_f \|' < c/2$ for any $c > 0$, for f sufficiently near T. Write $g_\delta = g_{G_\delta}$. Then for $\delta \geq \delta^*$ for some $\delta^* < 1$, we have $L(g_\delta) \leq \sup \| Dg_\delta \|' \leq c/2 < c$. Choose $c = b$ given in Lemma 14. Then there exists $\mu > 0$ such that given any $\bar{y}$ with $\| \bar{y} \|' < \mu$, then $\bar{y} = \tilde{g}(\bar{y})$ for some C^1 function $\tilde{g}$. Since $\tilde{g}(0) = 0$ and $\tilde{g}$ is continuous, we have $\| \tilde{y} \|' < \bar{\mu}$ for some $\bar{\mu} > 0$. Hence, $\| \tilde{y}_0 \|' < \bar{\mu}$ for some $\bar{\mu} > 0$. Since G_δ is a contraction in $B(\bar{\rho})$, we have $\| y_t(\tilde{y}_0) \|' \leq \| \tilde{y}_0 \|' < \bar{\mu}$ and $\lim_{t \to \infty} y_t(\tilde{y}_0) = 0$.

LEMMA 16. *Under assumptions A.1–A.9, there exists δ^* and μ, $\gamma > 0$, such that if $\| k_0 - k^\delta \|' < \mu$ and $1 \geq \delta \geq \delta^*$, there exists an optimal path $k_t(k_0, \delta)$ such that $\| k_t(k_0) \|' < \gamma$ and $\lim_{t \to \infty} k_t(k_0, \delta) = k^\delta$.*

Proof. Let $\bar{y} = k_0 - k^\delta$. By the previous lemma, there exists $\bar{\mu} > 0$ and $\bar{y}$ with $\| (\bar{y}, \bar{y}) \|' < \bar{\mu}$, such that $\lim_{t \to \infty} y_t(\tilde{y}_0) = 0$ and $\| y_t(\tilde{y}_0) \|' < \bar{\mu}$ where $\tilde{y}_0 = (\bar{y}, \bar{y})$. Let $k_t(k_0) = \Pi_1(y_t) + k^\delta$. Then for some $\gamma > 0$, $\| k_t(k_0, \delta) - k^\delta \|' < \gamma$ and $\lim_{t \to \infty} k_t(k_0, \delta) = k^\delta$.

Now suppose there exists $\bar{k}_t$ with $\bar{k}_0 = k_0$ such that

$$\limsup_{T \to \infty} \sum_0^T \delta^t V(\bar{k}_t, \bar{k}_{t+1}) > \sum_{t=0}^\infty \delta^t V(k_t, k_{t+1}),$$

where $k_t = k_t(k_0, \delta)$.[6] Hence, given any $T > 0$, there exists $\bar{t} > T$ such that

$$\sum_{t=0}^{\bar{t}} \delta^t V(\bar{k}_t, \bar{k}_{t+1}) > \sum_{t=0}^{\bar{t}} \delta^t V(k_t, k_{t+1}) + \epsilon$$

for some $\epsilon > 0$ independent of T. However,

$$\sum_{t=0}^{\bar{t}} \delta^t V(k_t, k_{t+1}) - \sum_{t=0}^{\bar{t}} \delta^t V(\bar{k}_t, \bar{k}_{t+1})$$

$$= \sum_{t=0}^{\bar{t}} \delta^t [V(k_t, k_{t+1}) - V(\bar{k}_t, \bar{k}_{t+1})]$$

$$> \sum_{t=0}^{\bar{t}} \delta^t \left[\frac{\partial V}{\partial y_1}(k_t, k_{t+1}) k_t + \frac{\partial V}{\partial y_2}(k_t, k_{t+1}) k_{t+1} \right.$$
$$\left. - \frac{\partial V}{\partial y_1}(k_t, k_{t+1}) \bar{k}_t - \frac{\partial V}{\partial y_2}(k_t, k_{t+1}) \bar{k}_{t+1} \right],$$

by concavity of V.

[6] What follows is basically the argument contained in Mangasarian [9].

Since

$$\delta \frac{\partial V}{\partial y_1}(k_t, k_{t+1}) + \frac{\partial V}{\partial y_2}(k_{t-1}, k_t) = 0,$$

we get

$$-\epsilon > \sum_{t=0}^{\bar{\imath}} \delta^t V(k_t, k_{t+1}) - \sum_{t=0}^{\bar{\imath}} \delta^t V(\bar{k}_t, \bar{k}_{t+1})$$

$$\geq \frac{\partial V}{\partial y_1}(k_0, k_1) k_0 + \delta^{\bar{\imath}} \frac{\partial V}{\partial y_2}(k_{\bar{\imath}}, k_{\bar{\imath}+1}) k_{\bar{\imath}+1}$$

$$- \frac{\partial V}{\partial y_1}(k_0, k_1) \bar{k}_0 - \delta^{\bar{\imath}} \frac{\partial V}{\partial y_2}(k_{\bar{\imath}}, k_{\bar{\imath}+1}) \bar{k}_{\bar{\imath}+1}$$

$$= \delta^{\bar{\imath}} \frac{\partial V}{\partial y_2}(k_{\bar{\imath}}, k_{\bar{\imath}+1})[k_{\bar{\imath}+1} - \bar{k}_{\bar{\imath}+1}].$$

Hence,

$$\epsilon < |\delta^{\bar{\imath}}| \left\| \frac{\partial V}{\partial y_2}(k_{\bar{\imath}}, k_{\bar{\imath}+1}) \right\| \| k_{\bar{\imath}+1} - \bar{k}_{\bar{\imath}+1} \| \tag{2.4}$$

By assumption A.3, we have $\| \bar{k}_{\bar{\imath}+1} \| < A$ for some $A > 0$, and since $\lim_{t \to \infty} k_t = k^\delta$ and $\partial V / \partial y_2$ is continuous, the right-hand side of (2.4) will become less than ϵ for any $\bar{\imath} > T'$ for some T'. Hence,

$$\lim_{T \to \infty} \sup \sum_{t=0}^{T} \delta^t V(\bar{k}_t, \bar{k}_{t+1}) \leq \sum_{t=0}^{\infty} \delta^t V(k_t, k_{t+1}). \qquad \text{Q.E.D.}$$

III. The Insensitivity of the Global Turnpike Result

We can now combine the "visit lemma" of Part I with the continuity results of Part II to establish that for δ close to one, the "global turnpike" theorem still holds.

THEOREM 3. *Given an optimal growth problem* $\mathrm{Max} \sum_{t=1}^{\infty} \delta^t V(k_t, k_{t+1})$ *where* $V: A \subset R_+^{2n} \to R$ *satisfying A.1 to A.9 above and an expansible* $\underline{k}$, *there exists* $\bar{\delta} < 1$ *such that if* $1 \geq \delta \geq \bar{\delta}$, *and* $k_0 \geq \underline{k}$, *there exists an optimal path* $k(t, k_0, \delta)$ *such that* $\lim_{t \to \infty} k(t, k_0, \delta) = k^\delta$ *where* k^δ *is the unique* OSS *associated with* δ.

Proof. Note that the "visit lemma" is true for any of the equivalent norms of R^{2n}. Hence, considering the constant $\mu > 0$ given by Lemma 16, there exists δ^1 such that for $1 \geq \delta \geq \delta^1$ and $k_0 \geq \underline{k}$, there exists $\bar{\imath}$ such that

$\| k(\bar{t}, k_0, \delta) - k^\delta \|' < \mu$, for any optimal path $k(t, k_0, \delta)$. Let $\bar{\delta} = \max\{\delta^1, \delta^*\}$ where δ^* is given by Lemma 16. Then for $1 \geqslant \delta \geqslant \bar{\delta}$, there exists a path $k(t, k(t, k_0, \delta), \delta)$ such that

$$\lim_{t \to \infty} k(t, k(\bar{t}, k_0, \delta), \delta) = k$$

and $k(t, k(\bar{t}, k_0, \delta), \delta)$ is optimal. Hence, $k(t + \bar{t}, k_0, \delta) = k(t, k(\bar{t}, k_0, \delta), \delta)$ is optimal, and we have

$$\lim_{t \to \infty} k(t, k_0, \delta) = \lim_{t \to \infty} k(t + \bar{t}, k_0, \delta) = k^\delta.$$

Although the theorem requires the choice of an expansible $\underline{k}$, this can be relaxed if one can show that there exists $\underline{k}$ expansible such that given any k_0 with $k_0{}^j > 0$, $j = 1,..., n$, any optimal path $k(t, k_0, \delta)$ has the property that there exists t such that $k(t, k_0, \delta) > \underline{k}$. This can be assured using "Inada"-type conditions.

It is interesting to consider how the counterexamples to the turnpike theorem in the literature fail to meet our hypothesis. Sutherland's [18] well-known example uses δ far from 1. However, Samuelson's paper [15] contains an example due to Martin Weitzman where the turnpike result fails for any $\delta < 1$. In our notation, Weitzman's example has $V(k_t, k_{t+1}) = k_t^{1/2}(1 - k_{t+1})^{1/2}$. Hence,

$$D^2V = \begin{bmatrix} -\tfrac{1}{4}k_t^{-3/2}(1 - k_{t+1})^{1/2} & -\tfrac{1}{4}k_t^{-1/2}(1 - k_{t+1})^{-1/2} \\ -\tfrac{1}{4}k_t^{-1/2}(1 - k_{t+1})^{-1/2} & -\tfrac{1}{4}k_t^{1/2}(1 - k_{t+1})^{-3/2} \end{bmatrix}$$

and $\det(D^2V) = 0$, and A.7 is not met.

The reader should notice that although our insensitivity result relates to the discount parameter, the same method can be used for arbitrary perturbations. This may prove useful in other contexts.

REFERENCES

1. C. BERGE, "Topological Spaces," Oliver and Boyd, Edinburgh, 1963.
2. W. BROCK, "Some Results on the Uniqueness of Steady States in Multi-sector Models of Optimal Growth When Future Utilities are Discounted," unpublished manuscript, University of Chicago, 1973.
3. D. GALE, On optimal development in a multi-sector economy, *Rev. Econ. Stud.* **34** (1967).
4. M. HIRSH AND C. PUGH, Stable manifolds and hyperbolic sets, *in* "Global Analysis" (S. Chern and S. Smale, Eds.), Proceedings of Symposia in Pure Mathematics, Vol. XIV, Amer. Math. Soc., Providence, Rhode Island, 1970.

5. K. HOFFMAN AND R. KUNZE, "Linear Algebra," Prentice Hall, Englewood Cliffs, N.J., 1961.
6. M. KURZ, Optimal economic growth and wealth effects, *Int. Econ. Rev.* **9** (1968).
7. S. LANG, "Analysis I," Addison Wesley, Reading, 1968.
8. D. LEVHARI AND N. LEVIATAN, On stability in the saddle point sense, *J. Econ. Theory* **4** (1972).
9. O. L. MANGASARIAN, Sufficient conditions for the optimal control of nonlinear systems, *J. SIAM Control* **4**, No. 1 (1966).
10. L. W. McKENZIE, The Dorfman–Samuelson–Solow turnpike theorem, *Int. Econ. Rev.* **4** (1963).
11. L. W. McKENZIE, Accumulation programs of maximum utility and the von Newmann facet, *in* "Value Capital and Growth, Papers in Honour of Sir John Hicks" (Wolfe, Ed.), Edinburgh Univ. Press, Edinburgh, 1968.
12. R. RADNER, Paths of economic growth that are optimal with regard only to final states, *Rev. Econ. Stud.* **28** (1961).
13. J. A. SCHEINKMAN, "On Optimal Steady States of *n*-Sector Growth Models When Utility is Discounted," Ph.D. dissertation, University of Rochester, 1973. Center for Mathematical Studies in Business and Economics, Report #7357, University of Chicago, Chicago (1973).
14. P. A. SAMUELSON, Reciprocal characteristic root property of discrete maxima, *Western Econ. J.* **6** (1968).
15. P. A. SAMUELSON, Optimality of profit, including prices under ideal planning, *Proc. Nat. Acad. Sci. U.S.A.* **70**, 2109–2111 (1973).
16. P. A. SAMUELSON, The general saddle-point property of optimal control motions, *J. Econ. Theory* **5** (1972).
17. P. A. SAMUELSON AND R. M. SOLOW, A complete capital model involving heterogeneous capital goods, *Quart. J. Econ.* **70** (1956).
18. W. R. S. SUTHERLAND, "On Optimal Development When Utility is Discounted," unpublished doctoral dissertation, Brown University, 1967.

ESSAY III

The Structure and Stability of Competitive Dynamical Systems

DAVID CASS AND KARL SHELL

1. INTRODUCTION AND SUMMARY

The theory of economic growth has itself developed at an enormous rate over the past twenty years. A careful reading of the major work in this extensive literature[1] leaves one quite definite impression: The analysis of the long-run behavior of idealized economies has been very uneven. On the one hand, quite general results are available concerning the theory of maximal growth, broadly defined to include the problem of production-maximal growth, as well as the closely related problem of consumption-optimal growth with zero (net) discounting. On the other hand, only a few simple examples and special cases have been examined in the theory of optimal growth with positive discounting, or of descriptive growth with linear saving–investment hypotheses.

In this paper we provide a general framework which encompasses these as well as many other problems in the theory of economic growth, or more broadly, the theory of economic dynamics. Our approach is to describe competitive dynamics as Hamiltonian dynamics, where the Hamiltonian can be written as a function of *present* output prices and current input stocks, and can be interpreted as the present value of net national product (equal, by duality, to the present value of net national income). Such a Hamiltonian dynamical system is competitive in the sense that it derives from the perfect-foresight, zero-profit, asset-market clearing equations

---

[1] Our references contain a large sample of the basic work concerned with global stability in economic growth, ranging from the early work on the "turnpike" theorem (e.g., [9, 18, 20, 23]), through the continuing work on optimal growth (e.g., [2, 11, 19, 24] for zero discounting, and [5, 15, 28, 35] for positive discounting) and on descriptive growth (e.g., [14, 32, 34, 36]), to the recent work on the "Hahn problem" (e.g., [4, 8, 12, 33]). We have not attempted to include systematic references to closely related topics, for example, local stability analysis.

arising in descriptive growth theory, and is consistent with (i) efficiency pricing conditions developed in the Malinvaud [17] tradition, and (ii) Euler's conditions or, more generally, Pontryagin's maximum principle (in either their usual continuous-time or their analogous discrete-time formulations), applying to production-maximal or consumption-optimal growth problems.

The problems we are interested in naturally lead to cases in which the Hamiltonian function is convex in present prices (the costate variables) and concave in current stocks (the state variables). Indeed, every convex technology is essentially characterized by such a convex–concave Hamiltonian function, and every convex–concave Hamiltonian function essentially represents a unique convex technology (see, for instance, the companion analysis of Lau [16], and related exposition of Cass [7]). Since our analysis originates in this duality, it is not surprising that we find the geometry of the Hamiltonian function to be the fundamental determinant of the long-run behavior of a competitive dynamical system.

It is customary and convenient in studying the dynamics of optimal growth to cast the analysis in terms of *current* output prices rather than present output prices. In the case with zero discounting, a (golden rule path) stationary point is also a saddlepoint of the current value Hamiltonian function. Thus, a simple assumption which insures uniqueness of the stationary input stocks is that the Hamiltonian be strictly concave in current input stocks. This strict concavity condition is unnecessarily strong. An assumption of "real Hamiltonian steepness" at the stationary point suffices to insure uniqueness. Moreover, a uniform strengthening of this steepness condition also allows us to establish convergence of the optimal path to the stationary input stocks. This stability analysis for consumption-optimal growth with zero discounting can be easily extended to apply to the case of production-maximal growth. In the latter case, our strengthened assumption of "real Hamiltonian steepness" at the von Neumann ray insures convergence to that ray, and is equivalent to Radner's assumption of bounded value-loss.

For optimal growth with constant, positive discounting, a (modified golden rule path) stationary point is not a saddlepoint of the Hamiltonian function. Nevertheless, when our strengthened "real Hamiltonian steepness" condition is modified by a term which depends on the discount rate, we again establish uniqueness of and convergence to the stationary input stocks. Furthermore, even when the discount rate is only asymptotically constant, some additional tightening of this modified steepness condition still permits us to establish global stability.

Our steepness conditions lead very naturally to a particular choice of Lyapunov function for the stability arguments. This particular function has been used previously by Samuelson [29] and Rockafellar [25] in analyzing the stability of consumption-optimal growth with zero discounting (and, under a liberal interpretation, by Radner [23] in analyzing the stability of production-maximal growth). Our extension of these earlier results provides both a coherent unification of the maximal growth models, as well as a powerful justification for our Hamiltonian approach to the analysis of competitive dynamical systems.

In the area of descriptive growth, the analysis of dynamical behavior has typically been limited to studying fairly specific examples. From our present perspective, the fundamental difficulty in obtaining definite results for more general models seems quite evident: Since the interest rate implicitly depends on the whole evolution of prices and quantities, there is no direct analog to our "real Hamiltonian steepness" conditions. Nonetheless, by exploiting the particular structure of descriptive growth under the Marxian saving–investment hypothesis, we are able to establish a broad class of circumstances in which similar conditions entail global stability. Thus, our Hamiltonian approach yields one of the first reasonably general results on the long-run performance of a decentralized, capital accumulation process. Extensions of this approach to cover a wider range of descriptive growth models appears to us an important and promising prospect.

We believe that our Hamiltonian approach has many further possibilities for application. In particular, even without complete convexity in the underlying model, the solutions to many other interesting optimal control problems must exhibit Hamiltonian dynamics of the sort we analyze in this paper, i.e., must obey dynamical laws derived from a convex–concave Hamiltonian function. Thus, for example, our results are immediately applicable to a fairly general version of the neoclassical investment model. On a broader tack, we also believe that our duality emphasis may be quite useful in investigating the various existence problems which are deliberately sidestepped in the present paper. For instance, the existence of solutions to the particular differential equations (or differential correspondences) we define as representing optimal growth would follow from a duality theorem for concave programming in some appropriate infinite-dimensional space. More speculatively, we think it may be possible to derive the solutions to particular descriptive growth models in a similar manner.

In either case, this casual conjecturing remains to be verified by further research, part of which we ourselves plan to undertake in the near future.

The extended Cambridge-versus-Cambridge debate has taught us that insights based on the aggregate production function are of only limited value for unifying models of heterogeneous capital accumulation. It is our hope that our Hamiltonian approach will, at least to some extent, provide the unifying principle that Cambridge, Massachusetts has been seeking.

2. The General Model

A. *Technology and Market*

Let

consumption-goods output (or sometimes "utility output") = $(c_1, ..., c_\mu) = c$,
net investment-goods output = $(z_1, ..., z_\nu) = z$,
capital stocks = $(k_1, ..., k_\nu) = k$,
primary factors = $(l_1, ..., l_\varepsilon) = l$, and
technology = $T \subset \{(c, z, -k, -l): (c, k, l) \geqslant 0\}$.

While the general tenor of our maintained assumptions about technology is quite conventional, there is some special structure which is either necessary or useful for accomplishing our specific goal of establishing global stability. Thus, while listing our maintained assumptions we also mix in comments about what purposes they serve (and what alternative assumptions would suffice).

Assumption (T1). Feasibility of nonnegative inputs. If $(k, l) \geqslant 0$, then there exists (c, z) such that $(c, z, -k, -l) \in T$.

This assumption simply states that, given a sign convention for measuring inputs, any input combination can be used. In conjunction with assumption (T8) below, it allows restriction of the Hamiltonian function to a simple domain of definition, the nonnegative orthant. This is merely convenient, and so (T1) could be replaced by a weaker regularity requirement concerning the projection of T onto the input space, for example, that this projection be closed.

Assumption (T2). Feasibility of boundary production. T is closed.

This assumption is a standard regularity requirement. Since so much of our analysis depends on it, directly or indirectly, it is difficult for us to see how it could be dispensed with.

Assumption (T3). Diminishing returns in production. T is convex.

While this assumption too is a standard regularity requirement, it is not indispensable. For instance, even with increasing returns to capital stock inputs, if production possibility sets are convex, then the technology is representable by a Hamiltonian function, and furthermore, an optimal growth path is describable by a Hamiltonian dynamical system. (The last requires some additional regularity to replace convexity; such regularity is implicitly assumed, for example, when the technology is specified in terms of industry or sectoral production functions together with input stock adding-up constraints.) Though we will not put much stress on this aspect of our analysis, the potential for handling such phenomena as increasing returns is a substantial reason for devoting serious attention to Hamiltonian dynamics, as well as an important area in the future development of economic dynamics.

ASSUMPTION (T4). Productivity of the technology. There exists $(c, z, -k, -l) \in T$ such that $(c, z) > 0$.

This assumption introduces the potential for balanced growth, since it means that, with appropriate endowments of initial capital stocks and primary factors, capital stocks can be maintained forever. While such an assumption is a common feature of most growth models, it is not at all innocuous, because it completely rules out the phenomenon of depletable resources. However, developing a general theory of the behavior of prescriptive or descriptive growth models when there are depletable resources is a major task in itself, and not one we even attempt here.

ASSUMPTION (T5). Constant returns to scale. T is a cone.

This assumption is primarily a convenience for expositing our Hamiltonian approach, since, when actual technological processes exhibit diminishing returns to scale, it is tantamount to introducing a fictitious input which "earns" residual income or accounting profit. In other words, because any set can be conceived as the projection of a cross-section of a cone in one higher dimension, there is absolutely no loss of generality in conducting analysis, when it is useful, in terms of such a cone plus its restriction. Of course some care must be taken in providing economic interpretation of this maneuver (partly amplified by the discussion in [6, pp. 273–76]). Thus, in particular, the reader should beware of a literal reading of our treatment of the optimal growth model; in our specification of that model, the "primary factor" typically summarizes both the influence of exogenous factor availability, as well as the influence of diminishing marginal utility.

ASSUMPTION (T6). Necessity of primary factors: If $(c, z, -k, -l) \in T$ and $l = 0$, then $c = 0$ and $z_i \{\leq\} 0$ according as $k_i \{\geq\} 0$ for $i = 1, 2, ..., v$.

This assumption parallels the no-free-lunch postulate of general equilibrium analysis, but is stronger, since it requires that gross outputs be zero when primary factor inputs are zero, even when some capital stock inputs are positive. The importance of the assumption is that, in conjunction with other of our assumptions, notably (T2), (T5) and (T7), it implies that too large capital stocks simply cannot be maintained over time. Because we also assume a bounded rate of depreciation (see (T7) immediately below), this upper bound on feasible capital stocks also provides an absolute bound on feasible produced outputs.[2] We will have need to refer to these implied restrictions later on in our analysis, and so at this point we somewhat prematurely formalize them in the following proposition (which implicitly appeals to both our maintained assumptions about technology and our special assumptions about exogenous factor availability; see (A1) and (A3) further below).

BOUNDEDNESS LEMMA. There is a finite bound $B < \infty$ such that every production point $(c, z, -k, -l) \in T$ which is replicable or feasible satisfies the boundedness restriction

$$\|(c, z, k)\| < B. \tag{B}$$

By way of further interpretation, it is interesting to observe that assumptions (T4) and (T6) play a role in our model analogous to that of the Inada conditions in the standard one-good model, and are crucial, for instance, in establishing the existence of stationary points which exhibit intertemporal consumption efficiency (modified golden rule paths).

ASSUMPTION (T7). Bounded rates of depreciation. There exists

$$\Lambda = \begin{bmatrix} \lambda_1 & & & 0 \\ & \cdot & & \\ & & \cdot & \\ & & & \cdot \\ 0 & & & \lambda_\nu \end{bmatrix}$$

[2] These assertions obviously presuppose that primary factors are scarce, that is, are available in limited amounts. Their proof is relatively straightforward if we restrict attention to production points $(c, z, -k, -l) \in T$ which (i) employ a unit level of primary factors $\|l\| = 1$, and (ii) yield nonnegative investment goods output $z \geq 0$, or which are *replicable*. In this special case, the standard argument based on assumptions (T2), (T5), and (T6) establishes that the set

$$\{(c, z, k): (c, z, -k, -l) \in T, z \geq 0 \text{ and } \|l\| = 1\}$$

is bounded. When we turn attention to production points which might be observed along a path achievable from given, finite initial capital stocks and primary factors, or, which are *feasible*, their proof is of explicitly dynamical character, as well as of significantly more complexity. The useful paper by Peleg and Ryder [22] contains a complete discussion for a particular discrete-time model. The related argument applying to our continuous- and discrete-time models is similar, though not identical.

with $\lambda_i \in (0, \infty)$ (continuous time) or $\lambda_i \in (0, 1]$ (discrete time) for $i = 1, 2, ..., \nu$ such that if $(c, z, -k, -l) \in T$, then $-\Lambda k \leq z$, and

ASSUMPTION (T8). *Free disposal in allocation.* If $(c, z, -k, -l) \in T$, $(c', z' + \Lambda(k' - k), -k', -l') \leq (c, z, -k, -l)$ and $(c', z') \geq (0, -\Lambda k')$, then $(c', z', -k', -l') \in T$.

Assumptions (T7) and (T8), taken together, are nothing more than an alternative statement of the standard assumptions of depreciation at constant (relative) rates plus free disposal of (gross) output and input. While there are several implications of these assumptions which are imporant for our analysis, here we will only emphasize one, that having to do with characterizing intertemporal consumption (or, more generally, net output) efficiency. Namely, (T8) (which only makes sense in light of (T7)) entails that output, both consumption-goods *and* investment-goods, must have associated nonnegative efficiency prices. (The reason for this is basically that (T8) means that having more capital stocks today does not require having less capital stocks, and, hence, less consumption-goods output, tomorrow.) This implication provides the rationale underlying our introduction of unlimited free disposal of output in the definition of the market M below, and is especially important in justifying our particular description of optimal growth as necessarily involving asymptotically zero or finite present value of capital stocks. While it seems likely that our results can be generalized to require somewhat less special structure than is imposed by (T7) and (T8) (for example, this is suggested by Rockafellar's [26] local analysis), the complete details of such extension remain to be seen.

Corresponding to the various commodities and the technology, define

output prices $= (p_1, ..., p_\mu, q_1, ..., q_\nu) = (p, q)$,
input rents $= (r_1, ..., r_\nu, w_1, ..., w_\xi) = (r, w)$, and
market $= M \subset \{(p, q, r, w): (p, q, w) \geq 0\}$.

M is dually related to T by

$$M = \{(p, q, r, w): pc' + qz' - rk - wl \leq 0$$
$$\text{for all} \quad (c', z') \leq (c, z), (c, z, -k, -l) \in T\}, \quad (1)$$

and, as noted above, contains all the price configurations which might appear in any snapshot of a competitive dynamical system. Even without assumptions (T1)–(T8), M is a closed convex cone having the additional properties of nonnegativity of output prices, if $(p, q, r, w) \in M$, then $(p, q) \geq 0$, and free disposal in valuation, if $(p, q, r, w) \in M$, $(p', -r', -w') \leq (p, -r, -w)$ and $p' \geq 0$, then $(p', q', -r', -w') \in M$.

B. *Accumulation and Growth*

Initial capital stocks and primary factors are given exogenously. Hence, letting bars denote this fact, all feasible paths of real variables must satisfy, in continuous time, $t \in [0, \infty)$,

$$(c(t), z(t), -k(t), -l(t)) \in T, \; \dot{k}(t) = z(t), \quad k(0) = \bar{k} \text{ and } l(t) = \bar{l}(t), \quad (2)$$

or, in discrete time, $t = 0, 1, ...,$

$$(c_t, z_t, -k_t, -l_t) \in T, \; k_{t+1} = k_t + z_t, \quad k_0 = \bar{k} \text{ and } l_t = \bar{l}_t . \quad (2')$$

In (2) it is understood that, for example, $\{z_i(t): 0 \leqslant t < \infty\}$ is summable, or $\{k_i(t): k_i(t) = k_i(0) + \int_0^t z_i(s) \, ds \text{ and } 0 \leqslant t < \infty\}$ is absolutely continuous on any finite interval $0 \leqslant t \leqslant t' < \infty$; a similar remark will apply to the corresponding price variables.

C. *Intertemporal Profit Maximization*

Parallel with (2) or (2'), all "feasible" paths of price variables must satisfy

$$(p(t), q(t), r(t), w(t)) \in M, \quad \dot{q}(t) = -r(t) \text{ and } q(0) \geqslant 0, \quad (3)$$

or

$$(p_t, q_t, r_t, w_t) \in M, \quad q_{t+1} = q_t - r_{t+1} \text{ and } q_{-1} \geqslant 0.[3] \quad (3')$$

We define paths satisfying, or solutions to (2) and (3) or (2') and (3'), to be a *competitive dynamical system*, provided, in addition, prices are nontrivial, for some t $(p(t), q(t), r(t), w(t)) \neq 0$ or $(p_t, q_t, r_t, w_t) \neq 0,[4]$ and there is static profit maximization,

$$p(t) \, c(t) + q(t) \, z(t) - r(t) \, k(t) - w(t) \, l(t) = 0, \quad (4)$$

---

[3] We note in passing that the notion of dual instability, prominent in the early literature concerning dynamic Leontief models, seems nothing more than a special case of the observation that (3) or (3') can be essentially converted into (2) or (2') by reversing the flow of time (e.g., considering $t \in [0, -\infty)$) and (ii) adding appropriate exogenous constraints (e.g., fixing $q(0) = \bar{q}$, $p(t) = \bar{p}(t)$).

It is worth stressing explicitly that, unlike feasible paths of real variables, "feasible" paths of price variables, that is, all paths affording at best zero profit opportunities, are not subject to exogenous constraints other than nonnegativity of initial investment goods prices (and this too is actually superfluous in the case of continuous time, given our particular definition of M).

[4] Paths of price variables which are identically zero are of little interest in either prescriptive or descriptive growth theory. In fact, the same is true of paths which are identically zero after some point in time; competitive dynamical systems with such prices correspond to finite-lived economics.

or

$$p_t c_t + q_t z_t - r_t k_t - w_t l_t = 0. \tag{4'}$$

Given the definition of M in (1), Eqs. (3)–(4) or (3')–(4') are nothing but the well-known perfect foresight, intertemporal profit maximization conditions.

D. *The Hamiltonian Representation*

Static profit maximization (at nonnegative output prices $(p, q) \geqslant 0$),

$$(c, z, -k, -l) \in T,$$

and

$$pc' + qz' - rk' - wl' \leqslant pc + qz - rk - wl = 0$$
$$\text{for all} \quad (c', z', -k', -l') \in T, \tag{5}$$

is equivalent to the conditions that $(c, z, -k, -l)$ is an optimal solution to the concave programming program,

$$\text{maximize } pc' + qz' \quad \text{subject to} \quad (c', z', -k, -l) \in T. \tag{NNP}$$

(p, q, r, w) is an optimal solution to the (dual) convex programming problem,

$$\text{minimize } r'k + w'l \quad \text{subject to} \quad (p, q, r', w') \in M, \tag{NNI}$$

and the values of NNP ($\equiv$ Net National Product) and NNI ($\equiv$ Net National Income) are equal,

$$\begin{aligned}
\text{value of NNP} &= pc + qz \\
&= \text{value of NNI} \\
&= rk + wl.
\end{aligned} \tag{6}$$

This equivalence suggests the potential usefulness of defining the *Hamiltonian function*

$$H(p, q, k, l) = \text{value of NNP}. \tag{7}$$

It is fairly straightforward to establish that H exhibits the following fundamental properties.

Property (H1). H is defined on the nonnegative orthant $\{(p, q, k, l): (p, q, k, l) \geqslant 0\}$.[5]

Property (H2). H is continuous in (p, q, k, l).

[5] Note that, though T is not compact, from assumptions (T2), (T6), and (T7), a cross-section like $\{(c', z', -k', -l'): (c', z', -k', -l') \in T \text{ and } (k', l') = (k, l)\}$ is compact. The parallel definition of H in terms of the value of NNI may run into difficulty when (k, l) is on the boundary of the projection of the technology set on the input space, i.e., when $(k, l) \not> 0$; see Footnote 7 below.

Property (H3).   *H* is nondecreasing in p and l.

Property (H4).   *H* is convex and linear homogeneous in (p, q), and concave and linear homogeneous in (k, l).

And, most important,

Property (H5). $\partial H(p, q, k, l)/\partial(p, q) = (c, z)$,[6] and, at least for $(k, l) > 0$,[7] $\partial H(p, q, k, l)/\partial(k, l) = (r, w)$.

Thus, the generalized gradients of *H* with respect to (p, q) are static profit-maximizing outputs (and conversely), while, for all practical purposes, the generalized gradients of *H* with respect to (k, l) are competitive input rents (and conversely).

Properties (H1)–(H5) follow directly from assumptions (T1)–(T7): Roughly speaking, for the purpose of analyzing static competitive or efficient allocation, every well-behaved technology set can be fully represented by a well-behaved Hamiltonian function.[8] Furthermore, given *H*, one can reconstruct *T* (if there is unlimited free disposal of output), or at least the critical "northeast" boundary of *T* (if there is not), completely.

---

[6] Here and after we use $\partial f(x, y)/\partial x$ to denote some (perhaps particular) or all generalized gradients of $f(x, y)$ with respect to x; e.g., when, for given y, the function $f(x, y)$ and its domain $D_x(y)$ are convex in x, some or all vectors $\partial f(x, y)/\partial x$ such that

$$f(x', y) - f(x, y) \geqslant (x' - x)\frac{\partial f(x, y)}{\partial x} \qquad \text{for all} \quad x' \in D_x(y).$$

[7] Some version of "constraint qualification"—here we use Slater's condition, the obvious choice for our problem—is required to insure that, in addition to (7),

$$H(p, q, k, l) = \text{value of NNI}.$$

(See the extended discussion of this point in [6, pp. 277–79]. We should emphasize that for the applications in this paper, whenever (5) obtains, (6) does also, so that by presumption boundary points present no difficulty (i.e., hypothesizing a solution to (2)–(4) or (2′)–(4′) already entails $\partial H(p, q, k, l)/\partial(k, l) = (r, w)$ without qualification).

[8] It is worth at least remarking on the relative merits of our Hamiltonian function representation vis-a-vis the more common production transformation representation, say, $F(c, z, k, l) = 0$, where *F* is defined implicitly by the "northeast" boundary of *T*. In general, the former has a distinct advantage over the latter: The domain of *H* is the fairly simple Cartesian product $\{(p, q): (p, q) \geqslant 0\} \times \{(k, l): (c, z, -k, -l) \in T\}$, while the domain of *F* is the more complicated boundary set $\{(c, z, k, l):(c, z, -k, -l) \in T$ and (c, z) is maximal in $\{(c', z'): (c', z', -k, -l) \in T\}\}$. In other words, in order to use *H*, one only needs to know all feasible input combinations, while in order to use *F*, one also needs to know all maximal output combinations, in effect, *T* itself. To our minds, this is a dominating superiority in most contexts where some functional representation of *T* is required.

This near equivalence between the T and H representations of convex[9] technologies is, as mentioned earlier, precisely stated and fully investigated in [7, 16].

For our objective here, it is more natural to represent the technology in terms of H rather than T. In particular, the equivalence between (5) and (6) together with the properties (H1)–(H5) mean that we can very succinctly rewrite the competitive dynamical system (2)–(4) or (2′)–(4′) as the *Hamiltonian dynamical system*

$$\begin{cases} \dot{k}(t) = \dfrac{\partial H(p(t), q(t), k(t), \bar{l}(t))}{\partial q}, & k(0) = \bar{k}, \\[2ex] \dot{q}(t) = -\dfrac{\partial H(p(t), q(t), k(t), \bar{l}(t))}{\partial k}, & q(0) \geqslant 0, \end{cases} \tag{8}$$

or

$$\begin{cases} k_{t+1} = k_t + \dfrac{\partial H(p_t, q_t, k_t, \bar{l}_t)}{\partial q}, & k_0 = \bar{k}, \\[2ex] q_{t+1} = q_t - \dfrac{\partial H(p_{t+1}, q_{t+1}, k_{t+1}, \bar{l}_{t+1})}{\partial k}, & q_{-1} \geqslant 0. \end{cases} \tag{8′}$$

The most striking feature of this formulation is its suggestion that *it is properties of the technology set as reflected in properties of the Hamiltonian function which are basic to the stability analysis of competitive dynamical systems*. This suggestion is amply borne out in the sequel. The representation (8) or (8′) just as obviously provides *a very convenient framework for constructing examples of competitive dynamical systems*, as we shall also clearly illustrate in the succeeding analysis.

E. *Simplifying Assumptions*

We now make some special assumptions in order to simplify the analysis that follows.

ASSUMPTION (A1). There is a single primary factor, $\xi = 1$, and it is unchanging in amount, $l(t) = \bar{l}(t) = 1$ or $l_t = \bar{l}_t = 1$, say. This assumption is made so that we can sensibly talk about stationary points. An essentially equivalent assumption would be that, however many, all primary factors grow asymptotically at the same constant rate (the "natural" growth rate).

---

[9] Since an output price system "convexifies" just the production possibility sets derived from a nonconvex technology, in that case one can only recover the union of the convex hulls of cross sections of the representation T, or its "northeast" boundary, from the representation H.

ASSUMPTION (A2). There is a single consumption good, $\mu = 1$. Since we can interpret output of this good as instantaneous utility, we are able to analyze most consumption-optimal growth problems treated in the literature. Here the single final utility output might be "produced" from a multi-dimensional vector of "intermediate" consumption-goods output.[10]

For descriptive growth theory, the assumption of a single consumption good is more restrictive, but we feel that inclusion of the general case would needlessly complicate out present analysis. Alternatively, we can simply duck this issue by postulating the existence of a sufficiently well-behaved consumption aggregate.

ASSUMPTION (A3). The initial endowment of each capital good is positive and finite $0 < \bar{k} < \infty$.

This assumption together with (T6) guarantees the existence of positive capital stocks for all time, $k(t) > 0$ or $k_t > 0$, a fact we use indirectly in analyzing optimal growth, directly in analyzing descriptive growth.

F. *Saving–Investment Behavior*

To close the Hamiltonian dynamical system, (8) or (8′), requires at a minimum, specification of initial prices of capital stocks, $q(0) = \bar{q}$ or $q_{-1} = \bar{q}$, and of dated prices of consumption-goods output, $p(t) = \bar{p}(t)$ or $p_t = \bar{p}_t$.

This may be accomplished directly or indirectly, depending on the particular problem under scrutiny. Consider, for example, the problem of optimal growth with constant, positive discounting. The maximand is

$$\int_0^\infty e^{-\rho t} c(t)\, dt, \tag{9}$$

or

$$\sum_{t=0}^\infty (1 + \rho)^{-t}\, c_t, \tag{9′}$$

where $c(t)$ or c_t is interpreted as utility output and ρ its associated time

---

[10] Even though T is assumed to be a cone, we could allow for diminishing returns in transforming "intermediate" consumption-goods output into the final utility output. Again, this follows from the fact that any convex set can be described as the projection of a cross-section of a convex cone of one higher dimension. In this situation, however, the interpretation of the fictitious input required for marginal productivity factor payment exhaustion of product is somewhat fanciful.

discount rate, the utility or "real" interest rate. Maximization of (9) or (9')
is constrained by technology and endowments (2) or (2'). For a feasible
path to be optimal, it must be efficient. Thus, it is required that there exist
nonnegative imputed prices, $(p(t), q(t)) \geqslant 0$ for all t or $(p_t, q_{t-1}) \geqslant 0$ for
all t, such that the laws of motion, (8) or (8'), hold along an optimal path.
But since, on an optimal path, the utility interest rate is assumed equal to
ρ, it is also required that the price of utility output be declining at this
rate, that is, that

$$-\frac{\dot{p}(t)}{p(t)} = \rho, \tag{10}$$

or

$$-\frac{(p_t - p_{t-1})}{p_t} = \rho. \tag{10'}$$

If we now choose initial utility as the numeraire commodity, $p(0) = 1$ or
$p_0 = 1$, then (10) or (10') becomes, in closed form,

$$p(t) = e^{-\rho t}, \tag{11}$$

or

$$p_t = (1 + \rho)^{-t}. \tag{11'}$$

Hence, for this problem, on the one hand, the dated prices of utility
output are directly specified, by the hypothesis of a constant utility rate of
interest, and the choice of initial utility as the numeraire commodity. On
the other hand, the initial prices of capital stocks (and thereby saving–
investment behavior) are only indirectly specified, by means of a so-called
transversality condition,

$$\lim_{t \to \infty} q(t) k(t) = 0 \quad \text{for} \quad \rho > 0, \tag{12}$$

or

$$\lim_{t \to \infty} q_t k_{t+1} = 0 \quad \text{for} \quad \rho > 0. \tag{12'}$$

In other words, it is finally required that on an optimal path, the present
value of the capital stocks tends to zero. Such a transversality condition has
been shown to be necessary for optimality in the discrete-time case; see
[21, 22, 37]. Under what circumstances it is also necessary for optimality in
the continuous-time case is at present an open question. In either case it
is clear that, in conjunction with perfect foresight, intertemporal profit
maximization (given dated prices of utility output), the transversality
condition amounts to a duality theorem for concave programming in some

appropriate infinite-dimensional space.[11] We plan in future research to investigate the necessity of the transversality condition in the continuous-time case by exploiting this duality characterization.

Formulation of the problem of optimal growth with zero discounting is much subtler, because for $\rho = 0$ no constrained maximum to (9) or (9') will exist. If the maximand is changed to

$$\int_0^\infty [c(t) - c^*] \, dt, \tag{13}$$

or

$$\sum_{t=0}^\infty (c_t - c^*), \tag{13'}$$

where c^* is golden rule utility output, then a maximum may exist. As before, the laws of motion for the optimal path are given by (8) or (8') and (11) or (11'). But now, the transversality condition, (12) or (12'), is no longer suitable. The condition appropriate to the maximand (13) or (13') (again based on duality considerations) is instead

$$\lim_{t \to \infty} q(t) \, k(t) = Q^* k^*, \tag{14}$$

or

$$\lim_{t \to \infty} q_t k_{t+1} = Q^* k^*, \tag{14'}$$

---

[11] Namely, that maximizing (9) or (9') subject to (2) or (2') yields the same value as minimizing

$$\int_0^\infty w(t)\bar{l}(t)dt + q(0)\bar{k} \quad \text{or} \quad \sum_{t=0}^\infty w_t \bar{l}_t + q_{-1}\bar{k}$$

subject to (3) or (3') plus the constraint (11) or (11'). That the two statements are equivalent is easily seen from analyzing the "feasible" behavior of

$$\int_0^T e^{-\rho t} c(t)dt + q(T)k(T) - \int_0^T w(t)\bar{l}(t)dt,$$

or

$$\sum_{t=0}^{T-1} (1 + \rho)^{-t}c_t + q_{T-1}k_T - \sum_{t=0}^{T-1} w_t \bar{l}_t, \quad \text{for} \quad T \geqslant 0.$$

Obviously, this particular duality theorem is only a special case of a general duality theorem involving arbitrary, exogenous specification of the weights attached to final output (e.g., terminal capital stocks as well as intermediate utility output).

In this connection, it should also be mentioned that our simplifying assumptions (A1) and (A3) play a role in this particular duality theorem similar to that of Slater's condition in the more familiar duality theorem for concave programming in Euclidean n-dimensional space, and can be weakened accordingly.

where $k*$ are the golden rule capital stocks, and $Q*$ the current investment goods prices (in terms of utility output) which support their maintenance.

As has been recognized for some time, the consumption-optimal growth with zero discounting and production-maximal growth models are very closely related, the differences being mainly in interpretation.[12] From our viewpoint, what is crucial is that both models yield canonical Hamiltonian dynamical systems, i.e., dynamical systems which are completely specified in terms of a time-autonomous Hamiltonian function. We have already seen that this is the case for consumption-optimal growth with zero discounting, since when $\rho = 0$, (11) or (11') yields $p(t) = 1$ or $p_t = 1$, while by assumption $\bar{l}(t) = 1$ or $\bar{l}_t = 1$. For production-maximal growth such time-autonomy derives from the assumptions that there is no consumption goods output and that there is no primary factor constraint, which in our technological framework can be explicitly characterized by $c(t) = 0$ or $c_t = 0$, or better yet, what amounts to the same thing (because of free disposal in allocation (T8) or property (H3)),

$$p(t) = 0, \tag{15}$$

or

$$p_t = 0, \tag{15'}$$

and $\bar{l}(t) = \infty$ or $\bar{l}_t = \infty$. It is interesting to observe that (15) or (15') already entails something like a transversality condition, since from (8) or (8') we now have (here appealing to constant returns to scale (T5) or property (H3))

$$q(t)\, k(t) = q(0)\, \bar{k}, \tag{16}$$

or

$$q_t k_t = q_{-1}\bar{k}. \tag{16'}$$

And, indeed, it does turn out that, in effect, the production-maximal growth model is closed merely by postulating (15) or (15'), at least from the perspective of the type of stability analysis we will present (see our Sections 3C and 3D, below).

An alternative method of relating these two models is simply to convert consumption-optimal growth into production-maximal growth. This can be accomplished by treating both cumulated utility output and primary factor input (the latter conceived as a stock yielding service flows) as produced stocks, an approach nicely elaborated by several authors,

---

[12] We have in mind here the infinite horizon version of the production-maximal growth model, as analyzed, for instance, by Furuya and Inada [10]. Also, our assumptions about technology would have to be modified somewhat in order to be consistent with the discussion below. In particular, capital stock inputs must be limitational for the production-maximal growth model to make any sense.

notably Atsumi [1] and McKenzie [19]. Of course, the resulting model has some characteristics peculiar to itself, that is, that are not commonly found in the standard production-maximal growth models, and thus requires some analysis peculiar to itself.

We will not pursue either line of inquiry involving production-maximal growth models in the present paper, mainly because these models have been so extensively treated in the literature already, but also because the requisite modification of our global stability analysis for optimal growth models is fairly obvious.

Saving–investment constraints like (11) and (12), (11) and (14), and (15) or (11′) and (12′), (11′) and (14′), and (15′) do in fact close the Hamiltonian dynamical system, (8) or (8′), in the following sense: The set of initial prices of capital stocks for which there exists a path satisfying both the Hamiltonian dynamical system and the saving–investment constraints is severely restricted.[13] While this restriction is only indirect, it turns out, as we shall show in Section 3, sufficiently well-specified to render the stability analysis of the optimal (and maximal) growth models in terms of our Hamiltonian formalism almost trivial, basically because of the simple form taken by the utility output prices, (11) or (11′) (and (15) or (15′)).[14]

In descriptive growth theory the Hamiltonian dynamical system,[15] (8) or (8′), is typically closed by appending an instantaneous saving–investment relation of the general form

$$S\left(p(t), -\frac{\dot{p}(t)}{p(t)}, q(t), k(t), \bar{l}(t)\right) = 0, \tag{17}$$

or

$$S\left(p_t, -\frac{p_t - p_{t-1}}{p_t}, q_t, k_t, \bar{l}_t\right) = 0. \tag{17′}$$

[13] Regarding optimal growth, the severest restriction occurs when, for instance, T is endowed with sufficient additional structure so that M exhibits the following properties: (i) if $(1, q, r, w) \in M$, then $w > 0$, and (ii) if $(1, q^i, r^i, w^i) \in M$ for $i = 1, 2$ are distinct, then $c + [\lambda q^1 + (1 - \lambda)q^2]z - [\lambda r^1 + (1 - \lambda)r^2]k - [\lambda w^1 + (1 - \lambda)w^2] < 0$ for all $0 < \lambda < 1$, $(c, z, -k, -1) \in T$. Then the initial prices of capital stocks are unique. Less onerous additional structure will also suffice for this result.

[14] What renders the analysis so simple is not so much the fact that the interest rate, $-\dot{p}(t)/p(t)$ or $-(p_t - p_{t-1})/p_t$, is constant, as the fact that it is exogenous, that is, is determined independently of output prices and input stocks, $(p(t), q(t), k(t), l(t))$ or (p_t, q_t, k_t, l_t). Indeed, at the end of Section 3 we describe how our results are easily modified to cover the case where the interest rate is only asymptotically constant, though still exogenous.

[15] That competitive dynamical systems can be explicitly represented as Hamiltonian dynamical systems has been more or less commonly recognized among capital theorists for a number of years, especially in relation to prescriptive growth theory. Hahn's fairly specialized version of this fact [13] is the only published use of such representation in descriptive growth theory of which we are aware, though there may well be others.

For global stability analysis, the most critical feature of (17) or (17′) is that the interest rate, $-(\dot{p}(t)/p(t))$ or $-(p_t - p_{t-1})/p_t$, is endogenous, and, hence, varies with the evolution of the economy. A familiar example of such a saving–investment relation is the "Keynesian" hypothesis,

$$q(t)\,z(t) = s[r(t)\,k(t) + w(t)\,\bar{l}(t)],\qquad(18)$$

or

$$q_t z_t = s[r_t k_t + w_t \bar{l}_t],\qquad(18')$$

where $0 < s < 1$ is the constant saving rate from NNI.[16] Another well-known example which can be cast in the form (17) or (17′) is the "Marxian" saving–investment hypothesis that wages are consumed, profits are reinvested,

$$q(t)\,z(t) = r(t)\,k(t),\qquad(19)$$

or

$$q_t z_t = r_t k_t .\qquad(19')$$

In Section 4, we closely examine the stability properties of the descriptive growth model which incorporates the behavior described by (19) or (19′).[17]

Both (18) or (18′) and (19) or (19′) are particular variants of the general linear saving–investment hypothesis

$$q(t)\,z(t) = s_r r(t)\,k(t) + s_w w(t)\,\bar{l}(t) - (1 - s_g)\,p(t)\,\frac{d[q(t)/p(t)]}{dt}\,k(t),\qquad(20)$$

or

$$q_t z_t = s_r r_t k_t + s_w w_t \bar{l}_t - (1 - s_g)\,p_t \left[\frac{q_t}{p_t} - \frac{q_{t-1}}{p_{t-1}}\right] k_t ,\qquad(20')$$

where $0 \leqslant s_r , s_w , s_g \leqslant 1$ are the constant saving rates from alternative functional income streams, including capital gains relative to consumption,

$$p(t)\,\frac{d[q(t)/p(t)]}{dt}\,k(t) = \left[\dot{q}(t) - \frac{\dot{p}(t)}{p(t)}\,q(t)\right] k(t),$$

---

[16] Some versions of (18) or (18′) are in terms of gross rather than net quantities; see, for example, [32, 34] Of course, such a specification requires an explicit formulation of the way depreciation occurs, as well as of the technology for producing gross outputs. The standard formulation postulates constant depreciation rates (parallel with the linear form of the saving–investment hypothesis itself).

[17] Notice that Marxian saving–investment behavior has the special property that it can be *entirely* described in terms of the Hamiltonian function. Thus, stability for this model can *only* involve properties of the Hamiltonian function, a special circumstance, which, together with the particular form of Marxian saving–investment behavior, greatly simplifies its analysis.

or

$$p_t \left[\frac{q_t}{p_t} - \frac{q_{t-1}}{p_{t-1}} \right] k_t = \left[(q_t - q_{t-1}) - \frac{p_t - p_{t-1}}{p_t} \frac{p_t}{p_{t-1}} q_t \right] k_t .$$

Shell, Sidrauski, and Stiglitz [32] give an extended discussion of the rationale behind including capital gains in perceived income, and its implications for capital accumulation.

Clearly, there are many other interesting specifications of (17) or (17′). In any case, the general role of such a saving–investment relation, like that of the saving–investment constraints for the optimal and maximal growth models, is to restrict the permissible solutions to the general Hamiltonian dynamical system, hopefully, enough so that definite qualitative properties can be ascertained. For the purpose of analyzing stability, we have found it useful to conceive of (17) or (17′) as possibly restricting (8) or (8′) in several different ways: (i) by providing a direct additional restriction on the domain of the Hamiltonian function (and, hence, Hamiltonian dynamical system),

$$(p, q, k, l) \in D = \{(p, q, k, l): S(p, i, q, k, l) = 0\}; \tag{21}$$

(ii) by providing a direct or indirect endogenous determination of the interest rate, i (or, because without loss of generality $p(0) = 1$ or $p_0 = 1$, of the price of consumption goods output),

$$i \in I(p, q, k, l) \qquad \text{for} \quad (p, q, k, l) \in D; \tag{22}$$

and (iii) by providing an additional indirect restriction on the initial prices of capital stocks,

$$q(0) \in \bar{Q}(0) \qquad \text{or} \qquad q_{-1} \in \bar{Q}_{-1} . \tag{23}$$

As compared to the optimal or maximal growth models, stability of the descriptive growth model is potentially easier to analyze on account of (21), harder to analyze on account of (22). In our experience with a few leading cases, we have usually found the complexities stemming from (22) to outweigh the simplifications stemming from (21).

3. STABILITY OF THE OPTIMAL GROWTH MODEL

A. *Preliminary Comments*

Our analysis of stability in the optimal growth model is conducted mainly in terms of continuous time; at the end of the section we briefly outline the parallel analysis in terms of discrete time. A substantial part of the underlying results, those concerning existence and uniqueness of stationary points, is common to both. When doing so will cause no confusion, we will simply suppress the time variable.

For the optimal growth model, it turns out to be most convenient to conduct the analysis in terms of *current* rather than present values. We denote current prices and rentals by upper case letters,

$$(Q(t), R(t), W(t)) \equiv \frac{(q(t), r(t), w(t))}{p(t)}, \tag{24}$$

or

$$(Q_t, R_t, W_t) \equiv \frac{(q_t, r_t, w_t)}{p_t}. \tag{24'}$$

Then bringing together (8), (11), and (12) or (14), or (8'), (11') and (12'), or (14'), and utilizing our other normalizing assumption (A1) along with this normalizing definition (24) or (24'), the competitive dynamical system for optimal growth can be written compactly as

$$\begin{cases} \dot{k} = \dfrac{\partial H(Q, k)}{\partial Q}, & k(0) = \bar{k}, \\[2mm] \dot{Q} = -\dfrac{\partial H(Q, k)}{\partial k} + \rho Q, & Q(0) \geqslant 0, \\[2mm] \lim_{t \to \infty} Q e^{-\rho t} k = 0 & \text{for} \quad \rho > 0, \\[1mm] \qquad\qquad\quad = Q^* k^* & \text{for} \quad \rho = 0, \end{cases} \tag{25}$$

or

$$\begin{cases} k_{t+1} = k_t + \dfrac{\partial H(Q_t, k_t)}{\partial H}, & k_0 = \bar{k}, \\[2mm] Q_{t+1} = Q_t - \dfrac{\partial H(Q_{t+1}, k_{t+1})}{\partial k} + \rho Q_t, & Q_{-1} \geqslant 0, \\[2mm] \lim_{t \to \infty} Q_t (1 + \rho)^{-t} k_{t+1} = 0 & \text{for} \quad \rho > 0, \\[1mm] \qquad\qquad\qquad\quad = Q^* k^* & \text{for} \quad \rho = 0, \end{cases} \tag{25'}$$

where we define the current value Hamiltonian function $H(Q, k) \equiv H(1, Q, k, 1) \equiv H(1, q/p, k, 1)$, the current value of imputed NNP (= the current value of imputed NNI).

B. *Stationary Points*

As done earlier in our discussion of transversality conditions, we denote the variables corresponding to stationary points for the system (25) or (25') with asterisks. Thus, in particular,

$$z^* = \frac{\partial H(Q^*, k^*)}{\partial Q} = 0,$$

$$-R^* + \rho Q^* = -\frac{\partial H(Q^*, k^*)}{\partial k} + \rho Q^* = 0. \tag{26}$$

Also, as is conventional, we will refer to stationary points, (Q^*, k^*), (and, occasionally and loosely, other of the variables corresponding to them, R^*, W^*, c^*, and z^*) as modified golden rule paths.

If the discount rate, ρ, is too high, then there may be no (nontrivial) modified golden rule path. However, utilizing our various assumptions about the technology it is fairly straightforward to establish the

EXISTENCE OF A MODIFIED GOLDEN RULE PATH. *Let*

$$\bar{\rho} = \sup\{\rho: (c, z, -k, -l) \in T, (c, z - \rho k) > 0\},$$

and suppose $\rho \in [0, \bar{\rho})$. *Then there exists* $(1, Q^*, R^*, W^*) \in M$ *and* $(c^*, z^*, -k^*, -1) \in T$ *such that* (i) $R^* = \rho Q^*$, (ii) $c^* > 0, z^* = 0$, *and* (iii) $c^* + Q^* z^* - R^* k^* - W^* = 0$.

Proof. The proof consists simply in carrying out the program outlined in [6, pp. 289–90]. In particular, we assert (without going into details) that (i) the mapping from the nonempty, compact, convex set $K = \{k: (c, z, -k, -l) \in T, \|(c, z, k)\| \leqslant B$ and $l \leqslant 1\}$ into itself defined by

$\Phi(k) = \{k': (c', z', -k', -l')$ is an optimal solution to
maximize c' subject to $(c', z', -k', -l') \in T, \|(c', z', k')\| \leqslant B,$
$z' - \rho k' \geqslant -\rho k, l' \leqslant 1\}$ for $k \in K$ (27)

is a nonempty, convex-valued, upper semicontinuous correspondence (so that Kakutani's fixed point theorem can be appealed to), and (ii) a fixed point of the mapping (27), say k^*, yields a (nontrivial) modified golden rule path as optimal solutions to the dual concave and convex programming problems

maximize c subject to $(c, z, -k, -l) \in T, z - \rho k \geqslant -\rho k^*, l \leqslant 1,$

and

minimize $W + \rho Q k^*$ subject to $(p, Q, R, W) \in M, R - \rho Q = 0, p = 1.$[18]

---

[18] It is worth noting, referring to the property (B), that only the bound associated with replicable production points is actually relevant to this argument. And this particular bound enters in two ways, first, to provide the compactness required for the application of Kakutani's theorem, and second, to permit dropping the constraint $\|(c, z, k)\| \leqslant B$, once the existence of a fixed point has been established.

Since, just to be able to talk about stability, we will require the existence of some (nontrivial) modified golden rule path, hereafter we simply hypothesize:

EXISTENCE ASSUMPTION. $\rho \in [0, \bar{\rho})$. (E)

Notice that, as in the one-good model satisfying Inada's conditions, $\bar{\rho} = \infty$ is possible.

We next take up the question of the uniqueness of *the* modified golden rule capital stocks, k^*, which in our approach turns out closely related to the question of the convergence of the optimal paths defined by (25) to *some* modified golden rule capital stocks, $k^*, k^{**}, \ldots$. Our strategy is to find conditions in terms of the geometry of the current value Hamiltonian, $H(Q, k)$, which insure both uniqueness and convergence, the two properties which together define global stability, or simply, stability.

Though the zero discount rate case has been quite extensively treated in the literature, we begin our discussion with a full account of that special case. We do so partly to provide a self-contained, complete analysis of stability for optimal growth, but mostly to provide an intuitive, heuristic motivation for our later discussion of the general case. We should expressly warn the reader at the outset that, aside from the statement and verification of various uniqueness and stability conditions, the balance of this subsection is mostly devoted to motivating, explaining and interpreting, in other words, to exposition, not analysis.

If $\rho = 0$, then a stationary point, (Q^*, k^*) (now referred to as a golden rule path), must be a saddle point of the current value Hamiltonian, $H(Q, k)$,

$$H(Q^*, k) \leqslant H(Q^*, k^*) \leqslant H(Q, k^*) \quad \text{for all} \quad (Q, k) \geqslant 0,$$

or

$$H(Q, k^*) - H(Q^*, k) \geqslant 0 \quad \text{for all} \quad (Q, k) \geqslant 0, \quad (28)$$

since it satisfies (26), and $H(Q, k)$ is convex in Q and concave in k. Now suppose k^* were not unique, i.e., that (28) were also to hold with (Q^{**}, k^{**}) in place of (Q^*, k^*), where $k^{**} \neq k^*$. Then (28) would also achieve its minimum value of zero at (Q^{**}, k^{**}) as well as (Q^*, k^*). This suggests that any reasonably general condition which guarantees that k^* is unique must also, in effect, guarantee that (28) is a strict inequality for $k \neq k^*$.[19] Thus, one obvious sufficient condition for uniqueness is simply

[19] As Lionel McKenzie has emphasized, there are many specific technologies for which the last is not true, and yet k^* is unique. Uzawa's two-sector model is perhaps the best known of these (see Footnote 31 below). The point is that what we are concerned with here are conditions which don't require more detailed specification of the technology, for example, that it has an industry or sectoral structure.

that $H(Q, k)$ be strictly concave in k (symmetrically, that $H(Q, k)$ be strictly convex in Q is a sufficient condition for uniqueness of Q^*; see, for example, [25]). However, this is clearly stronger than needed, since the equally obvious direct condition, possibly valid without strict concavity, works just as well.

UNIQUENESS ASSUMPTION FOR $\rho = 0$.

$$k \neq k^* \Rightarrow H(Q, k^*) - H(Q^*, k) > 0, \qquad (29)$$

or equivalently,[20]

$$k \neq k^* \Rightarrow (Q - Q^*) \frac{\partial H(Q, k)}{\partial Q} - \frac{\partial H(Q, k)}{\partial k} (k - k^*) > 0. \quad (U^0)$$

(U^0) can be aptly called the *real Hamiltonian steepness condition*, since (29) means that looking from (Q^*, k^*), the Hamiltonian function, $H(Q, k)$, has negative steepness in all directions $(0, k - k^*) \neq 0$, or alternatively, that when $k \neq k^*$, the convex function $H(Q, k^*) - H(Q^*, k)$ lies strictly above its horizontal support at $(Q, k) = (Q^*, k^*)$.

Convergence to the golden rule capital stocks, k^*, can be established if our real Hamiltonian steepness condition holds uniformly in k.

STABILITY ASSUMPTION FOR $\rho = 0$. For every $\epsilon > 0$, there is a $\delta > 0$ such that

$$\| k - k^* \| > \epsilon \Rightarrow (Q - Q^*) \frac{\partial H(Q, k)}{\partial Q} - \frac{\partial H(Q, k)}{\partial k} (k - k^*) > \delta. \quad (S^0)$$

The proof of this assertion will be a particular application of the proof for the general model when $\rho \geqslant 0$, presented in the next subsection.

---

[20] This equivalence rests heavily on the convexity–concavity of $H(Q, k)$. On the one hand, (29) implies (U^0), since

$$(Q - Q^*) \frac{\partial H(Q, k)}{\partial Q} - \frac{\partial H(Q, k)}{\partial k} (k - k^*) = \left[H(Q, k) + \frac{\partial H(Q, k)}{\partial k} (k^* - k) \right]$$

$$- \left[H(Q, k) + (Q^* - Q) \frac{\partial H(Q, k)}{\partial Q} \right]$$

$$\geqslant H(Q, k^*) - H(Q^*, k).$$

On the other hand, denial of (29) implies the denial of (U^0), since if $k' \neq k^*$ and $H(Q', k^*) - H(Q^*, k') = 0$, then $H(Q^*, k') = H(Q^*, k^*)$, $\partial H(Q^*, k')/\partial k = 0$, and $(Q^* - Q^*)(\partial H(Q^*, k')/\partial Q) - (\partial H(Q^*, k')/\partial k)(k - k^*) = 0$.

(U^0) and (S^0) can be interpreted in straightforward economic terms, and thereby related to the previous literature. Expanding the basic expression in both conditions yields

$$
\begin{aligned}
(Q - Q^*) &\frac{\partial H(Q, k)}{\partial Q} - \frac{\partial H(Q, k)}{\partial k}(k - k^*) \\
&= (Q - Q^*)\, z - R(k - k^*) \\
&= (Q - Q^*)(z - z^*) - (R - R^*)(k - k^*) \\
&\quad \text{(since by definition } z^* = R^* = 0) \\
&= (1 - 1)(c - c^*) + (Q - Q^*)(z - z^*) \\
&\quad - (R - R^*)(k - k^*) - (W - W^*)(1 - 1) \\
&= -(c + Q^*z - R^*k - W^*) - (c^* + Qz^* - Rk^* - W) \\
&\quad \text{(since by hypothesis} \\
&\quad c + Qz - Rk - W = c^* + Q^*z^* - R^*k^* - W^* = 0).
\end{aligned}
\tag{30}
$$

Now let $x = (c, z, -k, -1)$ denote any efficient production point and $\pi = (1, Q, R, W)$ its associated current competitive prices. Then the last line in (30) becomes

$$
-\pi x^* - \pi^* x, \tag{31}
$$

the sum of the potential losses from adopting the golden rule production point x^* at current competitive prices π plus those from adopting the efficient production point x at golden rule prices π^*. Thus, the conditions (U^0) or (S^0) are nothing more than the requirements that these potential losses be positive or uniformly positive, respectively, when an efficient production point does not utilize golden rule capital stocks. In particular, (S^0) is therefore seen to be nothing but a symmetric adaptation of Radner's bounded value-loss condition (introduced in [23, pp. 101–2]) to the present model.[21]

We now turn to consideration of the general optimal growth model with constant, nonnegative discounting, $\rho \geqslant 0$. As we have just seen, the

---

[21] For the same sort of reason that (U^0) and (29) are equivalent, (S^0) is also easily shown to be equivalent to a direct analog of Radner's bounded value-loss condition, namely

$$
\| k - k^* \| > \epsilon \Rightarrow \pi^* x > \delta.
$$

Indeed, if we convert the consumption-optimal growth model with $\rho = 0$ into a production-maximal growth model in the manner suggested earlier, then the latter condition is precisely the appropriate bounded value-loss condition (that is, after taking account of how this artificial variant differs from the standard formulation of the production-maximal growth model).

analysis of uniqueness and convergence when $\rho = 0$ hinges on the fact that then (Q^*, k^*) is a saddlepoint of $H(Q, k)$. When $\rho > 0$, this saddle-point property no longer obtains. Notice, however, that for the general model, a modified golden rule path, (Q^*, k^*), is *something like* a saddle-point for the modified current value Hamiltonian function, $H(Q, k) - \rho Q k$. That is, from (26) and convexity–concavity, we have

$$H(Q^*, k) - \rho Q^* k \leqslant H(Q^*, k^*) - \rho Q^* k^* \leqslant H(Q, k^*) - \rho Q^* k^*$$
$$\text{for all} \quad (Q, k) \geqslant 0,$$

or

$$H(Q, k^*) - \rho Q^* k^* - [H(Q^*, k) - \rho Q^* k] \geqslant 0 \quad \text{for all} \quad (Q, k) \geqslant 0,$$

or

$$H(Q, k^*) - H(Q^*, k) + \rho Q^*(k - k^*) \geqslant 0 \quad \text{for all} \quad (Q, k) \geqslant 0. \quad (32)$$

Obviously, the reason we say "something like" has to do with the asymmetry of terms involving ρ. Applying reasoning similar to that leading to (29) and (U⁰) now results in both strong and weak sufficient conditions for uniqueness of k^* (again because of asymmetry in terms involving ρ, which in effect makes the comparison involved in (Uˢ) below quantitative, rather than qualitative, as in that involved in (29) above.)

UNIQUENESS ASSUMPTION FOR $\rho \geqslant 0$ (STRONG VERSION).

$$k \neq k^* \Rightarrow H(Q, k^*) - H(Q^*, k) + \rho Q(k - k^*) > 0,$$

or $\qquad\qquad\qquad\qquad\qquad\qquad\qquad\qquad\qquad\qquad\qquad\qquad$ (Uˢ)

$$k \neq k^* \Rightarrow H(Q, k^*) - H(Q^*, k) + \rho Q^*(k - k^*) > -\rho(Q - Q^*)(k - k^*)$$

and

UNIQUENESS ASSUMPTION FOR $\rho \geqslant 0$.

$$k \neq k^* \Rightarrow (Q - Q^*)\frac{\partial H(Q, k)}{\partial Q} - \frac{\partial H(Q, k)}{\partial k}(k - k^*) + \rho Q^*(k - k^*) >$$
$$-\rho(Q - Q^*)(k - k^*). \quad (U)$$

We repeat for emphasis: By convexity-concavity, (Uˢ) implies (U), but the converse implication is generally false unless $\rho = 0$, in which case (U) simply reduces to (U⁰).

The geometric and economic interpretations of (U) are not nearly as transparent for $\rho > 0$ as they were for $\rho = 0$. Some idea of what (U) means geometrically can be gleaned from the observation that its strengthening (U^s) amounts to a modified real Hamiltonian steepness condition: When $k \neq k^*$, the convex function $H(Q, k^*) - H(Q^*, k) + \rho Q^*(k - k^*)$ lies strictly above the indefinite quadratic $-\rho(Q - Q^*)(k - k^*)$. This interpretation also reemphasizes the self-evident importance of variation in Q (as well as k) in the statement (and verification) of either (U^s) or (U). Notice especially that both conditions are automatically satisfied whenever $-\rho(Q - Q^*)(k - k^*) < 0$ because of convexity–concavity and (32).

Again reasoning from the case $\rho = 0$, some idea of the economic content of (U) can be gotten from repeating the exercise which yielded (30), and which here leads to exactly the same expression, since on a modified golden rule path $z^* = 0$ but $R^* = \rho Q^*$. Thus, the fundamental inequality in (U) can be expressed as

$$-\pi x^* - \pi^* x > -\rho(Q - Q^*)(k - k^*)$$

or

$$-\pi x^* - \pi^* x > \rho Q^*(k - k^*) + \rho Q(k^* - k), \tag{33}$$

"the sum of potential losses exceeds the sum of potential interest." The idea embodied in (33) seems to revolve around what it denies; figuratively speaking, if (33) were not true, then there would appear to be potential gains in trade away from the modified golden rule path. Or putting it another way, and getting a little bit ahead of our story (see (S) and the subsequent argument below), society may not countenance growth toward the modified golden rule capital stocks if, when once achieved, it would then appear that society could actually have done better elsewhere.[22]

We close this subsection by again remarking that all the foregoing discussion applies equally well to both continuous time and discrete time.

C. Stability Analysis

We suppose that a solution to (25) exists. Then, consider the behavior of the (Lyapunov) current valuation function

$$V = (Q - Q^*)(k - k^*). \tag{34}$$

---

[22] A more concrete interpretation may be possible. When $\rho = 0$, (S^0) can be used to show that *any* path converging to the golden rule capital stocks is superior to *all* paths which do not (see, for example, [11]). When $\rho > 0$, no such very crude comparison can be coaxed from (S), since, so to speak, the initial evolution of a path weighs much more heavily than its terminal evolution. It is an interesting, open question whether, nevertheless, some much more delicate but just as easily interpretable comparison can be developed on the basis of (S).

Direct calculation shows that

$$\frac{d(Ve^{-\rho t})}{dt} \sim \dot{V} - \rho V$$

$$= (Q - Q^*)\, \dot{k} + \dot{Q}(k - k^*) - \rho(Q - Q^*)(k - k^*)$$

$$= (Q - Q^*)\frac{\partial H(Q, k)}{\partial Q} - \left(\frac{\partial H(Q, k)}{\partial k} - \rho Q\right)(k - k^*)$$

$$\quad - \rho(Q - Q^*)(k - k^*)$$

$$= (Q - Q^*)\frac{\partial H(Q, k)}{\partial Q} - \left(\frac{\partial H(Q, k)}{\partial k} - \rho Q^*\right)(k - k^*)$$

$$\geqslant H(Q, k^*) - H(Q^*, k) + \rho Q^*(k - k^*)$$

$$\geqslant 0, \tag{35}$$

the last two inequalities again following from convexity–concavity of $H(Q, k)$ and the "saddlepoint" property of (Q^*, k^*), (32). Furthermore, the transversality condition in (25) requires that

$$\lim_{t \to \infty} Ve^{-\rho t} = \lim_{t \to \infty} (Q - Q^*)(k - k^*)\, e^{-\rho t}$$

$$\leqslant \lim_{t \to \infty} (Qe^{-\rho t}k + Q^*e^{-\rho t}k^*) \tag{36}$$

$$= 0 \qquad \text{for } \rho > 0$$

$$(= 2Q^*k^* \qquad \text{for } \rho = 0).$$

Hence, since $Ve^{-\rho t}$ is increasing and nonpositive for $\rho > 0$ (bounded for $\rho = 0$), V must have an upper bound, say, $V \leqslant V^* < \infty$. If, in addition, we knew that $k \neq k^*$ entails $\dot{V} > 0$ (with some uniformity in the relation between the size of $(k - k^*)$ and the size of $\dot{V}$), then a routine argument (the details of which are provided below) would establish that

$$\lim_{t \to \infty} k = k^*.\text{[23]}$$

[23] The reader may have begun to wonder why we focus on stability in terms of k rather than in terms of (Q, k). One reason is the fact that we don't even know for sure that Q is bounded (though $Qe^{-\rho t}$ likely is). Thus, the sort of analysis we present below concerning k cannot be carried out concerning Q. Perhaps a better (economic) reason is that we don't really care about the asymptotic behavior of prices in this context. The interesting aspect of the modified golden rule path is its real, not its price side, and we may well get convergence to the former even when Q^* is not unique. For example, the special model where $n = 1$ and $H(Q, k) = (1 + Q)f(k) - \lambda Qk$ can be employed to construct a solution to (25) on which, because k^* is, but Q^* is not unique, for given (Q^*, k^*), $\lim_{t \to \infty} k = k^*$, but $\lim_{t \to \infty} Q \neq Q^*$.

How do we insure the last? Casual inspection of the expressions in (35) suggests simply requiring that (U^s) or (U) hold uniformly in k.

STABILITY ASSUMPTION FOR $\rho \geqslant 0$ (STRONG VERSION).   For every $\epsilon > 0$, there is a $\delta > 0$ such that $\| k - k^* \| > \epsilon \Rightarrow$

$$H(Q, k^*) - H(Q^*, k) + \rho Q^*(k - k^*) >$$
$$-\rho(Q - Q^*)(k - k^*) + \delta. \quad \text{(S^s)}$$

and

STABILITY ASSUMPTION FOR $\rho \geqslant 0$.   For every $\epsilon > 0$, there is a $\delta > 0$ such that $\| k - k^* \| > \epsilon \Rightarrow$

$$(Q - Q^*)\frac{\partial H(Q, k)}{\partial Q} - \frac{\partial H(Q, k)}{\partial k}(k - k^*) + \rho Q^*(k - k^*) >$$
$$-\rho(Q - Q^*)(k - k^*) + \delta. \quad \text{(S)}$$

The reader may want to check for himself whether (S) holds in particular examples. Consider, for instance, the one-good model with a strictly concave intensive production function, $f(k) = F(k, 1)$, a constant depreciation rate, $f'(0) > \lambda > f'(\infty) \geqslant 0$, and utility output linear in consumption output, utility output $= c$ (without loss of generality). In this model $H(Q, k) = \max[1, Q] f(k) - \lambda Q k$, so that (S) holds when the discount rate, ρ, is sufficiently small. Notice that for this model, or its standard variants,[24] even our modified real Hamiltonian steepness condition (U) is far stronger than required for convergence. This is because, with a single capital good, the (Q, k) space is two-dimensional, while with both a single capital good and an intensive production technology which is strictly convex in capital intensity, the real side of an optimal path is unique. Thus, orbiting is not possible. Moreover, since the intensive production technology does not permit an unbounded capital intensity, the real side of an optimal path is also bounded. Hence, for such models, an optimal path must converge to *some* modified golden rule capital stock.

However, one should not be misled by these simple examples. In general, on optimal paths which are convergent, the valuation function, V, is also convergent, but not necessarily monotonically. This strongly suggests to us that any general argument for stability is going to require that V (or something very like it) be monotonically increasing, which in turn strongly

---

[24] See for example, [5, 15], or, for a pedagogic survey, [31]. A critical feature of all these models is that there is only a single capital good.

suggests that (S) (or something very like it) is the weakest general stability condition possible. Putting the matter another way, it seems very unlikely to us that, in more than two dimensions, orbiting on an optimal path can be ruled out unless some form of real Hamiltonian steepness obtains.[25]

Returning to the main point of this subsection, we now explicitly demonstrate the

STABILITY OF OPTIMAL GROWTH WITH CONSTANT, NONNEGATIVE DISCOUNTING.

Assumptions (E) *and* (S) *imply that the real side of the solutions to* (25) *converges to unique* (*nontrivial*) *modified golden rule capital stocks.*

Proof. To begin with, we have from the definition of V and the stability condition (S) that

$$\dot{V} = (Q - Q^*)\,\dot{k} + \dot{Q}(k - k^*)$$

$$= (Q - Q^*)\,\frac{\partial H(Q, k)}{\partial k} - \left(\frac{\partial H(Q, k)}{\partial k} - \rho Q\right)(k - k^*)$$

$$= \left[(Q - Q^*)\,\frac{\partial H(Q, k)}{\partial k} - \left(\frac{\partial H(Q, k)}{\partial k} + \rho Q^*\right)(k - k^*)\right]$$

$$\quad + \rho(Q - Q^*)(k - k^*)$$

$$\geqslant 0,$$

and from (35) and (36) that

$$V \leqslant V^* < \infty.$$

Hence, putting these together, we have that

$$\lim_{t \to \infty} V = V^\infty \leqslant V^* < \infty.$$

Suppose that $\lim_{t \to \infty} k = k^*$ were not true, i.e., that for some $\epsilon > 0$, there were a sequence of points $\{t_j\}$ such that $\| k(t_j) - k^* \| > 2\epsilon$. Then, since (B) and (T7) entail uniform continuity of $k(t)$ on the half line $[0, \infty)$, there would also have to be a sequence of intervals $\{[\underline{t}_j, \bar{t}_j]\}$ such $\bar{t}_j - \underline{t}_j >$

---

[25] Perhaps this is an appropriate place to point out that, when stripped of our particular interpretation, our stability argument applies to any sufficiently regular dynamical system of the form (25), with or without convexity, provided the right-hand side of the inequality in (S) is further strengthened to read $\max[0, -\rho(Q - Q^*)(k - k^*) + \delta]$. (This strengthening incorporates the one direct implication of convexity–concavity actually used in the stability argument, namely, the final inequality in (35).) Of course, without convexity, neither the transversality condition (more generally, boundedness) nor the steepness condition (more generally, definiteness) typically makes much sense, which for us significantly reduces possible interest in such generalization.

$\Delta t > 0$ and $\| k(t) - k^* \| > \epsilon$ for $t \in [\underline{t}_j, \bar{t}_j]$. But this would imply, now utilizing condition (S) to bound uniformly the derivative

$$\dot{V}(t) = \left[(Q(t) - Q^*) \frac{\partial H(Q(t), k(t))}{\partial Q} \right.$$
$$- \left(\frac{\partial [H(Q(t), k(t))]}{\partial k} + \rho Q^* \right) (k(t) - k^*) \right]$$
$$+ \rho(Q(t) - Q^*)(k(t) - k^*),$$

that there is a $\delta > 0$ such that

$$\dot{V}(t) > \delta \qquad \text{for} \quad t \in [\underline{t}_j, \bar{t}_j].$$

Hence, for sufficiently large t' we would have both $V^\infty - \delta \leqslant V(t) \leqslant V^\infty$ and

$$V(t) \geqslant V(t') + \sum_{t' \leqslant \underline{t}_j \leqslant \bar{t}_j \leqslant t} \delta(\bar{t}_j - \underline{t}_j)$$
$$\geqslant V(t') + [\max\{j : t' \leqslant \underline{t}_j \leqslant \bar{t}_j \leqslant t\} - \min\{j : t' \leqslant \underline{t}_j \leqslant \bar{t}_j \leqslant t\}] \delta \Delta t$$

for $t \geqslant t'$, which are inconsistent, and the theorem is proved.

It should be clear that stronger "$\epsilon - \delta$" conditions would suffice for our argument, for instance (S^s), or the conditions used by Rockafellar [26], or the conditions used by Brock and Scheinkman [3].

We close this discussion by commenting briefly on the optimal growth model with a discount rate, $\rho(t) = -\dot{p}(t)/p(t)$, which is only asymptotically constant and nonnegative, $\lim_{t \to \infty} \rho(t) = \rho \geqslant 0.$[26] For this model, we have

$$\dot{V} = (Q - Q^*) \frac{\partial H(Q, k)}{\partial Q} - \frac{\partial H(Q, k)}{\partial k} (k - k^*) + \rho(t) Q(k - k^*)$$
$$= (Q - Q^*) \frac{\partial H(Q, k)}{\partial Q} - \frac{\partial H(Q, k)}{\partial k} (k - k^*) + \rho Q^*(k - k^*)$$
$$+ \rho(Q - Q^*)(k - k^*) + (\rho(t) - \rho)(Q - Q^*)(k - k^*)$$
$$+ (\rho(t) - \rho) Q^*(k - k^*).$$

Since the last term in this expansion may be negative (the second to the last term may be negative too, but can eventually be safely neglected), our

---

[26] Symmetrically, we now assume that the valuation function, $V(t)$, is only uniformly bounded from above, $V(t) \leqslant V^* < \infty$ for all t. It is perhaps worth noting that this discussion applies equally well to any descriptive growth model for which these same properties, $\lim_{t \to \infty} \rho(t) = \rho \geqslant 0$ and $V(t) \leqslant V^* < \infty$ for all t, can be established.

argument above will not go through without some further strengthening of our modified real Hamiltonian steepness condition (U) beyond (S), basically to negate the effect of Q potentially being "too far" from Q^*. In particular, if we substitute the quantity $\max[\delta, -\delta(Q - Q^*)(k - k^*)]$ for the constant δ in the right-hand side of the inequality in (S), then the proof of stability involves only relatively minor modification, the details of which we omit.[27]

D. *Discrete Time*

Recall that the analysis of existence and uniqueness of stationary points is the same in either continuous time or discrete time. The reason for this fortunate circumstance is that, for an economy in balanced growth, currently compounding interest on this period's capital value (continuous time) is indistinguishable from accrued simple interest on last period's capital value (discrete time), provided both interest rates are the same. For the analysis of behavior away from stationary points, however, the intrinsic difference in the timing of interest calculations between continuous time and discrete time becomes of paramount importance.

In terms of modifying our analysis in the preceding subsection to accomodate discrete time, this shows up almost immediately once we write down the appropriate analogs to (34) and (35).

$$V_t = (Q_{t-1} - Q^*)(k_t - k^*) \tag{34'}$$

and

$$
\begin{aligned}
V_{t+1}(1 + \rho)^{-(t+1)} &- V_t(1 + \rho)^{-t} \\
&\sim V_{t+1} - (1 + \rho) V_t \\
&= (Q_t - Q^*)(k_{t+1} - k^*) - (1 + \rho)(Q_{t-1} - Q^*)(k_t - k^*) \\
&= (Q_t - Q^*) \left[\frac{\partial H(Q_t, k_t)}{\partial Q} + (k_t - k^*) \right] \\
&\quad - (1 + \rho) \left[\frac{1}{1 + \rho} \left(\frac{\partial H(Q_t, k_t)}{\partial k} + Q_t \right) - Q^* \right] (k_t - k^*) \\
&= (Q_t - Q^*) \frac{\partial H(Q_t, k_t)}{\partial Q} - \frac{\partial H(Q_t, k_t)}{\partial k} (k_t - k^*) - \rho Q^*(k_t - k^*) \\
&\geqslant H(Q_t, k^*) - H(Q^*, k_t) - \rho Q^*(k_t - k^*) \\
&\geqslant 0. \tag{35'}
\end{aligned}
$$

[27] Except to remark, for those interested in the details, that the essential difference comes in restricting attention to t sufficiently large so that

$$\max[|\,\rho(t) - \rho\,|, |\,\rho(t) - \rho\,|\,V^*, |\,(\rho(t) - \rho)Q^*(k - k^*)|] < \delta/3.$$

Equations (34') and (35') again lay a solid foundation for a routine argument establishing stability, provided only that the following inequality holds uniformly in $k_t \neq k^*$:

$$V_{t+1} - V_t = (Q_t - Q^*) \frac{\partial H(Q_t, k_t)}{\partial Q} - \frac{\partial H(Q_t, k_t)}{\partial k} (k_t - k^*)$$
$$+ \rho Q_{t+1}(k_t - k^*) > 0. \quad (37)$$

But notice the slippage of the time subscript in the last term of the middle expression! While this natural slippage highlights the fundamental character of the difference between continuous time and discrete time, the obvious method for getting around it also reemphasizes the central importance of both the price and quantity equations in our analysis. For, once more utilizing the second equation in (25'), we see that

$$\rho Q_{t+1}(k_t - k^*) = \frac{\rho}{1 + \rho} \left(\frac{\partial H(Q_t, k_t)}{\partial Q} + Q_t \right) (k_t - k^*). \quad (38)$$

Hence, substituting from (38) into (37), and carrying out some algebraic rearrangement yields the direct analog of (S) for discrete time.

STABILITY ASSUMPTION FOR $\rho \geqslant 0$ (DISCRETE TIME). For every $\epsilon > 0$, there is a $\delta > 0$ such that $\| k - k^* \| > \epsilon \Rightarrow$

$$(1 + \rho)(Q - Q^*) \frac{\partial H(Q, k)}{\partial Q} - \frac{\partial H(Q, k)}{\partial k} (k - k^*) + \rho Q^*(k - k^*) >$$
$$-\rho(Q - Q^*)(k - k^*) + \delta. \quad (S')$$

But now notice the addition of the factor $1 + \rho$ in the first term of the lefthand side!

Some brief reflection on the distinction between the stability conditions (S') and (S) is revealing. Evidently, they will generally coincide only with a zero discount rate, $\rho = 0$. For a given current Hamiltonian function, $H(Q, k)$, and positive discount rate, $\rho > 0$, both, just one or the other, or neither may hold. Hence, in particular, (S') may hold when (U), and, therefore, (S) as well, does not; in other words, for the system (25'), establishing convergence may be possible when establishing stability is not.[28] For example, in the one-good model mentioned in the last sub-

---

[28] Thus, it would be more accurate to refer to (S') as a convergence, rather than a stability condition. However, we have yet to find a simple example in which (S') holds, (U) does not, and there are actually several stationary capital stocks.

The reader should beware the fact that the comparison we are making here is somewhat artificial, since we are considering both continuous- and discrete-time conditions in terms of the *same* Hamiltonian function.

section, (S') is in fact slightly weaker than (S). For another example, consider the (mathematically simplest) quadratic Hamiltonian model where $\nu = 1$ and $H(Q, k) = (\alpha/2)(Q - Q^*)^2 + \gamma(Q - Q^*)(k - k^*) - (\beta/2)(k - k^*)^2 + \rho Q^*(k - k^*)$ with $\alpha, \beta > 0$. Here (S') amounts to the requirement that $4\alpha\beta > [(1 + \gamma)^2/(1 + \rho)] \rho^2$, but (U) or (S) to the requirement that $4\alpha\beta > \rho^2$. Clearly, since $-1 \leqslant \gamma \leqslant \infty$ entails $0 \leqslant (1 + \gamma)^2/(1 + \rho) \leqslant \infty$, any one of the four combinations of validity for these two parametric conditions is possible.

But then we really should not be surprised that the alternative treatments of time are just not the same. On the one hand, as we demonstrated earlier in the paper, the standard single capital good models must eventually converge to some modified golden rule capital stock in continuous time. On the other hand, Sutherland's illuminating example [35, example on p. 588] taught us some time ago that these same models may forever orbit in discrete time. (Incidentally, Sutherland's particular model essentially reduces to the quadratic Hamiltonian model with parameter values such that $4\alpha\beta = 23/16 < [(1 + \gamma)^2/(1 + \rho)] \rho^2 = 121/48 < \rho^2 = 4$.)

The general problem of relating results for continuous time with those for discrete time seems to us worth further, detailed investigation.

4. STABILITY OF THE DESCRIPTIVE GROWTH MODEL WITH MARXIAN SAVING–INVESTMENT BEHAVIOR

A. Preliminary Comments

It was our original hope that our Hamiltonian approach would provide a basis for unifying the stability analysis of maximal, optimal, and descriptive growth models. While we have not yet given up that hope, we are also not yet prepared to handle anything like the descriptive growth model with a general saving–investment relation (17) or (17'). Instead, the discussion of this section deals only with the Marxian saving–investment hypothesis, and that only in continuous time.

To the experienced capital theorist, it comes, of course, as no surprise that stability for descriptive growth models is much more fragile, that is, requires much more structure, than stability for optimal growth models. Even with a single capital good, perpetual orbiting in a descriptive growth setting is not an uncommon phenomenon. Just consider, for instance, the special saving–investment hypothesis (19) or (19') we shall later concentrate attention on. Right away we have to contend with the well-known example of Inada [14], based on Uzawa's [36] famous two-sector model, which shows that orbiting may arise whenever the investment-goods sector is more capital intensive than is the consumption-goods sector. Moreover, we must also contend with the fact that, in discrete time, even the one-good model with Marxian saving–investment behavior is likely to exhibit orbiting.[29]

In purely technical terms, there are major obstacles to simply extending the analysis of the previous section to descriptive growth models. For example, when the interest rate is endogenous and depends on the state of the economy, what particular value of the interest rate should form the basis for our stability condition (S)? We have seen that even the seemingly slight change from an exogenous, interest rate which is constant to one which is only asymptotically constant required some additional tightening of that condition. Or, for another example, what economic forces will insure boundedness of our valuation function in a decentralized, competitive dynamical system? There seems to be no intrinsic reason why every such system should mimic even a sufficiently constrained optimization problem, and therefore exhibit this more complete form of duality.

The worked-out examples of descriptive growth models all seem to have two distinctive characteristics: The underlying technology is simple enough so that it can be completely parameterized, while the saving–investment relation (typically it too can be completely parameterized) is special enough so that it severely restricts the domain of solutions to the Hamiltonian dynamical system. These special properties are then heavily exploited to show directly that paths which do not converge must eventually leave the permissible domain of solutions. Can these arguments even be systematically extended to a general model using our Hamiltonian approach? At the end of the section we will briefly comment on the extent of our success relative to the worked-out examples with Marxian saving–investment behavior (expecially [8, 14, 33, 36]), and on the possible future directions for applying our Hamiltonian approach to descriptive growth models with more general saving–investment behavior.

B. *The Formal Model*

In this section the choice of numeraire is fairly complicated. In general, the prices will be present values, but with the numeraire implicitly chosen so that the initial value of capital stocks equals the (constant) current value of capital stocks along the golden rule path. The express motivation

---

[29] In fact, given any three capital intensities, $0 < k_0 < k^* < k_1 < \infty$, it is easy to construct a strictly increasing, strictly concave intensive production function such that the golden rule capital stock is k^*, but the only solution for $k = k_0$ is

$$k_{2t} = k_0, k_{2t+1} = k_1 \qquad \text{for} \quad t = 0, 1, \dots.$$

for this particular choice, like that for the subsequent analysis, is that our results generalize particular properties intrinsic to the worked-out examples mentioned above. However, at several points in the discussion (notably, in the statement of uniqueness and stability conditions) it will be convenient to revert to current values (recalling that $(Q, R, W) \equiv (q, r, w)/p$). Also, we will find it convenient to alternate freely between the Hamiltonian and conventional representations of the model. Finally, because we are only analyzing the model in continuous time, we will suppress the time variable.

The complete competitive dynamical system incorporating all of our maintained assumptions about technology, resources, and behavior can be written concisely as

$$
\begin{cases}
\dot{k} = \dfrac{\partial H(p, q, k, 1)}{\partial q} = \dfrac{\partial H(Q, k)}{\partial Q} = z, \qquad k(0) = \bar{k} > 0, \\[2ex]
\dot{q} = -\dfrac{\partial H(p, q, k, 1)}{\partial k} = -p\dfrac{\partial H(Q, k)}{\partial k} = -r, \qquad q(0) \geqslant 0, \text{ (39)} \\[2ex]
p\dfrac{\partial H(p, q, k, 1)}{\partial p} = pc = \dfrac{\partial H(p, q, k, 1)}{\partial l} 1 = w,
\end{cases}
$$

where again we use $H(Q, k) \equiv (H(1, q/p, k, 1)$. Since this model would not be a very interesting description of an economy otherwise, we append one further restriction on its solutions, that

$$w > 0, \tag{40}$$

the present wage rate, and, hence, current consumption output and its present value are all positive. The basis of our whole analysis is the simple observation that, because of linear homogeneity of H in (p, q) and the last equation in (39),

$$(\dot{qk}) = q\dot{k} + \dot{q}k = q\dfrac{\partial H(p, q, k, 1)}{\partial q} - \dfrac{\partial H(p, q, k, 1)}{\partial k} k = qz - rk =$$

$$(pc + qz - rk - w) - (pc - w) = -(pc - w) = 0$$

or

$$qk = q(0)\,\bar{k}, \text{ a constant.} \tag{41}$$

C. Stationary Points

As in our earlier discussion of optimal growth, we are interested in stationary points defined in terms of current values (even though our competitive dynamical system is defined in terms of present values). The only stationary points of this sort which are consistent with (39)–(40) are those at which either the present value of investment-goods output is zero, i.e., the interest rate is not zero, or at which all present values are constant, i.e., the interest rate is zero. Existence of the latter, that is, of a golden rule path, is guaranteed by our earlier argument. Thus, for our purposes now, we need a somewhat different uniqueness assumption, namely the

POSITIVITY AND UNIQUENESS ASSUMPTION. (i) $Q^*k^* > 0$, and (ii)

$$k \neq k^* \Rightarrow (Q - Q^*) \frac{\partial H(Q, k)}{\partial Q} - \frac{\partial H(Q, k)}{\partial k} (k - k^*) =$$

$$(Q - Q^*) z - R(k - k^*) > 0 \quad \text{(P)}$$

when $Q(\partial H(Q, k)/\partial Q) = Qz = (\partial H(Q, k)/\partial k) k = Rk$.

Various additional restrictions on the technology (having to do with the necessity and productivity of capital) would entail positivity $Q^*k^* > 0$. The second part of (P) is essentially a weakening of (U^0) which focuses on just those perturbations satisfying the saving–investment hypothesis; it would obviously be satisfied whenever (U^0) is.

Given the first part of (P), if $q(0) \bar{k} > 0$, then the price side of the solutions to (39) can be normalized so that $qk = q(0) \bar{k} = Q^*k^*$.[30] Thus, we have either

$$qk = 0 \qquad \text{or} \qquad qk = Q^*k^* > 0. \qquad (42)$$

D. *Stability Analysis*

Here, we focus our attention on a current valuation function, $v = (q - Q^*)(k - k^*)$. For this system, from (42), v is bounded by

$$v = (q - Q^*)(k - k^*) = qk - qk^* - Q^*k + Q^*k^* \leqslant 2Q^*k^* < \infty, \quad (43)$$

while, from (39) and (41), v behaves according to

$$\dot{v} = \dot{q}(k - k^*) + (q - Q^*) \dot{k}$$

$$= (\dot{q}k) - \dot{q}k^* - Q^*\dot{k}$$

$$= \frac{\partial H(p, q, k, 1)}{\partial k} k^* - Q^* \frac{\partial H(p, q, k, 1)}{\partial q}$$

$$= rk^* - Q^*z. \qquad (44)$$

[30] Otherwise any normalization, e.g., $p(0) = 1$, will do.

In order for $\dot{v}$ to be sufficiently positive to guarantee convergence of k to k^*, we also need a somewhat different stability assumption than before, namely, the

INTENSITY AND STABILITY ASSUMPTION. (i) $(p, q, r, w) \in M$, $(c, z, -k, -l) \in T$, $pc + qz - rk - w = 0$, $pc = w > 0$, and $qk = Q^*k^* > 0 \Rightarrow rk^* \{\gtreqless\} 0$ according as $p \{\gtreqless\} 1$, or $rk^* \geqslant Rk^*$, and (ii) for every $\epsilon > 0$ there is a $\delta > 0$ such that $\| k - k^* \| > \epsilon \Rightarrow$

$$(Q - Q^*) \frac{\partial H(Q, k)}{\partial Q} - \frac{\partial H(Q, k)}{\partial k} (k - k^*) =$$
$$(Q - Q^*) z - R(k - k^*) > \delta \quad (\text{I})$$

when $Q(\partial H(Q, k)/\partial Q) = Qz = (\partial H(Q, k)/\partial k) k = Rk$.

We should emphasize that it is the first part of (I) which is really fundamental, since it entails that (44) can be bounded below by

$$rk^* - Q^*z \geqslant Rk^* - Q^*z, \quad (45)$$

and in that condition, the normalization $qk = Q^*k^*$ which is really crucial, since, without it, finding fairly general stability conditions seems an almost impossible task. Again, this particular normalization was suggested by careful scrutiny of the worked-out examples, especially the one- and two-sector models. Notice, by way of interpretation, that the conclusion of the first part of (I) can be restated as (because $Qk \{\gtreqless\} Q^*k^*$ according as $p \{\gtreqless\} 1$ when $qk = Q^*k^*$)

$$Rk^* \{\gtreqless\} 0 \qquad \text{according as} \quad Qk \{\gtreqless\} Q^*k^*, \quad (46)$$

"aggregate" net rentals are positive or negative depending on whether "aggregate" capital intensity is less or greater than its golden rule path value.

A reader steeped in the tradition of neoclassical growth theory might plausibly conjecture that (46) is closely related to the condition that

$$c \{\gtreqless\} c^* \qquad \text{according as} \quad Qk \{\gtreqless\} Q^*k^*, \quad (47)$$

aggregate consumption is less or greater than its golden rule path value depending on whether "aggregate" capital intensity is. Unfortunately, neither (46) nor (47) implies the other. It is interesting to notice, however, that (47) can be strengthened to provide an alternative stability condition, since (44) can also be bounded below by

$$rk* - Q*z = -(pc* + qz* - rk* - w) - (c + Q*z - R*k - W*)$$
$$- (p - 1)(c - c*)$$
$$\geqslant -(p - 1)(c - c*). \tag{48}$$

By virtue of (48), (47) entails that (again because $Qk \{\lesseqgtr\} Q*k*$ according as $p \{\gtreqless\} 1$ when $qk = Q*k*$)

$$rk* - Q*z \{\geqq 0\} \qquad \text{according as} \quad Qk \{\lesseqgtr\} Q*k*, \tag{49}$$

a condition which can obviously be elaborated to yield $\dot{v}$ sufficiently positive to guarantee convergence of k to $k*$. In either case, (46) or (47), the parallel with intrinsic properties of the one-good model is self-evident.

We are now in a position to demonstrate the

STABILITY OF DESCRIPTIVE GROWTH WITH MARXIAN SAVING–INVEST- MENT BEHAVIOR. *Assumptions* (P) *and* (I) *imply that the real side of the solutions to* (39) *converges to unique (nontrivial) golden rule capital stocks.*

Proof. According to (42), there are two distinct cases to consider. (i) $qk = 0$: Here $k > 0$ implies $q = 0$ implies $r = 0$ (as $\dot{q} = -r$) implies $rk* = 0$. Hence, from (44) $\dot{v} = -Q*z$, while from just the second part of (I)

for every $\epsilon > 0$ there is a $\delta > 0$ such that $\| k - k* \| > \epsilon \Rightarrow -Q*z > \delta$.

Thus, by the sort of reasoning used in our earlier stability argument, (43) entails $\lim_{t \to \infty} k = k*$. (ii) $qk = Q*k* > 0$: Here, for any point along a solution to (39)–(40), the first part of (I) allows us to strengthen the second part to

for every $\epsilon > 0$ there is a $\delta > 0$ such that $\| k - k* \| > \epsilon \Rightarrow$
$$\dot{v} = rk* - Q*z \geqslant Rk* - Q*z > \delta.$$

Thus, as before, (43) entails $\lim_{t \to \infty} k = k*$.

E. *Worked-out Examples and Extensions*

It is fairly easy to show that (P) and (I) are satisfied in Uzawa's two-sector model, provided that the consumption-goods sector is more capital intensive than the investment-goods sector so that Inada's type of counter-example is excluded.[31] It is much less obvious whether our conditions

---

[31] We note in passing that this model does not satisfy a stronger uniqueness or stability assumption, like (U⁰) or (S⁰) of the last section. Many feasible allocations with $k \neq k*$ can be static profit maximizing at (modified) golden rule prices.

apply to the other worked-out examples. Thus far we have been able to show, by an extremely tedious argument, that the Shell–Stiglitz example [33] satisfies (P) and a weaker version of (I), which may imply stability as well, but at present it appears that it does not satisfy (I). We have not yet tackled the other worked-out examples (in particular, the Caton–Shell example [8]). Even for the descriptive growth model with Marxian saving–investment behavior, much more work needs to be done!

Analysis of this model is clearly simplified because the saving–investment hypothesis can be described entirely in terms of H, and because the only consistent, meaningful stationary points are golden rule paths. The next obvious candidate for analysis is a model with the Keynesian saving–investment hypothesis, which has neither of these special features. Our failure thus far to find general results for such a model seems to be related to our inability to see how to utilize the restrictions imposed by (18), if indeed they can be. In any case, the investigation of this, and further similar extensions, seem a fascinating and important task for future research.

Of course, it may well turn out that the stability notion used in our present analysis is simply far too rigid for any such contemplated extensions. For example, it may be more appropriate to ask whether there is some bounded set of capital stocks, perhaps exhibiting other special properties, which serves as a global attractor for the real side of the solutions to a Hamiltonian dynamical system. This broadened stability notion would then obviously accommodate such phenomena as arise in Sutherland's or Inada's examples. It might also be sufficient to completely dispel Hahn-like worries [12] about the "gross" inefficiency of capitalist development. However, on the other hand, it would definitely entail a significant loss in our ability to do meaningful comparative dynamics.

ACKNOWLEDGMENTS

Research on this paper was supported by National Science Foundation grants GS-33354 at Carnegie–Mellon University, GS-41494, SOC74-03974, and SOC74-19469 at the University of Pennsylvania, and GS-40104 at Stanford University. The work leading up to the paper was begun in earnest during the summer of 1972, and preliminary reports were presented at the Stanford IMSSS Summer Seminar in July 1973 and at the Buffalo Conference on Macroeconomics and Capital Theory in March 1974. The present version is an expansion of a note prepared for the latter conference. At various points in our research correspondence with R. T. Rockafellar was very helpful. Both his and L. W. McKenzie's thoughtful, detailed criticism of the first draft of the paper have led to significant improvement. We have also benefitted from conversations with W. A. Brock, R. E. Gaines, M. Magill, and J. A. Scheinkman.

REFERENCES

1. H. ATSUMI, Neoclassical growth and the efficient program of capital accumulation, *Rev. Econ. Stud.* **32** (1965), 127–136.
2. W. A. BROCK, On the existence of weakly maximal programmes in a multi-sector economy, *Rev. Econ. Stud.* **37** (1970), 275–280.
3. W. A. BROCK AND J. A. SCHEINKMAN, Global asymptotic stability of optimal control systems with applications to the theory of economic growth, *J. Econ. Theory* **12** (1976), 164–190. Reprinted as Essay VII in this volume.
4. E. BURMEISTER, C. CATON, A. R. DOBELL, AND S. ROSS, The "saddlepoint property" and the structure of dynamic heterogeneous capital good models, *Econometrica* **41** (1973), 79–95.
5. D. CASS, Optimum growth in an aggregative model of capital accumulation, *Rev. Econ. Stud.* **32** (1965), 233–240.
6. D. CASS, Duality: a symmetric approach from the economist's vantage point, *J. Econ. Theory* **7** (1974), 272–295.
7. D. CASS, The Hamiltonian representation of static competitive or efficient allocation, *in* "Essays in Modern Capital Theory" (M. Brown, K. Sato and P. Zarembka, Eds.), pp. 159-178, North–Holland, Amsterdam, 1976.
8. C. CATON AND K. SHELL, An exercise in the theory of heterogeneous capital accumulation, *Rev. Econ. Stud.* **38** (1971), 13–22.
9. R. DORFMAN, P. A. SAMUELSON, AND R. M. SOLOW, "Linear Programming and Economic Analysis," McGraw–Hill, New York, 1958.
10. H. FURUYA AND K. INADA, Balanced growth and intertemporal efficiency in capital accumulation, *Int. Econ. Rev.* **3** (1962), 94–107.
11. D. GALE, On optimal development in a multi-sector economy, *Rev. Econ. Stud.* **34** (1967), 1–18.
12. F. H. HAHN, Equilibrium dynamics with heterogeneous capital goods, *Quart. J. Econ.* **80** (1966), 633–646.
13. F. H. HAHN, On some equilibrium paths, *in* "Models of Economic Growth" (J. A. Mirrlees and N. H. Stern, Eds.), pp. 193–206, Macmillan, London, 1973.
14. K. INADA, On a two-sector model of economic growth: comments and a generalization, *Rev. Econ. Stud.* **30** (1963), 119–127.
15. M. KURZ, Optimal economic growth and wealth effects, *Int. Econ. Rev.* **9** (1968), 155–174.
16. L. LAU, A characterization of the normalized restricted profit function, *J. Econ. Theory* **12** (1976), 131–163. Reprinted as Essay VI in this volume.
17. E. MALINVAUD, Capital accumulation and efficient allocation of resources, *Econometrica* **21** (1953), 233–268.
18. L. W. MCKENZIE, Turnpike theorems for a generalized Leontief model, *Econometrica* **31** (1963), 165–180.
19. L. W. MCKENZIE, Accumulation programs of maximum utility and the von Neumann facet, *in* "Value, Capital and Growth" (J. Wolfe, Ed.), pp. 353–383, Edinburgh Univ. Press, Edinburgh, 1968.
20. M. MORISHIMA, Proof of a turnpike theorem: the "no joint production case," *Rev. Econ. Stud.* **28** (1961), 89–97.
21. B. PELEG, Efficiency prices for optimal consumption plans, *J. Math. Anal. Appl.* **29** (1970), 83–90.
22. B. PELEG AND H. E. RYDER, JR., On optimal consumption plans in a multi-sector economy, *Rev. Econ. Stud.* **39** (1972), 159–169.

23. R. RADNER, Paths of economic growth that are optimal with regard only to final states: a turnpike theorem, *Rev. Econ. Stud.* **28** (1961), 98–104.
24. F. P. RAMSEY, A mathematical theory of saving, *Econ. J.* **38** (1928), 543–559.
25. R. T. ROCKAFELLAR, Saddlepoints of Hamiltonian systems in convex problems of Lagrange, *J. Optimization Theory Appl.* **12** (1973), 367–390.
26. R. T. ROCKAFELLAR, Saddlepoints of Hamiltonian systems in convex Lagrange problems having a nonzero discount rate, *J. Econ. Theory* **12** (1976), 71–113. Reprinted as Essay IV in this volume.
27. H. E. RYDER, JR., Optimal accumulation in a two-sector neoclassical economy with non-shiftable capital, *J. Polit. Econ.* **77** (1969), 665–683.
28. H. E. RYDER, JR., AND G. M. HEAL, Optimum growth with intertemporally dependent preferences, *Rev. Econ. Stud.* **40** (1973), 1–31.
29. P. A. SAMUELSON, The general saddlepoint property of optimal-control motions, *J. Econ. Theory* **5** (1972), 102–120.
30. J. A. SCHEINKMAN, On optimal steady states of *n*-sector growth models when utility is discounted, *J. Econ. Theory* **12** (1976), 11–30. Reprinted as Essay II in this volume.
31. K. SHELL, Applications of Pontryagin's maximum principle to economics, *in* "Mathematical Systems Theory and Economics I" (H. W. Kuhn and G. P. Szegö, Eds.), pp. 241–292, Springer–Verlag, Berlin, 1969.
32. K. SHELL, M. SIDRAUSKI, AND J. E. STIGLITZ, Capital gains, income, and saving, *Rev. Econ. Stud.* **36** (1969), 15–26.
33. K. SHELL AND J. E. STIGLITZ, The allocation of investment in a dynamic economy, *Quart. J. Econ.* **81** (1967), 592–609.
34. R. M. SOLOW, A contribution to the theory of economic growth, *Quart. J. Econ.* **70** (1956), 64–95.
35. W. R. S. SUTHERLAND, On optimal development in a multi-sectoral economy: the discounted case, *Rev. Econ. Stud.* **37** (1970), 585–589.
36. H. UZAWA, On a two-sector model of economic growth, *Rev. Econ. Stud.* **28** (1961), 40–47.
37. M. L. WEITZMAN, Duality theory for infinite horizon convex models, *Management Sci.* **19** (1973), 783–789.

ESSAY IV

Saddle Points of Hamiltonian Systems in Convex Lagrange Problems Having a Nonzero Discount Rate

R. Tyrrell Rockafellar*

Problems are studied in which an integral of the form $\int_0^{+\infty} L(k(t), \dot{k}(t))e^{-\rho t}\, dt$ is minimized over a class of arcs k: $[0, +\infty) \to R^n$. It is assumed that L is a convex function on $R^n \times R^n$ and that the discount rate ρ is positive. Optimality conditions are expressed in terms of a perturbed Hamiltonian differential system involving a Hamiltonian function $H(k, q)$ which is concave in k and convex in q, but not necessarily differentiable. Conditions are given ensuring that, for ρ sufficiently small, the system has a stationary point, in a neighborhood of which one has classical "saddle point" behavior. The optimal arcs of interest then correspond to the solutions of the system which tend to the stationary point as $t \to +\infty$. These results are motivated by questions in theoretical economics and extend previous work of the author for the case $\rho = 0$. The case $\rho < 0$ is also covered in part.

1. Introduction

Let $L: R^n \times R^n \to (-\infty, +\infty]$ be convex, lower, semicontinuous, and not identically $+\infty$, and let $\rho \geqslant 0$. For each $c \in R^n$, let

$$\phi(c) = \inf \left\{ \int_0^{+\infty} L(k(t), \dot{k}(t))\, e^{-\rho t}\, dt \,\bigg|\, k(0) = c \right\}, \qquad (1.1)$$

where the infimum is over the class of all *arcs* (taken here to mean *absolutely continuous functions*) k: $[0, +\infty) \to R^n$ such that $e^{-\rho t}k(t)$ remains bounded as $t \to +\infty$. The integral in (1.1) has a classical value, possibly infinite, unless neither the positive nor the negative part of the integrand $L(k(t), \dot{k}(t))\, e^{-\rho t}$ (a measurable function of t) is summable over $[0, +\infty)$; in the latter case, we consider the integral to have the value $+\infty$ by convention. The convexity of L implies the convexity of ϕ as an extended-real-valued function on R^n.

Our interest lies in the existence and characterization of the arcs k, if any, for which the infimum in (1.1) is attained. An important aid in this

* Supported in part by Grant AFOSR-72-2269 at the University of Washington.

regard is the study of a generalized Hamiltonian subdifferential "equation"

$$(-e^{\rho t}\dot{w}(t), \dot{k}(t)) \in \partial H(k(t), e^{\rho t}w(t)) \qquad \text{a.e.,} \qquad (1.2)$$

which after the change of variables,

$$q(t) = e^{\rho t}w(t), \qquad (1.3)$$

can be rewritten in the autonomous form

$$(-\dot{q}(t) + \rho q(t), \dot{k}(t)) \in \partial H(k(t), q(t)) \qquad \text{a.e.} \qquad (1.4)$$

The Hamiltonian H is defined here by the conjugacy formula

$$H(k, q) = \sup\{z \cdot q - L(k, z) | z \in R^n\}. \qquad (1.5)$$

By virtue of the assumptions on L, $H(k, q)$ is concave in k, convex in q, and the inverse formula

$$L(k, z) = \sup\{z \cdot q - H(k, q) | q \in R^n\} \qquad (1.6)$$

is valid (cf. [3]). The set $\partial H(k, q)$ consists of the *subgradients* of H at (k, q), i.e., the pairs $(r, z) \in R^n \times R^n$ such that

$$H(k, q') \geqslant H(k, q) + (q' - q) \cdot z \qquad \text{for all} \quad q' \in R^n, \qquad (1.7)$$

$$H(k', q) \leqslant H(k, q) + (k' - k) \cdot r \qquad \text{for all} \quad k' \in R^n. \qquad (1.8)$$

Established theory (cf. [3]) tells us that if $k(t)$ and $q(t)$ satisfy the (perturbed) Hamiltonian system (1.4) over a real interval J, then for every bounded subinterval $[t_0, t_1]$ of J, the integral

$$\int_{t_0}^{t_1} L(k(t), \dot{k}(t)) e^{-\rho t} dt \qquad (1.9)$$

is minimized with respect to the class of all arcs over $[t_0, t_1]$ having the same endpoints as k at $t = t_0$ and $t = t_1$. At the same time, there is a dual property: for a certain function M, the integral

$$\int_{t_0}^{t_1} M(q(t), \dot{q}(t) - \rho q(t)) e^{-\rho t} dt \qquad (1.10)$$

is minimized with respect to the class of all arcs over $[t_0, t_1]$ having the same endpoints as q at $t = t_0$ and $t = t_1$. The function M is defined by

$$\begin{aligned} M(q, s) &= \sup\{k \cdot s + z \cdot q - L(k, z) | (k, z) \in R^n \times R^n\} \\ &= \sup\{k \cdot s + H(k, q) | k \in R^n\}, \end{aligned} \qquad (1.11)$$

and one has, reciprocally,

$$L(k, z) = \sup\{k \cdot s + z \cdot q - M(q, s)|(q, s) \in R^n \times R^n\}. \quad (1.12)$$

Indeed, in the terminology of [3] the Lagrangians

$$\tilde{L}(t, k, z) = L(k, z) e^{-\rho t}, \quad (1.13)$$

$$\tilde{M}(t, w, v) = M(e^{\rho t}w, e^{\rho t}v) e^{-\rho t} \quad (1.14)$$

are dual to each other, whence the result [3, p. 213].

Henceforth, let $(\bar{k}, \bar{q})$ denote a pair in $R^n \times R^n$ such that

$$(\rho\bar{q}, 0) \in \partial H(\bar{k}, \bar{q}). \quad (1.15)$$

(We shall comment in Section 6 on the existence of such a pair $(\bar{k}, \bar{q})$.) Relation (1.15) means that $(\bar{k}, \bar{q})$ is a *stationary point* of the system (1.4), in the sense that the constant functions $k(t) \equiv \bar{k}$ and $q(t) \equiv \bar{q}$ satisfy the system over $J = (-\infty, +\infty)$. In a previous paper [2], we investigated for the case $\rho = 0$ the behavior of the system near such a stationary point, particularly the existence of solutions $(k(t), q(t))$ tending to $(\bar{k}, \bar{q})$ as $t \to +\infty$ or as $t \to -\infty$. This was shown to be closely related to question of optimality for the minimization problems in (1.1), as well as for a class of dual problems involving M. The analysis was carried out under the assumption that H was *strictly* concave–convex in a neighborhood of $(\bar{k}, \bar{q})$.

The purpose of the present paper is to extend some of the results to the case of sufficiently small $\rho > 0$, making use of a strengthened strict concavity–convexity assumption on H. Economic motivation may be found in the interesting paper of Cass and Shell [1], which contains certain related results based on a somewhat different set of technical assumptions.

It will be convenient to make a translation of variables,

$$x = k - \bar{k}, \quad p = q - \bar{q}, \quad (1.16)$$

so that the stationary point of the Hamiltonian system appears at the origin and the finiteness of certain integrals is more apparent. Specifically, let

$$H_0(x, p) = H(\bar{k} + x, \bar{q} + p) - H(\bar{k}, \bar{q}) - \rho x\bar{q}. \quad (1.17)$$

Then H_0 is a concave–convex function which, according to (1.15), satisfies

$$(0, 0) \in \partial H_0(0, 0), \quad (1.18)$$

or in other words, the minimax saddle point condition

$$H_0(x, 0) \leqslant H_0(0, 0) \leqslant H_0(0, p) \qquad \text{for all} \quad x \in R^n, p \in R^n. \quad (1.19)$$

Moreover, one has

$$H_0(0, 0) = 0. \qquad (1.20)$$

The (perturbed) Hamiltonian system

$$(-\dot{p}(t) + \rho p(t), \dot{x}(t)) \in \partial H_0(x(t), p(t)) \qquad (1.21)$$

is clearly equivalent to the previous system (1.4) under (1.16).

Let us also define

$$L_0(x, z) = L(\bar{k} + x, z) - L(\bar{k}, 0) - \bar{q} \cdot (z - \rho x), \qquad (1.22)$$

$$M_0(p, u) = M(\bar{q} + p, -\rho\bar{q} + u) - M(\bar{q}, -\rho\bar{q}) - \bar{k} \cdot u. \quad (1.23)$$

These formulas yield (by the theory of conjugate convex functions, cf. [3]) the relations

$$H_0(x, p) = \sup\{z \cdot p - L_0(x, z) \mid z \in R^n\}, \qquad (1.24)$$

$$L_0(x, z) = \sup\{z \cdot p - H_0(x, p) \mid p \in R^n\}, \qquad (1.25)$$

$$M_0(p, u) = \sup\{x \cdot u + z \cdot p - L_0(x, z) \mid (x, z) \in R^n \times R^n\}$$
$$= \sup\{x \cdot u + H_0(x, p) \mid x \in R^n\} \qquad (1.26)$$

$$L_0(x, z) = \sup\{x \cdot u + z \cdot p - M_0(p, u) \mid (p, u) \in R^n \times R^n\}, \quad (1.27)$$

inasmuch as (1.3) implies

$$-L(\bar{k}, 0) = H(\bar{k}, \bar{q}) = M(\bar{q}, -\rho\bar{q}) + \rho\bar{k} \cdot \bar{p}. \qquad (1.28)$$

Observe that

$$L_0(x, z) \geqslant L_0(0, 0) = 0 \qquad \text{for all} \quad (x, z) \in R^n \times R^n, \quad (1.29)$$

$$M_0(p, u) \geqslant M_0(0, 0) = 0 \qquad \text{for all} \quad (p, u) \in R^n \times R^n. \quad (1.30)$$

Let us say that a finite function h on a convex set $C \subset R^n$ is α-convex, where $\alpha \in R$, if for all $x \in R^n$, $x' \in R^n$ and $\lambda \in [0, 1]$, it is true that

$$h((1 - \lambda) x + \lambda x') \leqslant (1 - \lambda) h(x) + \lambda h(x') - \tfrac{1}{2}\alpha\lambda(1 - \lambda)| x - x' |^2, \qquad (1.31)$$

where $| \cdot |$ denotes the Euclidean norm. Obviously, this is ordinary convexity if $\alpha = 0$ and a form of strict convexity (*strong* convexity) if

$\alpha > 0$. One can verify that h is α-convex if and only if the function $h(x) - \frac{1}{2}\alpha \mid x \mid^2$ is convex. Thus, if C is open and h is twice differentiable, α-convexity is equivalent to the condition that

$$v \cdot Q(x)\, v \geqslant \alpha \mid v \mid^2 \qquad \text{for all} \quad x \in C,\, v \in R^n,$$

where $Q(x)$ is the matrix of second partial derivatives of h at x. Another easily derived characterization, for C open, is that h is α-convex if and only if for each $z \in C$, there exists $y \in R^n$ such that

$$h(x') \geqslant h(x) + (x' - x) \cdot y + \tfrac{1}{2}\alpha \mid x' - x \mid^2 \qquad \text{. for all} \quad x' \in C. \quad (1.32)$$

At all events, if h is α-convex on C (not necessarily open) and $y \in \partial h(x)$, then (1.32) holds.

We shall say h is α-*concave* if, in place of (1.31), we have

$$h((1 - \lambda)\, x + \lambda x') \geqslant (1 - \lambda)\, h(x) + \lambda h(x') + \tfrac{1}{2}\alpha\lambda(1 - \lambda) \mid x - x' \mid^2.$$
$$(1.33)$$

CURVATURE ASSUMPTION. *We suppose throughout this paper that, for certain values $\alpha > 0$ and $\beta > 0$, the Hamiltonian H is locally α-concave-β-convex near the stationary point $(\bar{k}, \bar{q})$, or in other words, that there exists a convex neighborhood $U \times V$ of $(0, 0)$ in $R^n \times R^n$ such that $H_0(x, p)$ is (finite and) α-concave in $x \in U$ for each $p \in V$ and β-convex in $p \in V$ for each $x \in U$. Moreover, the discount rate $\rho > 0$ is small enough so that*

$$\rho^2 < 4\alpha\beta. \quad (1.34)$$

Let K_+ denote the set of all pairs $(a, b) \in R^n \times R^n$ such that the Hamiltonian system (1.21) has a solution $(x(t), p(t))$ over $[0, +\infty)$ satisfying

$$(x(0), p(0)) = (a, b), \quad (1.35)$$

$$e^{-\rho t}x(t) \cdot p(t) \to 0 \text{ as } t \to +\infty. \quad (1.36)$$

The first of our main results is the following.

THEOREM 1. *There is an open neighborhood $U_+ \times V_+$ of $(0, 0)$ (arbitrarily small, with $U_+ \subset U$ and $V_+ \subset V$) such that $K_+ \cap (U_+ \times V_+)$ is the graph of a homeomorphism of U_+ onto V_+, and for each $(a, b) \in K_+ \cap (U_+ \times V_+)$ the solution to the system (1.21) over $[0, +\infty)$ satisfying (1.35) and (1.36) is unique, remains in $K_+ \cap (U_+ \times V_+)$ and converges to $(0, 0)$ as $t \to +\infty$.*

To give an interpretation to the set K_+, we introduce the functions

$$f_+(a) = \inf \left\{ \int_0^{+\infty} L_0(x(t), \dot{x}(t)) e^{-\rho t} \, dt \,\middle|\, x(0) = a \right\}, \qquad (1.37)$$

$$g_+(b) = \inf \left\{ \int_0^{+\infty} M_0(p(t), \dot{p}(t) - \rho p(t)) e^{-\rho t} \, dt \,\middle|\, p(0) = b \right\}, \qquad (1.38)$$

where each infimum is taken over the class of *all* arcs (absolutely continuous R^n-valued functions) defined on $[0, +\infty)$ and satisfying the endpoint condition in question. Note that the integrals are well-defined (possibly $+\infty$), due to the lower semicontinuity and nonnegativity of the functions L_0 and M_0. In fact, (1.29) and (1.30) imply that the functions f_+ and g_+ on R^n are nonnegative and vanish at 0. Of course, these functions are all convex; this follows immediately from the convexity of L_0 and M_0.

For $a = c - \bar{k}$, the minimization problem in (1.37) is equivalent to the one defining the value $\phi(c)$ at the beginning of our introduction, as will be demonstrated in the next section (Proposition 2). This equivalence could fail if one were to drop from the definition of $\phi(c)$ the restriction to arcs k such that $e^{-\rho t}k(t)$ remains bounded as $t \to +\infty$; see Example 2 in Section 6.

THEOREM 2. *Let U_+ and V_+ be neighborhoods of 0 with the properties in Theorem 1. Then f_+ is finite and continuously differentiable on U_+, g_+ is finite and continuously differentiable on V_+, and for $(a, b) \in U_+ \times V_+$, one has*

$$f_+(a) + g_+(b) \geqslant -a \cdot b, \qquad (1.39)$$

with

$$\begin{aligned} (a, b) \in K_+ &\Leftrightarrow f_+(a) + g_+(b) = -a \cdot b \\ &\Leftrightarrow b = -\nabla f_+(a) \Leftrightarrow a = -\nabla g_+(b). \end{aligned} \qquad (1.40)$$

Moreover, if $(x(t), p(t))$ is the solution to the Hamiltonian system (1.21) over $[0, +\infty)$ corresponding to $(a, b) \in K_+ \cap (U_+ \times V_+)$ as in Theorem 1, then the arc x uniquely furnishes the minimum in the definition (1.37) of $f_+(a)$, while the arc p uniquely furnishes the minimum in the definition (1.38) of $g_+(b)$.

Complementary results are obtainable for behavior over the interval $(-\infty, 0]$. These are of less interest for economic applications, but they do shed further light on the qualitative nature of the Hamiltonian dynamical system. They can also be interpreted equivalently, under a reversal of time, as results over $[0, +\infty)$ for a *negative discount rate ρ*.

Let K_- denote the set of all pairs $(a, b) \in R^n \times R^n$ such that the system (1.21) has a solution $(x(t), p(t))$ over $(-\infty, 0]$ satisfying (1.35), and

$$e^{-\rho t} x(t) \cdot p(t) \to 0 \text{ as } t \to -\infty. \tag{1.41}$$

Define

$$f_-(a) = \inf \left\{ \int_{-\infty}^0 L_0(x(t), \dot{x}(t)) \, e^{-\rho t} \, dt \, \middle| \, x(0) = a \right\}, \tag{1.42}$$

$$g_-(b) = \inf \left\{ \int_{-\infty}^0 M_0(p(t), \dot{p}(t) - \rho p(t)) \, e^{-\rho t} \, dt \, \middle| \, p(0) = b \right\}. \tag{1.43}$$

The functions f_- and g_- are nonnegative, convex, and they vanish at 0.

THEOREM 1'. *There is an open neighborhood $U_- \times V_-$ of $(0, 0)$ (arbitrarily small, with $U_- \subset U$ and $V_- \subset V$) such that $K_- \cap (U_- \times V_-)$ is the graph of a homeomorphism of U_- onto V_-, and for each $(a, b) \in K_- \cap (U_- \times V_-)$ the solution to the system (1.21) over $(-\infty, 0]$ satisfying (1.35) and (1.41) is unique, remains in $K_- \cap (U_- \times V_-)$ and converges to $(0, 0)$ as $t \to -\infty$. Moreover,*

$$K_+ \cap K_- = \{(0, 0)\}. \tag{1.44}$$

THEOREM 2'. *Let U_- and V_- be neighborhoods of 0 with the properties in Theorem 1'. Then f_- is finite and continuously differentiable on U_-, g_- is finite and continuously differentiable on V_-, and for $(a, b) \in U_- \times V_-$, one has*

$$f_-(a) + g_-(b) \geqslant a \cdot b, \tag{1.45}$$

with

$$(a, b) \in K_- \Leftrightarrow f_-(a) + g_-(b) = a \cdot b$$
$$\Leftrightarrow b = \nabla f_-(a) \Leftrightarrow a = \nabla g_-(b). \tag{1.46}$$

Moreover, if $(x(t), p(t))$ is the solution to the Hamiltonian system (1.21) over $(-\infty, 0]$ corresponding to $(a, b) \in K_- \cap (U_- \times V_-)$ as in Theorem 1', then the arc x uniquely furnishes the minimum in the definition (1.42) of $f_-(a)$, while the arc p uniquely furnishes the minimum in the definition (1.43) of $g_-(b)$.

Theorems 1 and 1' say that the behavior of the system (1.21) near the rest point $(0, 0)$ resembles that of a classical saddlepoint in the theory of differential equations. At least locally, K_+ and K_- are n-dimensional manifolds intersecting only at $(0, 0)$, and comprised, respectively, of the trajectories that tend to $(0, 0)$ as $t \to +\infty$ and as $t \to -\infty$.

Theorem 2 will be derived from Theorem 1 in Section 2, while Theorem 1 itself will be established at the end of Section 4. The proofs of Theorem 1′ and 2′ are parallel, but in certain respects simpler; they will be treated in Section 5. Various examples and a result about the existence of points $(\bar{k}, \bar{q})$ satisfying the stationary point condition (1.15) will be treated in Section 6. In Section 3, we develop some facts which enable us, in Section 4, to deduce the local results from more special theorems based on a *global* assumption of α-concavity–β-convexity.

2. LOCAL BEHAVIOR AND OPTIMALITY

We start by establishing some bounds that, as a by-product, make clear the equivalence of the original class of variational problems defining the values $\phi(c)$ and the notationally more convenient ·class of "translated" problems defining the values $f_+(a)$.

PROPOSITION 1.   *The convex function L_0 is finite on a neighborhood of* $(0, 0)$, *and there exist real numbers $\mu_0 > 0$ and μ_1 such that*

$$L_0(x, z) \geqslant \mu_0[|x| + |z - \rho x|] - \mu_1 \qquad for\ all \quad (x, z) \in R^n \times R^n. \quad (2.1)$$

Similarly, the convex function M_0 is finite on a neighborhood of $(0, 0)$, *and there exist real numbers $\nu_0 > 0$ and ν_1 such that*

$$M_0(p, s - \rho p) \geqslant \nu_0[|p| + |s - \rho p|] - \nu_1 \qquad for\ all \quad (p, x) \in R^n \times R^n. \quad (2.2)$$

Proof.   According to our curvature assumption, the convex function $H_0(0, \cdot)$ is finite and strictly convex in a neighborhood of $p = 0$. It follows from this and the minimax property (1.19) that the supremum in formula (1.25) is uniquely attained at $p = 0$. But $H_0(0, \cdot)$ is conjugate to $L_0(0, \cdot)$ by (1.24), so this implies 0 is the unique subgradient of $L_0(0, \cdot)$ at $z = 0$ [5, Theorem 23.5]. Hence, $L_0(0, \cdot)$ is finite on a neighborhood of 0 (since otherwise the subgradient set would have to be unbounded or empty [5, Theorem 23.4]). Thus, the convex set

$$\operatorname{dom} L_0 = \{(x, z) \in R^n \times R^n \mid L_0(x, z) < +\infty\} \quad (2.3)$$

contains $(0, z)$ for all z sufficiently near 0. On the other hand, the image of dom L_0 under the projection $(x, z) \rightarrow x$ consists of all x such that the convex function $L_0(x, \cdot)$ is not identically $+\infty$, or what is equivalent in view of the conjugacy relation (1.24), such that the convex function $H_0(x, \cdot)$ nowhere takes the value $-\infty$. This image therefore contains the neighborhood U in our curvature assumption, since a convex function cannot take on the value $-\infty$ anywhere if it is finite on some nonempty open set [5, Theorem 7.2]. Thus 0 lies in the interior of the x-projection of dom L_0, while 0 is also in the interior of the z-cross-section of dom L_0 corresponding to $x = 0$. These properties imply that $(0, 0)$ is an interior point of dom L_0 [5, Theorem 7.8], or in other words that L_0 is finite on a neighborhood of $(0, 0)$. Of course, L_0 is then continuous near $(0, 0)$ by convexity. Thus there exist $\nu_0 > 0$ and ν_1 such that

$$L_0(x, z) \leqslant \nu_1 \qquad \text{if} \quad |x| \leqslant \nu_0 \text{ and } |z| \leqslant \nu_0.$$

Applying this to formula (1.26) (for M_0 in terms of L_0), we obtain

$$
\begin{aligned}
M_0(p, u) &\geqslant \sup\{x \cdot p + z \cdot u - \nu_1 \,||\, |x| \leqslant \nu_0, |z| \leqslant \nu_0\} \\
&= \nu_0 |p| + \nu_0 |u| - \nu_1,
\end{aligned}
$$

which is the desired inequality (2.2).

By a parallel argument, the concave function $H_0(\cdot, 0)$ is finite and strictly concave on a neighborhood of $x = 0$, so that by (1.19), the supremum in formula (1.26) (for M_0 in terms of H_0) is attained uniquely for $x = 0$. Since this formula expresses the convex function $M_0(0, \cdot)$ as the conjugate of $-H(\cdot, 0)$, we are able to conclude, just as above, that 0 is the unique subgradient of $M_0(0, \cdot)$ at 0, and, hence, that $M_0(0, \cdot)$ is finite on a neighborhood of 0. The convex set

$$\text{dom } M_0 = \{(p, u)\,|\, M_0(p, u) < +\infty\} \tag{2.4}$$

therefore contains $(0, u)$ for all u sufficiently near 0. The p-projection of dom M_0 also contains the neighborhood V of 0 in our curvature assumption, because of (1.26). We deduce from this that $(0, 0)$ is an interior point of dom M_0 and consequently a point in a neighborhood of which M_0 is finite and continuous. Let the numbers $\mu > 0$, $\mu' > 0$, and μ_1 be such that

$$M_0(p, u) \leqslant \mu_1 \qquad \text{if} \quad |p| \leqslant \mu \text{ and } |u| \leqslant \mu'.$$

We then have from (1.27) that

$$
\begin{aligned}
L_0(x, z) &\geqslant \sup\{x \cdot u + p \cdot z - \mu_1 \,||\, |p| \leqslant \mu, |u| \leqslant \mu'\} \\
&= \mu |x| + \mu' |z| - \mu_1.
\end{aligned}
$$

Using the fact that

$$|z| \geqslant |z - \rho x| - \rho |x|,$$

we get

$$L_0(x, z) \geqslant (\mu - \rho\mu')|x| + \mu'|z - \rho x| - \mu_1.$$

The desired inequality (2.1) therefore holds for

$$\mu_0 = \min\{\mu - \rho\mu', \mu'\},$$

provided μ' is taken small enough so that this value is positive.

The next proposition is the one specifically establishing the asserted equivalence between the minimization problems defining $\phi(c)$ in (1.1) (where $e^{-\rho t}k(t)$ is bounded) and $f_+(a)$ in (1.37) for $x = k - \bar{k}$, $a = c - \bar{k}$. (In the problem for $f_+(a)$, it is not stipulated in advance that $e^{-\rho t}x(t)$ be bounded, but this turns out to be a consequence of the finiteness of the integral.)

PROPOSITION 2.   (a) *If the arc* $x : [0, +\infty) \to R^n$ *is such that* $L_0(x(t),$ $\dot{x}(t))$ $e^{-\rho t}$ *is summable in t over* $[0, +\infty)$, *then*

$$\lim_{t \to +\infty} e^{-\rho t}x(t) = 0, \tag{2.5}$$

and for $k(t) = \bar{k} + x(t)$, *we have* $L(k(t), \dot{k}(t))$ $e^{-\rho t}$ *summable in t, with*

$$\int_0^{+\infty} L(k(t), \dot{k}(t)) \, e^{-\rho t} \, dt$$
$$= \int_0^{+\infty} L_0(x(t), \dot{x}(t)) \, e^{-\rho t} \, dt - [H(\bar{k}, \bar{q})/\rho] - x(0) \cdot \bar{q}. \tag{2.6}$$

On the other hand, if $L(k(t), \dot{k}(t))$ $e^{-\rho t}$ *is majorized by a summable function of t over* $[0, +\infty)$, *and also*

$$\limsup_{t \to +\infty} e^{-\rho t}k(t) \cdot \bar{q} > -\infty, \tag{2.7}$$

then $L_0(x(t), \dot{x}(t))$ $e^{-\rho t}$ *is indeed summable over* $[0, +\infty)$. (b) *If the arc* $p : [0, +\infty) \to R^n$ *is such that* $M_0(p(t), \dot{p}(t) - \rho p(t))$ $e^{-\rho t}$ *is summable in t over* $[0, +\infty)$, *then*

$$\lim_{t \to +\infty} e^{-\rho t}p(t) = 0, \tag{2.8}$$

and for $q(t) = \bar{q} + p(t)$, *we have* $M(q(t), \dot{q}(t) - \rho q(t))$ $e^{-\rho t}$ *summable in t, with*

$$\int_0^{+\infty} M(q(t), \dot{q}(t) - \rho q(t)) \, e^{-\rho t} \, dt$$
$$= \int_0^{+\infty} M_0(p(t), \dot{p}(t) - \rho p(t)) \, e^{-\rho t} \, dt - [H(\bar{k}, \bar{q})/\rho] + k \cdot q(0). \tag{2.9}$$

On the other hand, if $M(q(t), \dot{q}(t) - pq(t)) e^{-pt}$ is majorized by a summable function of t over $[0, +\infty)$, and also

$$\limsup_{t \to +\infty} e^{-pt} q(t) \cdot \bar{k} > -\infty, \qquad (2.10)$$

then $M_0(p(t), \dot{p}(t) - pp(t)) e^{-pt}$ is summable over $[0, +\infty)$.

Proof. If $L_0(x(t), \dot{x}(t)) e^{-pt}$ is summable, then by virtue of inequality (2.1) in Proposition 1, we have

$$\int_0^{+\infty} | x(t) | e^{-pt} dt < +\infty \qquad \text{and} \qquad \int_0^{+\infty} | \dot{x}(t) - x(t) | e^{-pt} dt < +\infty. \qquad (2.11)$$

Setting $v(t) = e^{-pt} x(t)$, so that

$$\dot{v}(t) = [\dot{x}(t) - \rho x(t)] e^{-pt},$$

we see from (2.11) that

$$\int_0^{+\infty} | v(t) | dt < +\infty \qquad \text{and} \qquad \int_0^{+\infty} | \dot{v}(t) | dt < +\infty.$$

The finiteness of the second integral shows that $v(t)$ tends to a limit as $t \to +\infty$, while the finiteness of the first integral shows that the limit is 0. Thus (2.5) is true. Since

$$L(k(t), \dot{k}(t)) e^{-pt} = L_0(x(t), \dot{x}(t)) e^{-pt}$$
$$- H(\bar{k}, \bar{q}) e^{-pt} + (d/dt) e^{-pt} x(t) \cdot \bar{q}$$

by (1.22) and (1.28), we then have (2.6) and the summability of $L(k(t), \dot{k}(t)) e^{-pt}$. Conversely, if the latter expression is majorized by a summable function of t, then so is $(d/dt) e^{-pt} x(t) \cdot \bar{q}$ by (2.12), since $L_0 \geqslant 0$. This implies that $e^{-pt} x(t) \cdot \bar{q}$ tends to a certain limit other than $+\infty$ as $t \to +\infty$. The limit cannot be $-\infty$ by assumption (2.7), and, therefore, it is finite. In other words, $(d/dt) e^{-pt} x(t)$ is actually summable, which leads via (2.12) to the conclusion that $L(k(t), \dot{k}(t)) e^{-pt}$ also majorizes a summable function (the right side of (2.12) with the L_0 term deleted) and, hence, is summable. But then by (2.12), $L_0(x(t), \dot{x}(t)) e^{-pt}$ must likewise be summable.

The proof of part (b) of Proposition 2 is much the same.

COROLLARY. $\phi(\bar{k} + a) = f_+(a) - [H(\bar{k}, \bar{q})/\rho] - a \cdot \bar{q}$.

A fundamental fact about "truncated" variational problems over the finite interval $[0, T]$ will now be stated. Much of our analysis of the problems over $[0, +\infty)$ is dependent on limit arguments concerning what happens to this case as $T \to +\infty$.

PROPOSITION 3. *For arbitrary arcs* $x : [0, T] \to R^n$ *and* $p : [0, T] \to R^n$
with $0 < T < +\infty$, *one has*

$$\int_0^T L_0(x(t), \dot{x}(t)) \, e^{-\rho t} \, dt + \int_0^T M_0(p(t), \dot{p}(t) - \rho p(t)) \, e^{-\rho t} \, dt$$
$$\geqslant e^{-\rho T} x(T) \cdot p(T) - x(0) \cdot p(0). \tag{2.13}$$

Furthermore, equality holds in (2.13) *if and only if* x *and* p *satisfy the Hamiltonian system* (1.21) *over* [0, T].

Proof. Formula (1.26) tells us that

$$L_0(x, z) + M_0(p, u) \geqslant x \cdot u + z \cdot p, \tag{2.14}$$

with equality if and only if

$$(u, p) \in \partial L_0(x, z), \tag{2.15}$$

or equivalently (cf. [5, Theorem 37.5])

$$(-u, z) \in \partial H_0(x, p). \tag{2.16}$$

Therefore,

$$L_0(x(t), \dot{x}(t)) \, e^{-\rho t} + M_0(p(t), \dot{p}(t) - \rho p(t)) \, e^{-\rho t}$$
$$\geqslant e^{-\rho t}[x(t) \cdot \dot{p}(t) + \dot{x}(t) \cdot p(t) - \rho x(t) \cdot p(t)]$$
$$= (d/dt) \, e^{-\rho t} x(t) \cdot p(t),$$

with equality if and only if (1.21) holds. The result is then immediate.

COROLLARY. *For arbitrary arcs* $x : [0, +\infty) \to R^n$ *and* $p : [0, +\infty) \to R^n$
such that $e^{-\rho t} x(t) \cdot p(t) \to 0$ *as* $t \to +\infty$, *one has*

$$\int_0^{+\infty} L_0(x(t), \dot{x}(t)) \, e^{-\rho t} \, dt + \int_0^{+\infty} M_0(p(t), \dot{p}(t) - \rho p(t)) \, e^{-\rho t} \, dt$$
$$\geqslant -x(0) \cdot p(0), \tag{2.17}$$

with equality if and only if x *and* p *satisfy the Hamiltonian system* (1.21)
over $[0, +\infty)$. *In particular,*

$$K_+ \subset \{(a, b) | f_+(a) + g_+(b) + a \cdot b \leqslant 0\}. \tag{2.18}$$

Proof of Theorem 2 using Theorem 1. Fix any $(a, b) \in K_+$. Let x and

p denote the corresponding unique solution to the system (1.21) over $[0, +\infty)$ satisfying (in line with Theorem 1)

$$(x(0), p(0)) = (a, b), \tag{2.19}$$

$$(x(t), p(t)) \to (0, 0) \text{ as } t \to +\infty. \tag{2.20}$$

Then equality holds in (2.17) by the corollary immediately above, so that

$$+\infty > \int_0^{+\infty} L_0(x(t), \dot{x}(t)) \, e^{-\rho t} \, dt$$

$$= -a \cdot b - \int_0^{+\infty} M_0(p(t), \dot{p}(t) - \rho p(t)) \, e^{-\rho t} \, dt. \tag{2.21}$$

If $x' : [0, +\infty)$ is any other arc with $x'(0) = a'$, say, and

$$+\infty > \int_0^\infty L_0(x(t), \dot{x}'(t)) \, e^{-\rho t} \, dt,$$

we have

$$\lim_{t \to +\infty} e^{-\rho t} x'(t) \cdot p(t) = 0$$

by (2.20) and property (2.5) of Proposition 2. Therefore, again by the corollary to Proposition 3,

$$\int_0^{+\infty} L_0(x'(t), \dot{x}'(t)) \, e^{-\rho t} \, dt$$

$$\geqslant -a' \cdot b - \int_0^{+\infty} M_0(p(t), \dot{p}(t) - \rho p(t)) \, e^{-\rho t} \, dt. \tag{2.22}$$

Focusing attention on the case where $a' = a$, we see from (2.21) and (2.22) that

$$\int_0^{+\infty} L_0(x(t), \dot{x}(t)) \, e^{-\rho t} \, dt = f_+(a). \tag{2.23}$$

Similar reasoning establishes that

$$\int_0^{+\infty} M_0(p(t), \dot{p}(t) - \rho p(t)) \, e^{-\rho t} \, dt = g_+(b), \tag{2.24}$$

and in consequence, by way of (2.21),

$$f_+(a) = -a \cdot b - g_+(b). \tag{2.25}$$

We conclude further from (2.22) and the corollary to Proposition 3 that if x' were any arc with $x'(0) = a'$ and

$$\int_0^{+\infty} L_0(x'(t), \dot{x}'(t)) \, e^{-\rho t} \, dt = -a' \cdot b - g_+(b),$$

then (x', p) would have to satisfy the Hamiltonian system over $[0, +\infty)$, which by the uniqueness assertion in Theorem 1 would necessitate $x'(t) \equiv x(t)$. In particular, taking $a' = a$, we observe that the arc x uniquely gives the minimum in the definition of $f_+(a)$; in fact, the relation

$$f_+(a') \geqslant -a' \cdot b - g_+(b) \tag{2.26}$$

holds, with equality uniquely when $a' = a$. Analogously, the arc p uniquely gives the minimum in the definition of $g_+(b)$, and one has

$$g_+(b') \geqslant -a \cdot b' - f_+(a)$$

for all $b' \in R^n$. Combining (2.25) and (2.26), we get the subgradient relation

$$f_+(a') \geqslant f_+(a) - (a' - a) \cdot b \qquad \text{for all} \quad a' \in R^n, \tag{2.27}$$

or symbolically, $-b \in \partial f_+(a)$. By the same token, we have

$$g_+(b') \geqslant g_+(b) - (b' - b) \cdot a \qquad \text{for all} \quad b' \in R^n, \tag{2.28}$$

or in other words $-a \in \partial g_+(b)$. This establishes all of Theorem 2 except for the differentiability assertion. For the latter, let θ denote the homeomorphism whose graph is $K_+ \cap (U_+ \times V_+)$; thus, $(a, \theta(a)) \in K_+$ for all $a \in U_+$. Then $-\theta(a) \in \partial f_+(a)$, and since θ is continuous, we must actually have $-\theta(a) = \nabla f_+(a)$ [5, Theorems 25.1, 25.5, and 25.6]. Thus, f_+ is continuously differentiable on U_+; similarly, g_+ is continuously differentiable on V_+. This completes the proof.

In the next two sections, Theorem 1 itself will be proved, but for this purpose a further consequence of Proposition 3 will eventually be required. We state it now for convenience. For $0 < T < +\infty$, let

$$f_T(a, a') = \inf \left\{ \int_0^T L_0(x(t), \dot{x}(t)) \, e^{-\rho t} \, dt \, \Big| \, x(0) = a, \, x(T) = a' \right\}, \tag{2.29}$$

$$g_T(b, b') = \inf \left\{ \int_0^T M_0(p(t), \dot{p}(t) - \rho p(t)) \, e^{-\rho t} \, dt \, \Big| \, p(0) = b, \, p(T) = b' \right\}, \tag{2.30}$$

where again the infima are over all arcs (absolutely continuous R^n-valued functions on $[0, T]$) satisfying the given terminal constraints. It is evident from (1.29) and (1.30) that the functions f_T and g_T on $R^n \times R^n$ are convex, nonnegative, and vanish at $(0, 0)$.

PROPOSITION 4. *One has*

$$f_T(a, a') + g_T(b, b') \geqslant e^{-\rho T} a' \cdot b' - a \cdot b \quad \text{for all} \quad (a, a') \text{ and } (b, b'). \quad (2.31)$$

If $(x(t), p(t))$ satisfies the Hamiltonian system (1.21) over $[0, T]$ with $(x(0), p(0)) = (a, b)$ and $(x(T), p(T)) = (a', b')$, then equality holds in (2.31), x yields the minimum in the definition of $f_T(a, a')$, and p yields the minimum in the definition of $g_T(b, b')$. The converse implication is also true.

Proof. This is obvious from Proposition 3.

3. REDUCTION FROM THE LOCAL TO THE GLOBAL CASE

The next results will be used ultimately to show that, for the purpose of proving Theorem 1, our basic curvature assumption can just as well be cast in a global form. Certain facts about uniqueness of solutions to the Hamiltonian system are also implied by these results.

PROPOSITION 5. *If $(x_1(t), p_1(t))$ and $(y_2(t), p_2(t))$ are solutions to the Hamiltonian system (1.21) over an interval J, then the inequality*

$$(d/dt) e^{-\rho t}(x_1(t) - x_2(t)) \cdot (p_1(t) - p_2(t)) \geqslant 0 \quad \text{a.e.} \quad (3.1)$$

holds on J, with strict inequality over portions of J where $(x_1(t), p_1(t)) = (x_2(t), p_2(t))$ and at least one of the two solutions lies in the neighborhood $U \times V$ in the curvature assumption.

Over portions of J where $(x_1(t), p_1(t)) \neq (x_2(t), p_2(t))$ and both of the solutions lie in $U \times V$, one actually has

$$(d/dt) e^{-\rho t}(x_1(t) - x_2(t)) \cdot (p_1(t) - p_2(t))$$
$$\geqslant \sigma_0 \mid e^{-\rho t}(x_1(t) - x_2(t)) \cdot (p_1(t) - p_2(t)) \mid \quad \text{a.e.,} \quad (3.2)$$

where

$$\sigma_0 = 2 \min\{\alpha, \beta\} > 0, \quad (3.3)$$

as well as

$$(d/dt)(x_1(t) - x_2(t)) \cdot (p_1(t) - p_2(t))$$
$$\geqslant \sigma_1[\mid x_1(t) - x_2(t)\mid + \mid p_1(t) - p_2(t)\mid]^2 \quad \text{a.e.} \quad (3.4)$$

where

$$\sigma_1 = (4\alpha\beta - \rho^2)/4(\alpha + \beta + \rho) > 0. \tag{3.5}$$

Proof. We have by definition of ∂H_0 that

$$H_0(x_1(t), p_2(t)) \geqslant H_0(x_1(t), p_1(t)) + \dot{x}_1(t) \cdot (p_2(t) - p_1(t)), \tag{3.6}$$

$$H_0(x_2(t), p_1(t)) \leqslant H_0(x_1(t), p_1(t)) + (-\dot{p}_1(t) + \rho p_1(t)) \cdot (x_1(t) - x_2(t)), \tag{3.7}$$

$$H_0(x_2(t), p_1(t)) \geqslant H_0(x_2(t), p_2(t)) + \dot{x}_2(t) \cdot (p_1(t) - p_2(t)), \tag{3.8}$$

$$H_0(x_1(t), p_2(t)) \leqslant H_0(x_2(t), p_2(t)) + (-\dot{p}_2(t) + \rho p_2(t)) \cdot (x_2(t) - x_1(t)). \tag{3.9}$$

These inequalities yield

$$(\dot{x}_1(t) - \dot{x}_2(t)) \cdot (p_1(t) - p_2(t)) + (x_1(t) - x_2(t)) \cdot (\dot{p}_1(t) - \dot{p}_2(t))$$
$$-\rho(x_1(t) - x_2(t)) \cdot (p_1(t) - p_2(t)) \geqslant 0 \qquad \text{a.e.} \tag{3.10}$$

Multiplying the latter by $e^{-\rho t}$, we get (3.1). If $(x_1(t), p_1(t))$, say, lies in $U \times V$, where H_0 is in particular strictly concave–convex, we have strict inequality in (3.6) unless $p_1(t) = p_2(t)$, as well as strict inequality in (3.7) unless $x_1(t) = x_2(t)$. In this context, therefore, strict inequality holds in (3.10), and hence, in (3.1), unless $(x_1(t), p_1(t)) = (x_2(t), p_2(t))$.

Over subintervals where both solutions lie in $U \times V$, we can improve the argument by adding the term $\frac{1}{2}\beta \mid p_1(t) - p_2(t)\mid^2$ to the right sides of (3.6) and (3.8), while subtracting $\frac{1}{2}\alpha \mid x_1(t) - x_2(t)\mid^2$ from the right sides of (3.7) and (3.9). In this way, (3.10) is strengthened to

$$(\dot{x}_1(t) - \dot{x}_2(t)) \cdot (p_1(t) - p_2(t)) + (x_1(t) - x_2(t)) \cdot (\dot{p}_1(t) - \dot{p}_2(t))$$
$$- \rho(x_1(t) - x_2(t)) \cdot (p_1(t) - p_2(t)) \geqslant \alpha \mid x_1(t) - x_2(t)\mid^2$$
$$+ \beta \mid p_1(t) - p_2(t)\mid^2 \qquad \text{a.e.} \tag{3.11}$$

Using the fact that

$$\mid u \mid^2 + \mid v \mid^2 \geqslant 2 \mid u \cdot v \mid,$$

we see that

$$\alpha \mid x_1(t) - x_2(t)\mid^2 + \beta \mid p_1(t) - p_2(t)\mid^2$$
$$\geqslant \sigma_0 \mid (x_1(t) - x_2(t)) \cdot (p_1(t) + p_2(t))\mid. \tag{3.12}$$

When (3.12) is juxtaposed with (3.11) and both sides are multiplied by

$e^{-\rho t}$, we obtain (3.2). In establishing (3.4), the first thing to record is that (3.11) also implies

$$(d/dt)(x_1(t) - x_2(t)) \cdot (p_1(t) - p_2(t))$$

$$\geqslant \alpha \mid x_1(t) - x_2(t) \mid^2 + \rho(x_1(t) - x_2(t)) \cdot (p_1(t) - p_2(t))$$

$$+ \beta \mid p_1(t) - p_2(t) \mid^2$$

$$\geqslant \alpha \mid x_1(t) - x_2(t) \mid^2 - \rho \mid x_1(t) - x_2(t) \mid \mid p_1(t) - p_2(t) \mid$$

$$+ \beta \mid p_1(t) - p_2(t) \mid^2 \qquad \text{a.e.}$$

$$(3.13)$$

The proof of (3.4) can be completed by showing that for all real numbers $\lambda \geqslant 0$ and $\mu \geqslant 0$, one has

$$\alpha \lambda^2 - \rho \lambda \mu + \beta \mu^2 \geqslant \sigma_1 (\lambda + \mu)^2. \qquad (3.14)$$

This inequality is trivial of course if $\lambda = 0 = \mu$, so we can suppose that $\lambda + \mu > 0$ and rewrite (3.14) as

$$\alpha \theta^2 - \rho \theta (1 - \theta) + \beta (1 - \theta)^2 \geqslant \sigma_1, \qquad (3.15)$$

where $\theta = \lambda / (\lambda + \mu)$. The validity of (3.15) for all $\theta \in [0, 1]$ is seen by calculating the minimum value of the left side of (3.15) as a quadratic (convex) function of $\theta \in (-\infty, +\infty)$ and showing that it in fact equals σ_1, which is positive by assumption (1.34).

COROLLARY 1.   *If $(x_1(t), p_1(t))$ and $(x_2(t), p_2(t))$ are solutions to the Hamiltonian system over an interval J, then the expression*

$$\theta(t) = e^{-\rho t}(x_1(t) - x_2(t)) \cdot (p_1(t) - p_2(t)) \qquad (3.16)$$

is nondecreasing over J, in fact strictly increasing over those portions of J where $(x_1(t), p_1(t)) = (x_2(t), p_2(t))$ and at least one of the solutions $U \times V$.
   Over portions of J where $(x_1(t), p_1(t)) = (x_2(t), p_2(t))$ and both of the solutions lie in $U \times V$, one has $e^{-\sigma_0 t}\theta(t)$ nondecreasing where $\theta(t) > 0$, and $e^{\sigma_0 t}\theta(t)$ nondecreasing where $\theta(t) < 0$.

   Proof.   The function θ is absolutely continuous, so it is nondecreasing over intervals where $\dot{\theta}(t) \geqslant 0$ almost everywhere, and it is strictly increasing over intervals where $\dot{\theta}(t) > 0$ almost everywhere. The justification of the final assertion of the corollary is seen by rewriting (3.2) as

$$\dot{\theta}(t) - \sigma_0 \mid \theta(t) \mid \geqslant 0 \qquad \text{a.e.}$$

Multiplying both sides of this by $e^{-\sigma_0 t}$, one finds that

$$(d/dt)\, e^{-\sigma_0 t} \theta(t) \geq 0 \qquad \text{where} \quad \theta(t) > 0,$$

$$(d/dt)\, e^{\sigma_0 t} \theta(t) \geq 0 \qquad \text{where} \quad \theta(t) < 0.$$

COROLLARY 2. *If among the solutions to the Hamiltonian system* (1.21) *over* $[0, +\infty)$ *satisfying*

$$(x(0), p(0)) = (a, b) \in U \times V, \tag{3.17}$$

$$\lim_{t \to +\infty} e^{-\rho t} x(t) \cdot p(t) = 0, \tag{3.18}$$

there is one such that $(x(t), p(t))$ *remains bounded and in* $U \times V$ *as* $t \to +\infty$, *then it is the unique solution to the system over* $[0, +\infty)$ *having either* $x(0) = a$ *or* $p(0) = b$.

Proof. Let $(x'(t), p'(t))$ also satisfy (3.18) with either $x'(0) = a$ or $p'(0) = b$. The corollary to Proposition 3 gives us

$$\int_0^{+\infty} L_0(x'(t), \dot{x}'(t))\, e^{-\rho t}\, dt + \int_0^{+\infty} M_0(p'(t), \dot{p}'(t) - \rho p'(t))\, e^{-\rho t}\, dt$$
$$= -x'(0) \cdot p'(0) < +\infty, \tag{3.19}$$

and, hence, by Proposition 2, we have

$$\lim_{t \to +\infty} e^{-\rho t} x'(t) = \lim_{t \to +\infty} e^{-\rho t} p'(t) = 0. \tag{3.20}$$

By virtue of the boundedness of $(x(t), p(t))$, the expression

$$\theta(t) = e^{-\rho t}(x'(t) - x(t)) \cdot (p'(t) - p(t)) \tag{3.21}$$

therefore satisfies

$$\lim_{t \to +\infty} \theta(t) = 0 = \theta(0). \tag{3.22}$$

This implies via Corollary 1 that $x'(t) = x(t)$ and $p'(t) = p(t)$ for all $t \in [0, +\infty)$.

Corollary 2 is the basis for the uniqueness assertion in Theorem 1. The rest of Theorem 1 relates only to the local behavior of H_0 and the corresponding Hamiltonian system near $(0, 0)$. In the proof, therefore, there is no harm in replacing H_0 by any more convenient function that agrees with it on a neighborhood of $(0, 0)$. The proposition below will allow us in this manner to derive Theorem 1 by way of results that are more global in nature.

PROPOSITION 6. *Let $C \times D$ be any compact convex neighborhood of $(0, 0)$ contained in the neighborhood $U \times V$ in the curvature assumption on H_0. Then there exists a function H_1 on $R^n \times R^n$ agreeing with H_0 on $C \times D$, such that $H_1(x, p)$ is everywhere finite, α-concave in x, and β-concave in p.*

Moreover, H_1 can be constructed in such a manner that the corresponding convex Lagrangians

$$L_1(x, z) = \sup\{p \cdot z - H_1(x, p) | \, p \in R^n\}, \tag{3.23}$$

$$M_1(p, u) = \sup\{u \cdot x + H_1(x, p) | \, x \in R^n\}, \tag{3.24}$$

are finite throughout $R^n \times R^n$.

Proof. Let

$$\bar{H}_0(x, p) = H_0(x, p) + \tfrac{1}{2}\alpha \, | \, x \, |^2 - \tfrac{1}{2}\beta \, | \, p \, |^2. \tag{3.25}$$

Then H_0 is concave–convex on $U \times V$. The construction given in [2, Proof of Proposition 3.1] furnishes a finite, concave–convex function $\bar{H}_1$ on $R^n \times R^n$ agreeing with H_0 on $C \times D$. Let

$$H_1(x, p) = \bar{H}_1(x, p) - \tfrac{1}{2}\alpha \, | \, x \, |^2 + \tfrac{1}{2}\beta \, | \, p \, |^2. \tag{3.26}$$

Then $H_1(x, p)$ is everywhere finite, α-concave in x, β-convex in p, and $H_1(x, p) = H_0(x, p)$ for (x, p) in $C \times D$. Moreover

$$\lim_{\lambda \to +\infty} H_1(x, \lambda p)/\lambda = +\infty, \tag{3.27}$$

$$\lim_{\lambda \to +\infty} H_1(\lambda x, p)/\lambda = -\infty, \tag{3.28}$$

so that the functions L_1 and M_1 in (3.23) and (3.24) must be finite everywhere [5, Corollary 13.3.1].

4. GLOBAL RESULTS

In view of Proposition 6, there is no loss of generality if in the rest of the development of the proof of Theorem 1 we invoke the following.

GLOBAL CURVATURE ASSUMPTION. *The function H_0 is actually finite and α-concave-β-convex throughout $R^n \times R^n$, i.e., the earlier curvature assumption is valid with $U \times V = R^n \times R^n$. Furthermore, the functions L_0 and M_0 are finite throughout $R^n \times R^n$.*

A crucial consequence of this assumption is the following property.

PROPOSITION 7. *Under the global curvature assumption, if $(x(t), p(t))$
satisfies the Hamiltonian system (1.21) over $[0, +\infty)$, then either*

$$\lim_{t \to +\infty} e^{-\rho t} x(t) \cdot p(t) = +\infty, \qquad (4.1)$$

or one has

$$\lim_{t \to +\infty} (x(t), p(t)) = (0, 0). \qquad (4.2)$$

Proof. We first apply Corollary 1 of Proposition 5 to $(x_1(t), p_1(t)) \equiv
(x(t), p(t))$ and $(x_2(t), p_2(t)) \equiv (0, 0)$ to see that the function

$$\theta(t) = e^{-\rho t} x(t) \cdot p(t)$$

is nondecreasing, and in fact $e^{-\sigma_0 t} \theta(t)$ is nondecreasing on subintervals
where $\theta(t) > 0$. Thus (4.1) holds unless $\theta(t) \leqslant 0$ for all $t \geqslant 0$. Suppose
now that the latter is true, so that also

$$x(t) \cdot p(t) \leqslant 0 \qquad \text{for all} \quad t \geqslant 0. \qquad (4.3)$$

From Proposition 5 we have at the same time

$$(d/dt) x(t) \cdot p(t) \geqslant \sigma_1 [|x(t)| + |p(t)|]^2 \geqslant \sigma_1 |(x(t), p(t))|^2 \qquad \text{a.e.} \qquad (4.4)$$

Hence, for all $T > 0$,

$$\sigma_1 \int_0^T |(x(t), p(t))|^2 \, dt \leqslant x(T) \cdot p(T) - x(0) \cdot p(0) \leqslant -x(0) \cdot p(0). \qquad (4.5)$$

This yields

$$\int_0^{+\infty} \zeta(t) \, dt < +\infty, \qquad \text{where} \quad \zeta(t) = |(x(t), p(t))|^2. \qquad (4.6)$$

Since the concave–convex function H_0 is everywhere finite, its subdifferential multifunction ∂H_0 is bounded on bounded sets [6, Lemma 4], so
that in particular there is a number λ such that the elements of the set
$\partial H_0(a, b)$ are bounded in norm by λ when $|(a, b)| \leqslant 1$. Then, since $(x(t),
p(t))$ satisfies the system (1.21), we have

$$|(x(t), p(t))| \leqslant \lambda + \rho \qquad \text{whenever} \quad |(x(t), p(t))| \leqslant 1. \qquad (4.7)$$

For $\zeta(t)$ as in (4.6), this means that

$$\dot{\zeta}(t) \leqslant 2(\lambda + \rho) \qquad \text{whenever} \quad \zeta(t) \leqslant 1. \qquad (4.8)$$

We proceed now to show that (4.6) and (4.8) imply

$$\lim_{t \to +\infty} \zeta(t) = 0, \tag{4.9}$$

a property equivalent, of course, to the desired conclusion (4.2). Fix any $\epsilon \in (0, 1)$ and let

$$S = \{t \in [0, +\infty)| \ \zeta(t) \leqslant \epsilon/2\}.$$

The set S is closed by the continuity of $\zeta(t)$, so its complement in $[0, +\infty)$ is the union of a sequence of intervals. The finiteness of the integral in (4.6) ensures that the intervals among these having length $\epsilon/2(\lambda + \rho)$ or greater are all contained in $[0, T]$ for some T sufficiently large. Then for every $t > T$, there exists $t_0 \in S$ such that $| t - t_0 | < \epsilon/4(\lambda + \rho)$. But (4.8) implies

$$\zeta(t) \leqslant \zeta(t_0) + 2(\lambda + \rho)| \ t - t_0 | \qquad \text{if} \quad t_0 \in S \text{ and } 2(\lambda + \rho)| \ t - t_0 | \leqslant \epsilon/2. \tag{4.10}$$

Thus $\zeta(t) \leqslant \epsilon$ if $t > 0$. Since ϵ can be taken arbitrarily small, (4.9) is indeed correct.

We next state a result for the functions f_T and g_T in (2.29) and (2.30) that does not make fullest use of the global curvature assumption, although the latter will enter via Proposition 7 when we argue later by taking the limit as $T \to +\infty$.

THEOREM 3. *Under the global curvature assumption, the function f_T for $0 < T < +\infty$ is everywhere continuously differentiable and strictly convex on $R^n \times R^n$, and the infimum in its definition is always attained by a unique arc. The same properties hold for g_T . Furthermore, one has the conjugacy relations*

$$g_T(b, b') = \max_{(a,a')} \{e^{-\rho T}a' \cdot b' - a \cdot b - f_T(a, a')\} = f_T{}^*(-b, e^{-\rho T}b'), \tag{4.11}$$

$$f_T(a, a') = \max_{(b,b')} \{e^{-\rho T}a' \cdot b' - a \cdot b - g_T(b, b')\} = g_T{}^*(-a, e^{-\rho T}a'), \tag{4.12}$$

and the gradient relation

$$(-b, e^{-\rho T}b') = \nabla f_T(a, a') \Leftrightarrow (-a, e^{-\rho T}a') = \nabla g_T(b, b'). \tag{4.13}$$

The conditions in (4.13) are satisfied if and only if

$$f_T(a, a') + g_T(b, b') = e^{-\rho T}a' \cdot b' - a \cdot b. \tag{4.14}$$

Proof. Relations (4.11) and (4.12) in "sup" form, and the existence of minimizing arcs, follow from [4, Corollary 2 of Theorem 1] and the global finiteness of the functions L_0 and M_0. This finiteness also implies from the definitions (2.29) and (2.30) that f_T and g_T are finite everywhere, and hence that "sup" can be strengthened to "max" in passing to the conjugate functions f_T^* and g_T^* [5, pp. 217–218]. In view of (4.11) and (4.12), we have the subdifferential relation

$$(-b, e^{-\rho T}b') \in \partial f_T(a, a') \Leftrightarrow (-a, e^{-\rho T}a') \in \partial g_T(b, b'), \qquad (4.15)$$

these conditions being equivalent to (4.14). Suppose now for $i = 1, 2$ that (a_i, a_i') and (b_i, b_i') are such that these conditions hold, and let $x_i(t)$ and $p_i(t)$ be corresponding arcs over $[0, T]$ furnishing the minima in the definition of $f_T(a_i, a_i')$ and $g_T(b_i, b_i')$. Then, according to the converse part of Proposition 4, $(x_i(t), p_i(t))$ satisfies the system (1.21) with

$$(x_i(0), p_i(0)) = (a_i, b_i) \qquad \text{and} \qquad (x_i(T), p_i(T)) = (a_i', b_i'). \qquad (4.16)$$

Invoking Corollary 1 of Proposition 5, we see that the function θ in (3.16) satisfies $\theta(T) > \theta(0)$, unless $(x_1(t), p_1(t)) = (x_2(t), p_2(t))$ for all $t \in [0, T]$. But

$$\theta(0) = (a_1 - a_2) \cdot (b_1 - b_2), \qquad \theta(T) = e^{-\rho T}(a_1' - a_2') \cdot (b_1' - b_2'). \qquad (4.17)$$

Therefore, the equation $(a_1, a_1') = (a_2, a_2')$ implies $(b_1, b_1') = (b_2, b_2')$, and conversely. This shows that the subdifferential multifunctions ∂f_T and ∂g_T are actually one-to-one functions, so that f_T and g_T must be differentiable and strictly convex [5, Corollary 26.3.1]. The argument also shows the uniqueness of the minimizing arcs over $[0, T]$, and the proof of Theorem 3 is, therefore, complete.

The first consequence of Theorem 3 which we derive concerns the existence of minimizing arcs in the definitions of the functions f_+ and g_+.

PROPOSITION 8. *Under the global curvature assumption, the convex function f_+ is everywhere finite on R^n, and for each $a \in R^n$, there is a unique arc p over $[0, +\infty)$ furnishing the minimum in the definition of $f_+(a)$.*

Proof. Since L_0 is finite and has the properties (1.29), it is evident that

$$0 \leqslant f_+(a) \leqslant f_T(a, 0) < +\infty \qquad \text{for all} \quad T > 0. \qquad (4.18)$$

Hence, f_+ is finite. Now fix any $a \in R^n$. The definitions of f_+ and f_T yield the identity

$$f_+(a) = \inf_{a' \in R^n} \{f_T(a, a') + e^{-\rho T}f_+(a')\} \qquad \text{for all} \quad T > 0. \qquad (4.19)$$

We know from Theorem 3 that f_T is finite, strictly convex, and cofinite (i.e., has an everywhere-finite conjugate function f_T*). In particular, this implies that, as a function of a', $f_T(a, a')$ is strictly convex and satisfies the growth condition

$$\lim_{\lambda \to +\infty} [f_T(a, a' + \lambda a'') - f_T(a, a')]/\lambda = +\infty \qquad \text{whenever} \quad a'' \neq 0 \quad (4.20)$$

[5, Corollary 13.3.1]. The convexity of f_+ ensures, of course, that the difference quotient $[f_+(a' + \lambda a'') - f_+(a')]/\lambda$ is always nondecreasing in λ, so it follows that for each $T > 0$, the function

$$h_T(a') = f_T(a, a') + e^{-\rho T} f_+(a') \qquad (4.21)$$

is everywhere finite on R^n, strictly convex and satisfies

$$\lim_{\lambda \to +\infty} [h_T(a' + \lambda a'') - h_T(a')]/\lambda = +\infty \qquad \text{whenever} \quad a'' \neq 0. \quad (4.22)$$

Therefore, h_T attains its minimum over R^n at a unique point [5, Theorem 27.2]. Let us denote this point by $x(T)$, defining also $x(0) = a$. We then have the identiy

$$f_+(a) = f_T(a, x(T)) + e^{-\rho T} f_+(x(T)) \qquad \text{for all} \quad T > 0. \quad (4.23)$$

Note that this identity would also have to be satisfied by any arc giving the minimum in the definition of $f_+(a)$, so the function $x : [0, +\infty) \to R^n$ that we have constructed is the unique candidate for such an arc. To verify that x is absolutely continuous, we temporarily fix T and let y denote the unique arc over $[0, T]$ giving the minimum in the definition of $f_T(a, x(T))$ (cf. Theorem 3). For all $S \in (0, T)$, it is true that

$$f_T(a, x(T)) = f_S(a, y(S)) + e^{-\rho S} f_{T-S}(y(S), x(T)), \qquad (4.24)$$

$$f_+(y(S)) \leqslant f_{T-S}(y(S), x(T)) + e^{-\rho(T-S)} f_+(x(T)). \qquad (4.25)$$

combining (4.24) and (4.25) with (4.23), we obtain

$$f_+(a) \geqslant f_S(a, y(S)) + e^{-\rho S} f_+(y(S)). \qquad (4.26)$$

On the other hand, the formula

$$f_+(a) = \min_{a' \in R^n} \{f_S(a, a') + e^{-\rho S} f_+(a')\} \qquad (4.27)$$

holds, with the minimum attained uniquely at the point $x(S)$. Therefore (4.26) implies $y(S) = x(S)$. This is true for all $S \in (0, T)$, so the arcs x and

y coincide over $[0, T]$. Thus x is absolutely continuous, and for every $T > 0$ we have

$$f_T(a, x(T)) = \int_0^T L_0(x(t), \dot{x}(t))\, e^{-\rho t}\, dt. \qquad (4.28)$$

Plugging the latter into (4.23), we get

$$f_+(a) \geqslant \int_0^T L_0(x(t), \dot{x}(t))\, e^{-\rho t}\, dt \qquad \text{for all} \quad T > 0,$$

and, therefore,

$$f_+(a) \geqslant \int_0^{+\infty} L_0(x(t), \dot{x}(t))\, e^{-\rho t}\, dt. \qquad (4.29)$$

Thus x must give the minimum in the definition of $f_+(a)$ and is the unique arc to do so.

The argument establishing the assertions of Proposition 8 about g_+ is entirely parallel.

PROPOSITION 9. *Under the global curvature assumption, we have*

$$f_+(a) = \lim_{T \to +\infty}\, [\min_{a' \in R^n}\, f_T(a, a')], \qquad (4.30)$$

$$g_+(b) = \lim_{T \to +\infty}\, [\min_{b' \in R^n}\, g_T(b, b')]. \qquad (4.31)$$

Proof. Let

$$\psi_T(a) = \min_{a' \in R^n}\, f_T(a, a'). \qquad (4.32)$$

(The "min", in place of "inf", is appropriate because of the growth property of f_T displayed in (4.20).) The identity

$$f_T(a, a') = \inf_{c \in R^n}\, \{f_S(a, c) + e^{-\rho S} f_{T-S}(c, a')\} \qquad \text{for} \quad 0 < S < T \quad (4.33)$$

shows that

$$f_T(a, a') \geqslant \inf_{c \in R^n}\, f_S(a, c) = \psi_S(a), \qquad (4.34)$$

and it is true, therefore, that

$$\psi_T(a) \geqslant \psi_S(a) \qquad \text{for} \quad 0 < S < T < +\infty. \qquad (4.35)$$

At the same time we have

$$f_+(a) \leqslant \psi_T(a) \qquad \text{for all } T > 0 \qquad (4.36)$$

by (4.21) and the nonnegativity of f_+ . Hence, the limit

$$\psi_+(a) \triangleq \lim_{t \to +\infty} \psi_T(a) \tag{4.37}$$

exists and satisfies

$$0 \leqslant \psi_+(a) \leqslant f_+(a) < +\infty. \tag{4.38}$$

We must show that also $\psi_+(a) \geqslant f_+(a)$. The convexity of f_T implies that of the functions ψ_T and, hence, that of ψ_+. The next step consists of demonstrating that ψ_+, like f_+, satisfies

$$\psi_+(a) = \min_{a' \in R^n} \{f_T(a, a') + e^{-\rho T}\psi_+(a')\} \qquad \text{for all} \quad T > 0. \tag{4.39}$$

Certainly the definitions imply

$$\psi_{T+S}(a) = \inf_{a' \in R^n} \{f_T(a, a') + e^{-\rho T}\psi_S(a')\} \tag{4.40}$$

for all $T > 0, S > 0$. In particular, then, we have

$$\psi_{T+S}(a) \leqslant f_T(a, a') + e^{-\rho T}\psi_S(a') \qquad \text{for all} \quad a' \in R^n, \tag{4.41}$$

and passing to the limit as $S \to +\infty$, we get

$$\psi_+(a) \leqslant f_T(a, a') + e^{-\rho T}\psi_+(a') \qquad \text{for all} \quad a' \in R^n. \tag{4.42}$$

On the other hand, let us fix any $a \in R^n$ and $T > 0$, and consider the function

$$k_S(a') = f_T(a, a') + e^{-\rho T}\psi_S(a'). \tag{4.43}$$

Since ψ_S is finite and convex, while f_T is strictly convex with the growth property (4.20), we have k_S strictly convex with

$$\lim_{\lambda \to +\infty} [k_S(a' + \lambda a'') - k_S(a')]/\lambda = +\infty \qquad \text{if} \quad a'' \neq 0. \tag{4.44}$$

It follows that k_S attains its minimum over R^n at a unique point a_S' . Then

$$\psi_{T+S}(a) = f_T(a, a_S') + e^{-\rho T}\psi_S(a_S'). \tag{4.45}$$

Observe that this relation entails

$$f_T(a, a_S') \leqslant \psi_{T+S}(a) \leqslant \psi_+(a),$$

and, hence,

$$a_S' \in B = \{a' \in R^n \mid f_T(a, a') \leqslant \psi_+(a)\}. \tag{4.46}$$

The set B is bounded, by virtue of the growth property (4.20) [5, Theorems 8.4 and 27.1(f)], so that (4.46) implies the existence of a cluster point of a_S' as $S \to +\infty$. Since the functions ψ_S are convex and converge pointwise to ψ_+ on R^n, they actually converge uniformly on all bounded sets [5, Theorem 10.8]. Therefore, in passing to the limit as $S \to +\infty$ in (4.45), we have

$$\psi_+(a) = f_T(a, a') + e^{-\rho T}\psi_+(a'), \tag{4.47}$$

where a' is any cluster point of a_s' as $s \to +\infty$. Thus, equality does hold in (4.42) for some a', and (4.39) is correct.

We next apply to (4.39) the same argument we applied in the proof of Proposition 8 to the parallel formula for f_+. This yields the existence for each $a \in R^n$ of an arc x over $[0, +\infty)$ satisfying $x(0) = a$,

$$\psi_+(a) = f_T(a, x(T)) + e^{-\rho T}\psi_+(x(T)), \tag{4.48}$$

$$f_T(a, x(T)) = \int_0^T L_0(x(t), \dot{x}(t)) e^{-\rho t}\, dt, \tag{4.49}$$

for all $T > 0$. But then

$$\psi_+(a) \geqslant \int_0^{+\infty} L_0(x(t), \dot{x}(t)) e^{-\rho t}\, dt \geqslant f_+(a). \tag{4.50}$$

This completes the proof of Proposition 9, the argument for g_+ being parallel.

PROPOSITION 10. *Let F_+ and G_+ be the functions defined like f_+ and g_+ in (1.37) and (1.38), but with the infima taken only over arcs which are bounded over $[0, +\infty)$. Then*

$$\lim_{T \to +\infty} f_T(a, a') = F_+(a) \qquad \text{for all} \quad a' \in R^n, \tag{4.51}$$

$$\lim_{T \to +\infty} g_T(b, b') = G_+(b) \qquad \text{for all} \quad b' \in R^n. \tag{4.52}$$

Proof. The properties (1.29) of L_0 imply that $f_T(a, 0)$ is nonincreasing as a function of $T > 0$, and $f_T(a, 0) \geqslant F_+(a)$. (Any arc x over $[0, T]$ with $x(0) = a$ and $x(T) = 0$ can be continued over $[0, +\infty)$ by defining $x(t) = 0$ for all $t > T$.) Thus, the function

$$\tilde{F}_+(a) \triangleq \lim_{T \to +\infty} f_T(a, 0) \geqslant F_+(a) \tag{4.53}$$

is well defined. For $T > S > 0$, we have

$$f_{T+S}(a, 0) \leqslant f_T(a, a') + e^{-\rho T} f_S(a', 0), \tag{4.54}$$

$$f_T(a, a') \leqslant f_{T-S}(a, 0) + e^{-\rho(T-S)} f_S(0, a'). \tag{4.55}$$

Taking the limit in these inequalities as $T \to +\infty$ for fixed S and a', we obtain, respectively,

$$\tilde{F}_+(a) \leqslant \lim_{T \to +\infty} \inf f_T(a, a'), \tag{4.56}$$

$$\lim_{T \to +\infty} \sup f_T(a, a') \leqslant \check{F}_+(a), \tag{4.57}$$

and, hence,

$$\lim_{T \to +\infty} f_T(a, a') = \check{F}_+(a). \tag{4.58}$$

We finish the proof of (4.51) by showing that $\tilde{F}_+(a) \leqslant F_+(a)$. Fix $a \in R^n$ and $\epsilon > 0$, and let x be a bounded arc over $[0, +\infty)$ such that $x(0) = a$ and

$$\int_0^\infty L_0(x(t), \dot{x}(t)) \, e^{-\rho t} \, dt < F_+(a) + \epsilon. \tag{4.59}$$

Then for all $T > 0$, it is true that

$$F_+(a) + \epsilon > \int_0^T L_0(x(t), \dot{x}(t)) \, e^{-\rho t} \, dt \geqslant f_T(a, x(T)). \tag{4.60}$$

According to (4.58), the functions $a' \to f_T(a, a')$ converge as $T \to +\infty$ to the constant function $a' \to \tilde{F}_+(a)$, and since the functions are convex, the convergence must be uniform on all bounded sets [5, Theorem 10.8], in particular on the set $\{x(T) | \, 0 \leqslant T < +\infty\}$ Therefore,

$$\lim_{T \to +\infty} f_T(a, x(T)) = \tilde{F}_+(a), \tag{4.61}$$

and (4.60) thus implies $F_+(a) + \epsilon \geqslant \tilde{F}_+(a)$. Since $\epsilon > 0$ was arbitrary, we are able to conclude $F_+(a) \geqslant \tilde{F}_+(a)$ as aimed.

The argument for g_+ and G_+ is parallel.

Our main "global" result can now be treated.

THEOREM 4. *Under the global curvature assumption, the functions f_+ and g_+ are everywhere continuously differentiable and strictly convex on R^n, and they satisfy the conjugacy relations*

$$g_+(b) = \max_{a \in R^n} \{-a \cdot b - f_+(a)\} = f_+^*(-b), \tag{4.62}$$

$$f_+(a) = \max_{b \in R^n} \{-a \cdot b - g_+(b)\} = g_+^*(-a). \tag{4.63}$$

Furthermore, one has

$$(a, b) \in K_+ \Leftrightarrow f_+(a) + g_+(b) + a \cdot b = 0$$
$$\Leftrightarrow b = -\nabla f_+(a) \Leftrightarrow a = -\nabla g_+(b). \tag{4.64}$$

For each $(a, b) \in K_+$, there is a unique solution $(x(t), p(t))$ to the Hamiltonian system (1.21) over $[0, +\infty)$ satisfying (1.35) and (1.36), and it tends to $(0, 0)$ as $t \to +\infty$. In fact, x is the unique arc furnishing the minimum in the definition of $f_+(a)$, while p is the unique arc furnishing the minimum in the definition of $g_+(b)$.

Proof. Defining ψ_T as in (4.32), we have from Theorem 3 the relation

$$g_T(b, 0) = \max_{(a,a')} \{-a \cdot b - f_T(a, a')\}$$

$$= \max_a \{-a \cdot b - \psi_T(a)\} = \psi_T^*(-b). \tag{4.65}$$

As $T \to +\infty$, the convex functions ψ_T converge pointwise to f_+ by Proposition 9, while the convex functions $b \to g_T(b, 0)$ converge pointwise to G_+ by Proposition 10. Thus ψ_T and the conjugate ψ_T^* converge to finite limit functions as $T \to +\infty$, implying that these limit functions must be conjugate to each other (cf. [6; 7; 5, Theorem 10.8]). Therefore, $G_+(b) = f_+^*(-b)$, so that (again by virtue of the finiteness of the two functions)

$$G_+(b) = \max_{a \in R^n} \{-a \cdot b - f_+(a)\} \tag{4.66}$$

and, reciprocally,

$$f_+(a) = \max_{b \in R^n} \{-a \cdot b - G_+(b)\}. \tag{4.67}$$

The next thing to note is that G_+ satisfies the identity

$$G_+(b) = \inf_{b' \in R^n} \{g_T(b, b') + e^{-\rho T} G_+(b')\} \qquad \text{for all} \quad T > 0. \tag{4.68}$$

This is evident from the definition of G_+ in Proposition 10. The same argument used in connection with Formula (4.19) in the proof of Proposition 8 shows for each $b \in R^n$ the existence of a unique arc p over $[0, +\infty)$ satisfying $p(0) = b$ and

$$G_+(b) = g_T(b, p(T)) + e^{-\rho T} G_+(p(T)) \qquad \text{for all} \quad T > 0, \tag{4.69}$$

$$g_T(b, p(T)) = \int_0^T M_0(p(t), \dot{p}(t) - \rho p(t)) e^{-\rho t} \, dt \qquad \text{for all} \quad T > 0. \tag{4.70}$$

Now fix any $a \in R^n$ and let x be the unique arc over $[0, +\infty)$ giving the minimum in the definition of $f_+(a)$, as exists by Proposition 8. Then

$$f_+(a) = f_T(a, x(T)) + e^{-\rho T} f_+(x(T)) \qquad \text{for all} \quad T > 0, \tag{4.71}$$

$$f_T(a, x(T)) = \int_0^T L_0(x(t), \dot{x}(t)) e^{-\rho t} \, dt \qquad \text{for all} \quad T > 0. \tag{4.72}$$

Let b be such that the maximum in (4.67) is attained, and let p be a corresponding arc over $[0, +\infty)$ with $p(0) = b$ satisfying (4.69) and (4.70). We then have from (4.69) and (4.71) that

$$
\begin{aligned}
0 &= f_+(a) + G_+(b) + a \cdot b \\
&= f_T(a, x(T)) + g_T(b, p(T)) + e^{-\rho T}[f_+(x(T)) + G_+(p(T))] + a \cdot b \\
&= f_T(a, x(T)) + g_T(b, p(T)) - e^{-\rho T}x(T) \cdot p(T) + a \cdot b \\
&\quad + e^{-\rho T}[f_+(x(T)) + G_+(p(T)) + x(T) \cdot p(T)],
\end{aligned}
\tag{4.73}
$$

and, consequently, by virtue of the conjugacy relations (4.66) and (4.11),

$$
f_T(a, x(T)) + g_T(b, p(T)) - e^{-\rho T}x(T) \cdot p(T) + a \cdot b = 0 \qquad \text{for all} \quad T > 0,
\tag{4.74}
$$

$$
f_+(x(T)) + G_+(p(T)) + x(T) \cdot p(T) = 0 \qquad \text{for all} \quad T > 0.
\tag{4.75}
$$

Substituting (4.70) and (4.72) into (4.74) and applying Proposition 3, one sees that $(x(t), p(t))$ is a solution to the Hamiltonian system (1.21). Moreover, (4.74) implies in conjunction with (4.69) and (4.71) that

$$
\begin{aligned}
\limsup_{T \to +\infty} e^{-\rho T}x(T) \cdot p(T) &= \limsup_{T \to +\infty} [f_T(a, x(T)) + g_T(b, p(T)) + a \cdot b] \\
&\leqslant f_+(a) + G_+(b) + a \cdot b < +\infty,
\end{aligned}
\tag{4.76}
$$

and, hence, via Proposition 7, that

$$
\lim_{t \to +\infty} (x(t), p(t)) = (0, 0).
\tag{4.77}
$$

The minimizing arc x is thus bounded over $[0, +\infty)$, and therefore $f_+(a) = F_+(a)$. This has been verified for an arbitrary $a \in R^n$, so actually $f_+ \equiv F_+$.

A parallel argument shows that likewise $g_+ \equiv G_+$. Thus, the formulas derived above for f_+ and G_+ are actually valid for f_+ and g_+; both (4.62) and (4.63) are valid, and for each (a, b) in the set

$$
\begin{aligned}
K_+' &= \{(a, b) | f_+(a) + g_+(b) + a \cdot b = 0\} \\
&= \{(a, b) | f_+(a) + g_+(b) + a \cdot b \leqslant 0\} \\
&= \{(a, b) | -b \in \partial f(a)\} = \{(a, b) | -a \in \partial g_+(b)\},
\end{aligned}
\tag{4.78}
$$

there exists a solution to the system (1.21) over $[0, +\infty)$ with $(x(0), p(0)) = (a, b)$, satisfying (4.77) and (by (4.75))

$$
(x(T), p(T)) \in K_+' \qquad \text{for all} \quad T > 0.
\tag{4.79}
$$

But this implies $K_+' \subset K_+$, whereas on the other hand, the inclusion $K_+ \subset K_+'$ follows from the corollary to Proposition 3. Therefore, $K_+' = K_+$, and for each $(a, b) \in K_+$, there is a solution to the system (1.21) over $[0, +\infty)$ with $(x(0), p(0)) = (a, b)$ which remains in K_+ and tends to $(0, 0)$ as $t \to +\infty$. Corollary 2 of Proposition 5 tells us this must be the unique solution to (1.21) satisfying

$$\lim_{t \to \infty} e^{-\rho t} x(t) \cdot p(t) = 0,$$

and having either $x(0) = a$ or $p(0) = b$. Hence, for each $a \in R^n$, there is no more than one $b \in R^n$ with $(a, b) \in K_+$, and for each $b \in R^n$ there is no more than one $a \in R^n$ with $(a, b) \in K_+$. Since $K_+ = K_+'$, this says that the subgradient sets $\partial f_+(a)$ and $\partial g_+(b)$ never contain more than one element. It follows that f_+ and g_+ are continuously differentiable [5, Theorems 23.4, 25.1, and 25.5] and in view of their conjugacy relationship, also strictly convex [5, Theorem 26.3].

COROLLARY.   *Under the global curvature assumption, one has $F_+ = f_+$ and $G_+ = g_+$.*

Proof of Theorem 1.   As already has been noted, there is no loss of generality if the global curvature assumption is invoked in the proof of Theorem 1. (The uniqueness assertion is covered by Corollary 2 of Proposition 3.) Thus, we can place ourselves in the context of Theorem 4, according to which K_+ is the graph of a homeomorphism from R^n onto R^n (namely the mapping $-\nabla f_+$, whose inverse is $-\nabla g_+$). The task is to show that, given any neighborhood $U \times V$ of $(0, 0)$ in $R^n \times R^n$, there exists an open neighborhood $U_+ \times V_+$ of $(0, 0)$ such that $K_+ \cap (U_+ \times V_+)$ is the graph of a homeomorphism from U_+ onto V_+, and for each $(a, b) \in K_+ \cap (U_+ \times V_+)$, the solution to the system (1.21) starting at (a, b) and tending to $(0, 0)$ stays entirely within $K_+ \cap (U_+ \times V_+)$. Since K_+ is already the graph of a global homeomorphism, the local homeomorphism property will certainly be satisfied if U_+ and V_+ are taken to be of the form

$$U_+ = \{a \mid \exists b \quad \text{with} \quad (a, b) \in K_+ \cap W\},$$
$$V_+ = \{b \mid \exists a \quad \text{with} \quad (a, b) \in K_+ \cap W\}, \tag{4.80}$$

where W is some open neighborhood of $(0, 0)$; one then has

$$K_+ \cap (U_+ \times V_+) = K_+ \cap W. \tag{4.81}$$

Thus the proof is reduced to showing that every neighborhood $U \times V$ of

$(0, 0)$ contains an open neighborhood W of $(0, 0)$ such that, for each $(a, b) \in K_+ \cap W$, the solution to the system (1.21) starting at (a, b) and tending to $(0, 0)$ stays entirely within $K_+ \cap W$. Actually, such a solution $(x(t), p(t))$ remains in K_+ by definition and, hence, by Theorem 4, it satisfies

$$f_+(x(t)) + g_+(p(t)) + x(t) \cdot p(t) = 0 \qquad \text{for all} \quad t > 0. \qquad (4.82)$$

Moreover, $x(t) \cdot p(t)$ is nondecreasing in t; this follows from Proposition 5 in the case of $(x_1(t), p_1(t)) = (x(t), p(t))$ and $(x_2(t), p_2(t)) \equiv (0, 0)$. Hence, the expression $f_+(x(t)) + g_+(p(t))$ is nonincreasing. This indicates that the desired properties can be obtained by taking W to be of the form

$$W = \{(a, b) \mid f_+(a) + g_+(b) < \epsilon\}, \qquad (4.83)$$

provided this set is indeed, for $\epsilon > 0$ sufficiently small, an open neighborhood of $(0, 0)$ contained in whatever neighborhood $U \times V$ has been specified. But the latter properties follow from the fact that f_+ and g_+ are finite, strictly convex functions (hence, continuous) satisfying by definition

$$f_+(a) \geqslant f_+(0) = 0 \qquad \text{and} \qquad g_+(b) \geqslant g_+(0) = 0 \qquad (4.84)$$

(cf. [5, Theorem 27.2]).

5. RESULTS FOR THE INTERVAL $(-\infty, 0]$

Most of the results for $[0, +\infty)$ can easily be derived in a parallel form for $(-\infty, 0]$ but with some important simplifications. In building up to the proofs of Theorems 1' and 2', we begin with facts corresponding to those in Proposition 2.

PROPOSITION 2'. *The inequalities*

$$\int_{-\infty}^{0} L_0(x(t), \dot{x}(t)) \, e^{-\rho t} \, dt < +\infty$$

and $\qquad\qquad\qquad\qquad\qquad\qquad\qquad\qquad\qquad\qquad\qquad\qquad$ (5.1)

$$\int_{-\infty}^{0} M_0(p(t), \dot{p}(t) - \rho p(t)) \, e^{-\rho t} \, dt < +\infty$$

imply, respectively, that

$$\lim_{t \to -\infty} e^{-\rho t} x(t) = 0 \qquad \text{and} \qquad \lim_{t \to -\infty} e^{-\rho t} p(t) = 0. \qquad (5.2)$$

Proof. The argument is based on Proposition 1 and follows exactly the same lines as the first part of the proof of Proposition 2.

COROLLARY. *If* (5.1) *holds, then*

$$\lim_{t \to -\infty} e^{-\rho t} x(t) \cdot p(t) = 0. \tag{5.3}$$

PROPOSITION 3'. *For* $-\infty < T < 0$, *one always has*

$$\int_T^0 L_0(x(t), \overset{\circ}{x}(t)) \, e^{-\rho t} \, dt + \int_T^0 M_0(p(t), \dot{p}(t) - \rho p(t)) \, e^{-\rho t} \, dt$$

$$\geqslant x(0) \cdot p(0) - e^{-\rho T} x(T) \cdot p(T). \tag{5.4}$$

Furthermore, equality holds here if and only if $(x(t), p(t))$ *satisfies the Hamiltonian system* (1.21) *over* $[T, 0]$.

Proof. Same argument as for Proposition 3.

COROLLARY 1. *For arbitrary arcs x and p over* $(-\infty, 0]$, *one has*

$$\int_{-\infty}^0 L_0(x(t), \dot{x}(t)) \, e^{-\rho t} \, dt + \int_{-\infty}^0 M_0(p(t), \overset{\circ}{p}(t) - \rho p(t)) \, e^{-\rho t} \, dt$$

$$\geqslant x(0) \cdot p(0), \tag{5.5}$$

with equality if and only if $(x(t), p(t))$ *is a solution to system* (1.21) *over* $(-\infty, 0]$ *which satisfies* (5.3).

COROLLARY 2. *One has*

$$f_-(a) + g_-(b) \geqslant a \cdot b \qquad for \ all \quad (a, b) \in R^n \times R^n, \tag{5.6}$$

$$K_- \subset \{(a, b) | \ f_-(a) + g_-(b) = a \cdot b\}. \tag{5.7}$$

In fact, K_- *consists precisely of the pairs* (a, b) *belonging to the set on the right in* (5.7) *such that the infima in the definitions of* $f_-(a)$ *and* $g_-(b)$ *are both attained by arcs x and p, respectively; such pairs of arcs give the solutions* $(x(t), p(t))$ *to the system* (1.21) *described in the definition of* K_-, *and they always satisfy* (5.2) *and consequently*

$$\lim_{t \to -\infty} (x(t), p(t)) = (0, 0). \tag{5.8}$$

Note the absence in Corollary 1 of any assumption on $e^{-\rho t} x(t) \cdot p(t)$, which is justified by the corollary to Proposition 2'. This has produced the general inequality (5.6). We were able to derive the similar inequality for f_+ and g_+ only under the *global* curvature assumption.

Proof of Theorem 2′ Using Theorem 1′. This is obvious in view of Corollary 2 above, except for the assertions about ∇f_- and ∇g_-. The relations (5.6) and (5.7) do imply that

$$K_- \subset \{(a, b)| \ b \in \partial f_-(a)\}, \tag{5.9}$$

and, hence, the homeomorphism Θ in Theorem 1′ from U_- onto V_- whose graph is $K_- \cap (U_- \times V_-)$ satisfies

$$\Theta(a) \in \partial f_-(a) \qquad \text{for all} \quad a \in U_-. \tag{5.10}$$

But f_- is a convex function which is finite on U_-. Therefore, $\partial f_-(a)$ reduces almost everywhere on U_- to the gradient $\nabla f_-(a)$ [5, Theorem 25.5]. Moreover, at the remaining points $a \in U_-$, $\partial f_-(a)$ can be constructed as the convex hull of the limiting values of gradients $\nabla f_-(a')$ existing at points a' near a [5, Theorem 25.6]. The existence of a homeomorphism Θ satisfying (5.10) therefore implies that $\partial f_-(a)$ reduces everywhere on U_- to a single element, and this must then be the gradient $\nabla f_-(a)$. Thus (5.10) is equivalent to

$$\Theta(a) = \nabla f_-(a) \qquad \text{for all} \quad a \in U_-, \tag{5.11}$$

and in particular f_- is continuously differentiable on U_-. This, with a similar argument for g_-, justifies the second and third equivalences in (1.46).

The next result corresponds to Proposition 7 and Corollary 2 of Proposition 5.

PROPOSITION 11. *Let $(x(t), p(t))$ be a solution to the system* (1.21) *over* $(-\infty, 0]$ *with* $(x(t), p(t)) = (a, b)$. *Then either*

$$\lim_{t \to -\infty} e^{-\rho t} x(t) \cdot p(t) = -\infty \tag{5.12}$$

or one has (5.3), *and hence* $(a, b) \in K_+$. *If* (5.3) *holds and* $(x(t), p(t))$ *remains in* $U \times V$ (*the neighborhood of* (0, 0) *in the basic curvature assumption*) *for all* $t \in (-\infty, 0]$, *then any solution* $(x'(t), p'(t))$ *to* (1.21) *likewise with property* (5.3) *and having either* $x'(0) = a$ *or* $p'(0) = b$, *must satisfy*

$$(x'(t), p'(t)) = (x(t), p(t)) \qquad \text{for all} \quad t \in (-\infty, 0]. \tag{5.13}$$

Proof. From Proposition 3′, we have

$$e^{-\rho T}x(T) \cdot p(T) = x(0) \cdot p(0) - \int_T^0 L_0(x(t), \dot{x}(t)) e^{-\rho t} dt$$

$$- \int_T^0 M_0(p(t), \dot{p}(t) - \rho p(t)) e^{-\rho t} dt \qquad (5.14)$$

for all $T < 0$. If the limit of the right side of (5.11) is not $-\infty$, then (5.3) holds by the corollary to Proposition 2′, and indeed the stronger relations (5.2) are valid. If $(x'(t), p'(t))$ also has these properties and has either $x'(0) = a$ or $p'(0) = b$, the function

$$\theta(t) = e^{-\rho t}(x'(t) - x(t)) \cdot (p'(t) - p(t)) \qquad (5.15)$$

satisfies

$$\lim_{t \to -\infty} \theta(t) = 0 = \theta(0). \qquad (5.16)$$

Assuming that $(x(t), p(t)) \in U \times V$ for all $t\,(-\infty, 0]$, we must have (5.13) because of Corollary 1 of Proposition 5.

PROPOSITION 8′. *Under the global curvature assumption, the convex function f_- is everywhere finite on R^n, and for each $a \in R^n$, there is a unique arc x over $(-\infty, 0]$ furnishing the minimum in the definition of $f_-(a)$. Similarly, g_- is finite everywhere on R^n, and for each $b \in R^n$, there is a unique arc p over $(-\infty, 0]$ furnishing the minimum in the definition of $g_-(b)$.*

Proof. Closely parallel to Proposition 8. No new version of Theorem 3 need be stated for the intervals $[T, 0]$, since for $T < 0$, one has

$$\inf \left\{ \int_T^0 L_0(x(t), x(t)) e^{-\rho t} dt \,\middle|\, x(T) = a', x(0) = a \right\}$$
$$= e^{-\rho T}f_{-T}(a', a), \qquad (5.17)$$

$$\inf \left\{ \int_T^0 M_0(p(t), \dot{p}(t) - \rho p(t)) e^{-\rho t} dt \,\middle|\, p(T) = b', p(0) = b \right\}$$
$$= e^{-\rho T}g_{-T}(b', b). \qquad (5.18)$$

We next derive facts corresponding to Propositions 9 and 10.

PROPOSITION 12. *Under the global curvature assumption, one has*

$$\lim_{T \to -\infty} e^{-\rho T}f_{-T}(a', a) = f_-(a) \qquad \text{if} \quad a' = 0,$$
$$= +\infty \qquad \text{if} \quad a' \neq 0, \qquad (5.19)$$

$$\lim_{T \to -\infty} e^{-\rho T}g_{-T}(b', b) = g_-(b) \qquad \text{if} \quad b' = 0,$$
$$= +\infty \qquad \text{if} \quad b' \neq 0, \qquad (5.20)$$

and consequently also

$$\lim_{T \to -\infty} [\min_{a' \in R^n} e^{-\rho T} f_{-T}(a', a)] = f_-(a), \tag{5.21}$$

$$\lim_{T \to -\infty} [\min_{b' \in R^n} e^{-\rho T} g_{-T}(b', b)] = g_-(b). \tag{5.22}$$

Proof.   Note first from (5.14) that

$$e^{-\rho T} f_{-T}(0, a) \geqslant f_-(a) \qquad \text{for all} \quad T < 0, \tag{5.23}$$

where the left side is nonincreasing as $T \to -\infty$ and, hence, approaches a limit. To show that the limit is $f_-(a)$, select an arbitrary $\epsilon > 0$ and any arc x over $(-\infty, 0]$ such that $x(0) = a$ and

$$\int_{-\infty}^0 L_0(x(t), \dot{x}(t)) \, e^{-\rho t} \, dt < f_-(a) + \epsilon. \tag{5.24}$$

For all T sufficiently low, one will have

$$\int_{T+1}^0 L_0(x(t), \dot{x}(t)) \, e^{-\rho t} \, dt < f_-(a) + \epsilon. \tag{5.25}$$

Let $\bar{x}$ denote the arc corresponding to the minimum in the definition of $f_1(0, x(T+1))$ (as exists by Theorem 3), and define the arc x' over $[T, 0]$ by

$$\begin{aligned}
x'(t) &= \bar{x}(t - T) \qquad \text{for} \quad T \leqslant t \leqslant T + 1, \\
&= x(t) \qquad\quad\ \text{for} \quad T + 1 \leqslant t \leqslant 0.
\end{aligned} \tag{5.26}$$

Then, by (5.17),

$$\begin{aligned}
e^{-\rho T} f_{-T}(0, a) &\leqslant \int_T^0 L_0(x'(t), \dot{x}'(t)) \, e^{-\rho t} \, dt \\
&= \int_T^{T+1} L_0(\bar{x}(t), \dot{\bar{x}}(t)) \, e^{-\rho t} \, dt + \int_{T+1}^0 L_0(x(t), \dot{x}(t)) \, e^{-\rho t} \, dt \\
&= e^{-\rho T} f_1(0, x(T+1)) + \int_{T+1}^0 L_0(x(t), \dot{x}(t)) \, e^{-\rho t} \, dt. \tag{5.27}
\end{aligned}$$

On the other hand, since f_1 is convex with $0 = f_1(0, 0) = \min f_1$, it is true (for $T < 0$) that

$$0 \leqslant e^{-\rho T} f_1(0, x(T+1)) \leqslant f_1(0, e^{-\rho T} x(T+1)). \tag{5.28}$$

But (5.24) implies via Proposition 2′ that

$$\lim_{T \to -\infty} e^{-\rho T} x(T+1) = 0. \tag{5.29}$$

Hence,

$$\lim_{T \to -\infty} e^{-\rho T} f_1(0, x(T+1)) = 0, \tag{5.30}$$

because f_1 is continuous (Theorem 3). From this and inequalities (5.25) and (5.27), it is clear that one will have

$$e^{-\nu T} f_{-T}(0, a) < f_-(a) + \epsilon \tag{5.31}$$

for all T sufficiently low. The first limit assertion in (5.19) is thereby established. The second part of (5.19) follows from the fact that

$$\lim_{T \to -\infty} f_{-T}(a', a) = f_+(a') > 0 \qquad \text{if} \quad a' \neq 0, \tag{5.32}$$

which is valid because of Proposition 10 and the corollary to Theorem 4; since f_+ is nonnegative and strictly convex by Theorem 4, it cannot vanish except at the origin. The implication from (5.19) to (5.21) can be verified using the convexity of the expression $e^{-\rho T} f_{-T}(a', a)$ as a function of a' for fixed a.

The proofs of (5.20) and (5.22) are analogous.

THEOREM 4'. *Under the global curvature assumption, the functions f_- and g_- are everywhere continuously differentiable and strictly convex on R^n, and they satisfy the conjugacy relations*

$$g_-(b) = \max_{a \in R^n} \{a \cdot b - f_-(a)\} = f_-^*(b), \tag{5.33}$$

$$f_-(a) = \max_{b \in R^n} \{a \cdot b - g_-(b)\} = g_-^*(a). \tag{5.34}$$

Furthermore, one has

$$(a, b) \in K_- \Leftrightarrow f_-(a) + g_-(b) = a \cdot b$$
$$\Leftrightarrow b = \nabla f_-(a) \Leftrightarrow a = \nabla g_-(b). \tag{5.35}$$

For each $(a, b) \in K_-$, there is a unique solution $(x(t), p(t))$ to the Hamiltonian system (1.21) over $(-\infty, 0]$ satisfying $(x(0), p(0)) = (a, b)$ and (5.3), and it tends to $(0, 0)$ as $t \to -\infty$. In fact, x is the unique arc furnishing the minimum in the definition of $f_-(a)$, while p is the unique arc furnishing the minimum in the definition of $g_-(b)$.

Proof. Let

$$\phi_T(a) = \min_{a' \in R^n} e^{-\rho T} f_{-T}(a', a) \qquad \text{for} \quad T < 0. \tag{5.36}$$

Then ϕ_T is a finite convex function. Using the conjugacy relations in Theorem 3, we calculate that

$$\phi_T{}^*(b) = \max_{a \in R^n} \{a \cdot b - \phi_T(a)\}$$

$$= e^{-\rho T} \max_{(a,a')} \{e^{\rho T}a \cdot b - a \cdot 0 - f_{-T}(a', a)\} \qquad (5.37)$$

$$= e^{-\rho T}g_{-T}(0, b).$$

By Proposition 12, therefore, the functions ϕ_T converge pointwise to f_- as $T \rightarrow -\infty$, while their conjugates $\phi_T{}^*$ converge pointwise to g_-. Since f_- and g_- are finite everywhere (Proposition 8'), this implies that f_- and g_- are conjugate to each other (cf. [6, 7]), i.e., Formulas (5.33) and (5.34) are correct. (The finiteness justifies writing "max" in place of "inf" [5, Theorems 23.4 and 23.5].) Proposition 8' and Corollary 2 of Proposition 3' give us now the facts stated after (5.35), as well as the first equivalence in (5.35). Since f_- and g_- are conjugate to each other, we certainly have

$$f_-(a) + g_-(b) = a \cdot b \Leftrightarrow b \in \partial f_-(a) \Leftrightarrow a \in \partial g_-(b) \qquad (5.38)$$

[5, Theorem 23.5], and, hence,

$$K_- = \{(a, b)| \; b \in \partial f_-(a)\} = \{(a, b)| \; a \in \partial g_-(b)\}. \qquad (5.39)$$

The uniqueness properties in Proposition 11 assert that K_- is the graph of a one-to-one mapping, and it therefore follows that f_- and g_- are continuously differentiable and strictly convex [5, Corollary 26.3.1]. The proof of Theorem 4' is thereby finished.

Proof of Theorem 1'.   First we prove (1.44). It is clear that

$$(0, 0) \in K_+ \cap K_- ,$$

since the Hamiltonian system (1.21) is satisfied by $(x(t), p(t)) \equiv (0, 0)$. Suppose that also $(a, b) \in K_+ \cap K_-$. Then there is a solution $(x(t), p(t))$ to the Hamiltonian system over $(-\infty, +\infty)$ satisfying $(x(0), p(0)) = (a, b)$ and

$$0 = \lim_{t \to +\infty} \theta(t) = \lim_{t \to -\infty} \theta(t), \qquad \text{where} \quad \theta(t) = e^{-\rho t}x(t) \cdot p(t). \quad (5.40)$$

Applying Corollary 1 of Proposition 5 to $(x_1(t), p_1(t)) \equiv (x(t), p(t))$ and $(x_2(t), p_2(t)) \equiv (0, 0)$, we find that this implies $(x(t), p(t)) = (0, 0)$ for all $t \in (-\infty, +\infty)$. In particular, $(a, b) = (0, 0)$. Therefore (1.44) is correct.

The assertion in Theorem 1' about uniqueness of solutions is covered by Proposition 11. The rest of the proof is just like that of Theorem 1. We invoke the global curvature assumption and apply Theorem 4. The sets U_- and V_- are defined by

$$U_- = \{a \mid \exists b \quad \text{with} \quad (a, b) \in K_- \cap W\}, \tag{5.41}$$

$$V_- = \{b \mid \exists a \quad \text{with} \quad (a, b) \in K_- \cap W\}, \tag{5.42}$$

where

$$W = \{(a, b) \mid f_-(a) + g_-(b) \leqslant \epsilon\} \tag{5.43}$$

for ϵ sufficiently small. For each $(a, b) \in K_- \cap W$, the corresponding solution $(x(t), p(t))$ to the system (1.21) over $(-\infty, 0]$, as in the definition of K_-, remains in K_- and, hence, satisfies (by Theorem 4)

$$f_-(x(t)) + g_-(p(t)) = x(t) \cdot p(t) \qquad \text{for} \quad -\infty < t \leqslant 0. \tag{5.44}$$

But the right side of (5.44) is nondecreasing as a function of t by Proposition 5, and, hence, the left side is also nondecreasing. This shows that $(x(t), p(t))$ remains in W for all $t \in (-\infty, 0]$. The details of the proof can thus be effected as in the case of Theorem 1.

6. SOME COMPLEMENTARY RESULTS

We present now two counterexamples, as well as a theorem on the existence of a stationary point $(\bar{k}, \bar{q})$ in certain cases where the discount rate ρ is sufficiently small. For other existence results of somewhat different import, see [1].

EXAMPLE 1. This will demonstrate that strict concavity–convexity of H_0 near $(0, 0)$ is not enough to guarantee "saddle point behavior" of the dynamical system for a given $\rho > 0$, and that something like the inequality in the basic curvature assumption is necessary. Let $n = 1$ and

$$H(x, p) = -\tfrac{1}{2}x^2 + \tfrac{1}{2}p^2 + xp \qquad \text{for all} \quad (x, p) \in R \times R. \tag{6.1}$$

Then H is strictly concave in x and strictly convex in p, with $H(0, 0) = 0$ and $\nabla H(0, 0) = (0, 0)$. Thus $(\bar{k}, \bar{q}) = (0, 0)$ satisfies the rest-point condition (1.15), and we have $H_0 = H$. The perturbed Hamiltonian system (1.21) reduces to

$$\begin{bmatrix} \dot{x} \\ \dot{p} \end{bmatrix} = \begin{bmatrix} 1 & 1 \\ 1 & \rho - 1 \end{bmatrix} \begin{bmatrix} x \\ p \end{bmatrix}, \tag{6.2}$$

a differential equation whose behavior around $(0, 0)$ is easily analyzed. One finds that there is "saddle point behavior" if $0 \leqslant \rho < 2$, but if $\rho > 2$, then *all* solutions to (6.2) (other than $(x(t), p(t)) \equiv (0, 0)$) diverge from $(0, 0)$ as $t \to +\infty$.

EXAMPLE 2. The purpose of this example is to show that the problem in the definition (1.1) of $\phi(c)$, if deprived of the boundedness restriction on $e^{-\rho t}k(t)$, may fail to be reducible to the problem in the definition (1.37) of $f_+(a)$ as in Proposition 2 and its corollary. Taking $n = 1$, we define

$$L(k, z) = r(k) + r(z) + 4(z - \rho k) \qquad \text{for} \quad (k, z) \in R \times R, \qquad (6.3)$$

where

$$
\begin{aligned}
r(z) &= \tfrac{1}{2}z^2 && \text{if} \quad |z| \leqslant 1, \\
&= |z| && \text{if} \quad |z| \geqslant 1.
\end{aligned}
\qquad (6.4)
$$

Note that r is a differentiable convex function on the real line whose conjugate is

$$
\begin{aligned}
r^*(p) &= \tfrac{1}{2}|p|^2 && \text{if} \quad |p| \leqslant 1, \\
&= +\infty && \text{if} \quad |p| > 1.
\end{aligned}
\qquad (6.5)
$$

From the definition (1.5), we have

$$H(k, q) = -r(k) + r^*(q - 4) + 4\rho k. \qquad (6.6)$$

Thus, the rest point condition (1.15) is satisfied by $(\bar{k}, \bar{q}) = (0, 4)$, and H is α-concave-β-convex near $(\bar{k}, \bar{q})$ for $\alpha = \beta = 1$. The basic curvature condition is therefore fulfilled, assuming $0 < \rho < 2^{1/2}$.

We claim that $\phi(c)$ is finite for all $c \in R$, while the function $\tilde{\phi}$ obtained by dropping the boundedness restriction in the infimum defining $\phi(c)$ has in fact $\tilde{\phi}(c) = -\infty$ for all $c \in R$; thus, the boundedness restriction plays an essential role. To see this, consider first an arbitrary arc k over $[0, +\infty)$ with $k(0) = c$ and $e^{-\rho t}k(t)$ bounded. If $L(k(t), \dot{k}(t)) e^{-\rho t}$ is majorized by a summable function over $[0, +\infty)$, Proposition 2(a) implies that $L_0(k(t), \dot{k}(t)) e^{-\rho t}$ is summable over $[0, +\infty)$ (here $k(t) = x(t)$ because $\bar{k} = 0$), and furthermore $e^{-\rho t}k(t) \to 0$ as $t \to +\infty$. In consequence,

$$
\begin{aligned}
\int_0^{+\infty} &L(k(t), \dot{k}(t)) e^{-\rho t} \, dt \\
&= \int^{+\infty} [r(k(t)) + r(\dot{k}(t))] e^{-\rho t} \, dt + 4 \int_0^\infty (d/dt) e^{-\rho t}k(t) \, dt \\
&\geqslant -4k(0) = -4c.
\end{aligned}
\qquad (6.7)
$$

This demonstrates that

$$\phi(c) \geqslant -4c > -\infty \qquad \text{for all} \quad c \in R. \qquad (6.8)$$

On the other hand, the finiteness of L ensures that $\phi(c) < +\infty$. Therefore ϕ is indeed finite. Observe at the same time that $r(z) \leqslant |z|$ and, hence,

$$
\begin{aligned}
L(k, z) &\leqslant |k| + |z - \rho k + \rho k| + 4(z - \rho k) \\
&\leqslant (1 + \rho)|k| + |z - \rho k| + 4(z - \rho k).
\end{aligned}
\qquad (6.9)
$$

For the arc $k(t) = -e^{2\rho t}$ (which does *not* have $e^{-\rho t}k(t)$ bounded over $[0, +\infty)$), we obtain from (6.9) that

$$
\begin{aligned}
\int_0^{+\infty} L(k(t), \dot{k}(t)) \, e^{-\rho t} \, dt &\leqslant \int_0^{+\infty} [(1 + \rho) \, e^{2\rho t} + \rho e^{2\rho t} - 4\rho e^{2\rho t}] \, e^{-\rho t} \, dt \\
&= [1 - 2\rho] \int_0^{-\infty} e^{\rho t} \, dt = -\infty
\end{aligned}
\qquad (6.10)
$$

if $\rho > \frac{1}{2}$. In this case,

$$-\infty = \tilde{\phi}(k(0)) = \tilde{\phi}(-1),$$

and since $\tilde{\phi}$ is a convex function with $\tilde{\phi}(c) \leqslant \phi(c) < +\infty$, it follows that $\tilde{\phi}(c) = -\infty$ for all $c \in R$ [5, Theorem 7.2].

Thus if $\frac{1}{2} < \rho < 2^{1/2}$, we have $\phi(c) \neq \tilde{\phi}(c)$ for all c, even though the basic curvature assumption is fulfilled.

We conclude now with our theorem on the existence of stationary points for sufficiently small values of the discount rate ρ.

THEOREM 5. *Suppose that $(\bar{k}_0, \bar{q}_0)$ satisfies the stationary point condition (1.15) for $\rho = 0$ and that H is α-concave-β-convex in some neighborhood of $(\bar{k}_0, \bar{q}_0)$. Then for each $\rho > 0$ sufficiently small, there exists a unique pair $(\bar{k}_\rho, \bar{q}_\rho)$ satisfying the stationary point condition for that value of ρ, and one has*

$$\lim_{\rho \to 0} (\bar{k}_\rho, \bar{q}_\rho) = (0, 0). \qquad (6.11)$$

Proof. We know that H is globally concave–convex (since it is related to the convex function L by (1.5)), and our hypothesis entails the finiteness of H near $(0, 0)$. Therefore, H is continuous near $(0, 0)$ [5, Theorem 35.1]. Let $C \times D$ be a compact convex neighborhood of $(\bar{k}_0, \bar{q}_0)$ such that, on $C \times D$, $H(k, q)$ is finite and continuous, α-concave in k and β-convex in q. In particular, for each $q' \in R^n$ and $\rho \geqslant 0$ the function

$$(k, q) \to H(k, q) - \rho k q' \qquad (6.12)$$

is strictly concave–convex on $C \times D$ and has a unique saddle point relative to $C \times D$ (in the minimax sense), which, as is easy to see from the continuity of H and definition of "saddle point," must depend continuously on q' and ρ. Let

$$\Phi_\rho : C \times D \to C \times D \qquad (6.13)$$

be the continuous mapping which assigns to each $(k', q') \in C \times D$ the saddlepoint (k'', q'') of the function (6.12) relative to $C \times D$. Then Φ_ρ has at least one fixed point. Such fixed points are the pairs $(\bar{k}, \bar{q}) \in C \times D$ such that

$$H(\bar{k}, \bar{q}) - \rho k \cdot \bar{q} - \rho k \cdot q \leqslant H(\bar{k}, \bar{q}) - \rho \bar{k} \cdot \bar{q} \qquad \text{for all} \quad k \in C, \quad (6.14)$$

$$H(\bar{k}, q) - \rho \bar{k} \cdot \bar{q} \geqslant H(\bar{k}, \bar{q}) - \rho \bar{k} \cdot \bar{q} \qquad \text{for all} \quad q \in D. \quad (6.15)$$

Of course, the term $\rho \bar{k} \cdot \bar{q}$ can be dropped from both sides of (6.15). The theory of the minimum of a convex function informs us that (6.15) holds if and only if there is a vector $\bar{m}$ such that

$$\bar{m} \cdot q \leqslant \bar{m} \cdot \bar{q} \qquad \text{for all} \quad q \in D, \qquad (6.16)$$

$$H(\bar{k}, q) + \bar{m} \cdot q \geqslant H(\bar{k}, \bar{q}) + \bar{m} \cdot \bar{q} \qquad \text{for all} \quad q \in R^n \qquad (6.17)$$

(cf. [5, Theorem 27.4]). Likewise, (6.14) holds if and only if there exists a vector $\bar{n}$ such that

$$k \cdot \bar{n} \leqslant \bar{k} \cdot \bar{n} \qquad \text{for all} \quad k \in C, \qquad (6.18)$$

$$H(\bar{k}, \bar{q}) - \rho k \cdot \bar{q} - k \cdot \bar{n} \leqslant H(\bar{k}, \bar{q}) - \rho \bar{k} \cdot \bar{q} - \bar{k} \cdot \bar{n} \qquad \text{for all} \quad k \in R^n. \qquad (6.19)$$

Observe that (6.17) and (6.19) can be combined into

$$(\rho \bar{q} + \bar{n}_0 - \bar{m}) \in \partial H(\bar{k}, \bar{q}). \qquad (6.20)$$

If $\bar{n} = 0$ and $\bar{m} = 0$, as must be true by (6.16) and (6.17) if $(\bar{k}, \bar{q})$ is an interior point of $C \times D$, then (6.20) reduces to the stationary point condition (1.15).

We have seen that for each ρ there is at least one set of vectors $\bar{k}, \bar{q}, \bar{m}, \bar{n}$ with $(\bar{k}, \bar{q}) \in C \times D$ such that (6.16)–(6.19) are satisfied. To investigate this further, consider also another set of vectors $\bar{k}', \bar{q}', \bar{m}', \bar{n}'$ satisfying these conditions for a possibly different value ρ'. Since H is α-concave–β-convex on $C \times D$, (6.17) implies

$$H(\bar{k}, q) + \bar{m} \cdot q \geqslant H(\bar{k}, \bar{q}) + \bar{m} \cdot \bar{q} + \tfrac{1}{2}\beta \, |\, q - \bar{q} \,|^2 \qquad \text{for all} \quad q \in C, \quad (6.21)$$

while (6.19) implies

$$H(k, \bar{q}) - k \cdot (\rho\bar{q} + \bar{n})$$
$$\leqslant H(\bar{k}, \bar{q}) - k \cdot (\rho\bar{q} + \bar{n}) - \tfrac{1}{2}\alpha \mid k - \bar{k} \mid^2 \qquad \text{for all} \quad k \in D. \quad (6.22)$$

Therefore,

$$H(\bar{k}, \bar{q}') - H(\bar{k}, \bar{q}) \geqslant \bar{m} \cdot (\bar{q} - \bar{q}') + \tfrac{1}{2}\beta \mid \bar{q}' - \bar{q} \mid^2, \qquad (6.23)$$

$$H(\bar{k}, \bar{q}) - H(\bar{k}', \bar{q}) \geqslant (\bar{k} - \bar{k}') \cdot (\rho\bar{q} + \bar{n}) + \tfrac{1}{2}\alpha \mid \bar{k}' - \bar{k} \mid^2, \quad (6.24)$$

and dually,

$$H(\bar{k}', \bar{q}) - H(\bar{k}', \bar{q}') \geqslant \bar{m}' \cdot (\bar{q}' - \bar{q}) + \tfrac{1}{2}\beta \mid \bar{q} - \bar{q}' \mid^2, \qquad (6.25)$$

$$H(\bar{k}', \bar{q}') - H(\bar{k}, \bar{q}') \geqslant (\bar{k}' - \bar{k}) \cdot (\rho'\bar{q}' + \bar{n}') + \tfrac{1}{2}\alpha \mid \bar{k} - \bar{k}' \mid^2. \quad (6.26)$$

Adding the last four inequalities and using the fact that by (6.16) and (6.18),

$$\bar{m} \cdot (\bar{q} - \bar{q}') \geqslant 0, \qquad (\bar{k} - \bar{k}') \cdot \bar{n} \geqslant 0,$$
$$\bar{m}' \cdot (\bar{q}' - \bar{q}) \geqslant 0, \qquad (\bar{k}' - \bar{k}) \cdot \bar{n}' \geqslant 0,$$

we obtain

$$0 \geqslant (\bar{k} - \bar{k}')(\rho\bar{q} - \rho'\bar{q}') + \alpha \mid \bar{k}' - \bar{k} \mid^2 + \beta \mid \bar{q}' - \bar{q} \mid^2, \qquad (6.27)$$

or equivalently,

$$(\rho' - \rho)(\bar{k} - \bar{k}') \cdot \bar{q}' \geqslant \alpha \mid \bar{k}' - \bar{k} \mid^2 + \rho(\bar{k}' - \bar{k}) \cdot (\bar{q}' - \bar{q}) + \beta \mid \bar{q}' - \bar{q} \mid^2.$$
$$(6.28)$$

Defining

$$\gamma = \max \{ \mid (k - k') \cdot q' \mid \| k \in C, k' \in C, q' \in D \}, \qquad (6.29)$$

we can convert (6.28) into the bound

$$\gamma \mid \rho' - \rho \mid \geqslant \alpha \mid \bar{k}' - k \mid^2 - \rho \mid \bar{k}' - \bar{k} \mid \cdot \mid \bar{q}' - \bar{q} \mid + \beta \mid \bar{q}' - \bar{q} \mid^2$$
$$\geqslant \sigma_1 [\mid \bar{k}' - \bar{k} \mid^2 + \mid \bar{q}' - \bar{q} \mid]^2, \qquad (6.30)$$

where

$$\sigma_1 = (4\alpha\beta - \rho^2)/4(\alpha + \beta + \rho); \qquad (6.31)$$

the proof of the second inequality in (6.30) is given at the end of the proof of Proposition 5. Let us suppose that $\rho^2 < 4\alpha\beta$, so that $\sigma_1 > 0$. Then two conclusions are apparent from (6.30). First, if $\rho' = \rho$, then $\bar{k}' = \bar{k}$ and $\bar{q}' = \bar{q}$. In other words, $(\bar{k}, \bar{q})$ is *uniquely* determined by conditions (6.16)–(6.19). Second, taking $\rho' = 0$ and $(\bar{k}', \bar{q}') = (\bar{k}_0, \bar{q}_0)$, we see that as $\rho \downarrow 0$, the point $(\bar{k}, \bar{q})$ must tend to $(\bar{k}_0, \bar{q}_0)$. Hence, for ρ sufficiently small, $(\bar{k}, \bar{q})$ must be an interior point of $C \times D$, so that $\bar{m} = 0 = \bar{n}$ as already explained, and the stationary point condition (1.15) is actually satisfied. These two conclusions immediately yield the assertions in the theorem.

REFERENCES

1. D. CASS AND K. SHELL, The structure and stability of competitive dynamical systems, *J. Econ. Theory* **12** (1976), 31–70. Reprinted as Essay III in this volume.
2. R. T. ROCKAFELLAR, Saddle points of Hamiltonian systems in convex problems of Lagrange, *J. Optimization Theory Appl.* **12** (1973), 367–390.
3. R. T. ROCKAFELLAR, Conjugate convex functions in optimal control and the calculus of variations, *J. Math. Anal. Appl.* **32** (1970), 174–222.
4. R. T. ROCKAFELLAR, Existence and duality theorems for convex problems of Bolza, *Amer. Math. Soc.* **159** (1971), 1–40.
5. R. T. ROCKAFELLAR, "Convex Analysis," Princeton University Press, Princeton, N.J., 1970.
6. R. T. ROCKAFELLAR, Generalized Hamiltonian equations for convex problems of Lagrange, *Pacific J. Math.* **33** (1970), 411–427.
7. R. A. WIJSMAN, Convergence of sequences of convex sets and functions, *Bull. Amer. Math. Soc.* **70** (1964), 186–188.
8. R. A. WIJSMAN, Convergence of sequences of convex sets and functions, II, *Trans. Amer. Math. Soc.* **123** (1966), 32–45.

ESSAY V

Existence of Solutions to Hamiltonian Dynamical Systems of Optimal Growth

R. E. Gaines*

1. Introduction

Cass and Shell [3] have shown how a wide range of problems in the theory of economic dynamics may be formulated in terms of Hamiltonian dynamical systems. In particular they have studied the system modeling consumption–optimal growth with discount rate $\rho > 0$:

$$\dot{k} = \partial H(Q, k)/\partial Q,$$

$$\dot{Q} = -(\partial H(Q, k)/\partial k) + \rho Q,$$

$$k(0) = \bar{k} \geqslant 0,$$

$$\lim_{t \to +\infty} Q(t)\, e^{-\rho t} k(t) = 0, \tag{1}$$

$$Q(t) \geqslant 0,$$

$$k(t) \geqslant 0,$$

where

$$k = (k_1, ..., k_n) = \text{capital stocks},$$

$$Q = (Q_1, ..., Q_n) = \text{current prices of capital goods output},$$

and

$$H(Q, k) = \text{current value of imputed NNP}.$$

The Hamiltonian function $H(Q, k)$ is defined on the basis of certain assumptions about technology. For a detailed discussion of the manner in which the Hamiltonian function "captures" the essence of the techno-

* This research was carried out while the author was visiting at the Department of Economics, University of Pennsylvania, and the Institut Mathematique, University of Louvain, Belgium while on sabbatical leave from Colorado State University. Technical services were provided under NSF Grant SOC 74 — 19469 at the University of Pennsylvania.

114

logy, a discussion of the derivation and significance of the particular model (1), and an extensive bibliography we refer the reader to [3].

In this paper we present a set of conditions on the Hamiltonian function $H(Q, k)$ which are sufficient to guarantee that the system (1) has a nonnegative solution. These conditions, presented and briefly discussed in Section 2, include convexity–concavity and other properties that are consistent with or mimic the technological assumptions of Cass and Shell. Various implications of these conditions which are crucial to our existence analysis (and which are of some interest in their own right) are presented in Section 3. These include a priori bounds on solutions to a finite time problem associated with (1).

The existence proof, presented in Section 4, relies on a continuation principle from the theory of fixed points for multivalued mappings in infinite dimensional spaces and on the a priori information obtained in Section 3. The mathematical machinery we employ is described in the appendix.

The system (1) can be considered as necessary conditions arising from an associated optimization problem, i.e., the problem of maximizing the integral of discounted consumption over an infinite time horizon. For a study of (1) from this vantage point, we refer the reader to the excellent work of Rockafellar [8]. Using *only* convexity–concavity assumptions on $H(Q, k)$, Rockafellar obtains a remarkably complete qualitative theory for problem (1) including existence of solutions. He also shows that solutions to (1) are solutions to the optimization problem (if that problem is properly posed). Though we do not reproduce the machinery to state and analyze the optimization problem here, using the propositions developed by Rockafellar in [8, Section 2], it can be shown that *under our assumptions, solutions to* (1) (*whose* existence we establish) *are solutions to the optimization problem* (as posed by Rockafellar).

Our conditions described in Section 2 involve much weaker convexity–concavity on $H(Q, k)$ than Rockafellar's α-concave, β-convex condition, but on the other hand our methods require exploitation of structural features of $H(Q, k)$ (designed to mimic assumptions on the underlying technology) other than convexity–concavity. As a bonus from these additional assumptions we obtain various bounds on solutions; for example, nonnegativity of $(Q(t), k(t))$. We suspect, though to our knowledge the work has not been carried out, that our assumptions could be used in conjunction with the most general theorems of optimal control (see, for example, [6]) to prove existence of solutions to (1). (This observation was suggested by W. A. Brock.)

However, apart from our primary interest in developing an existence theory that exploits the underlying technological assumptions of Cass–

Shell and only those assumptions, our second primary objective is to develop machinery for investigating existence which is *independent of the associated optimization problem.* Our view is that (1) is a representative selected from a large class of models some of which are descriptive models where the associated optimization problem is only implicity defined, if it exists at all. The application of the kind of machinery developed here to those descriptive models is a subject for future research.

2. SUFFICIENT CONDITIONS FOR EXISTENCE

Existence of solutions to (1) will be established under the conditions (E1)–(E6) stated in this section. In the statements, if $x = (x_1, x_2, ..., x_n)$, then $\| x \| = (\sum_{i=1}^{n} x_i^2)^{1/2}$. Inequalities stated for set-valued functions hold for every member of the set. The Hamiltonian function $H(Q, k)$ of Cass and Shell is defined on the nonnegative orthant; i.e., on $\{(Q, k): Q \geqslant 0, k \geqslant 0\}$. To simplify our analysis we will assume that $H(Q, k)$ can be extended so that its domain is all of $R^n \times R^n$. Moreover, we assume that the extended function satisfies

(E.1) CONVEXITY–CONCAVITY.   *H is concave in k and convex in Q on* $R^n \times R^n$.

Under (E1) H possesses generalized gradients

$$\frac{\partial H(Q, k)}{\partial Q}, \frac{\partial H(Q, k)}{\partial k}$$

defined by

$$\frac{\partial H(Q, k)}{\partial Q} = \{z \in R^n: H(Q', k) \geqslant H(Q, k) + (Q' - Q) \cdot z, \forall Q' \in R^n\},$$

$$\frac{\partial H(Q, k)}{\partial k} = \{r \in R^n: H(Q, k') \leqslant H(Q, k) + (k' - k) \cdot r, \forall k' \in R^n\}.$$

It is these "set-valued derivatives" which appear in (1). Thus, to be completely accurate we should write in place of (1) the system

$$
\begin{aligned}
&k \in (\partial H(Q, k)/\partial Q), \\
&\dot{Q} \in -(\partial H(Q, k)/\partial k) + \rho Q, \\
&k(0) = \bar{k} \geqslant 0, \\
&\lim_{t \to +\infty} Q(t) e^{-\rho t} k(t) = 0, \\
&Q(t) \geqslant 0, \\
&k(t) \geqslant 0,
\end{aligned}
\tag{1'}
$$

involving differential correspondences or contingent equations. By a *solution* to the first two correspondences we will mean a pair of absolutely continuous functions $(Q(t), k(t))$ which satisfies the inclusion requirement almost everywhere on some interval.

The assumption of convexity–concavity of $H(Q, k)$ on *all* of $R^n \times R^n$ is made for convenience and can be replaced by the weaker assumption of convexity–concavity on the nonnegative orthant provided $\bar{k} > 0$ and $Q^* > 0$. The extension to the weaker case can be made by considering an appropriate sequence $\{H_m(Q, k)\}$ of functions concave–convex on $R^n \times R^n$ which converge to a nonextendable $H(Q, k)$ on the nonnegative orthant, applying the existence theory to each $H_m(Q, R)$, and considering convergence of the resulting sequence of solutions $\{(Q_m(t), k_m(t)\}$. Since we deal only with nonnegative solutions anyway, the stronger assumption is used only as a simple way to guarantee regularity of the generalized gradients on the boundary of the nonnegative orthant.

(E2) EXISTENCE OF A NONNEGATIVE STATIONARY POINT.   *There exists* $(Q^*, k^*) \geqslant (0, 0)$ *such that*

$$0 \in \partial H(Q^*, k^*)/\partial Q,$$

$$0 \in (\partial H(Q^*, k^*)/\partial k) + \rho Q^*.$$

Cass and Shell [3] establish the existence of such a stationary point as a natural consequence of assumptions on technology.

(E3) LIMITATION BY PRIMARY FACTORS.   *There exists* $K > 0$ *such that if* $Q \geqslant 0$, $k \geqslant 0$, $(k - k^*) \cdot (Q - Q^*) \leqslant 0$, *and* $\| k \| \geqslant K$, *then*

$$(\partial H(Q, k)/\partial Q) \cdot k < 0.$$

Since $\partial H(Q, k)/\partial Q$ has the economic interpretation of instantaneous net investment, this condition says, roughly speaking, that if capital stocks are sufficiently large the corresponding net investments must be nonpositive. Thus, this is a mathematically convenient manner of expressing the spirit of the condition (T6) in [3]. In fact, (E3) can be deduced from (T6) and the other assumptions on technology.

(E4) PRODUCTIVITY OF TECHNOLOGY.   *There exists* $\gamma > 0$ *such that if* $Q \geqslant 0$, $k \geqslant 0$, $\| k \| \leqslant \max [\| \bar{k} \|, K] \equiv K_0$, $(k - k^*) \cdot (Q - Q^*) \leqslant 0$, *and* $\| Q - Q^* \| \geqslant \gamma$, *then* $(\partial H(Q, k)/\partial Q) \cdot (Q - Q^*) > 0$.

The vector $\partial H(Q, k)/\partial Q$ represents those levels of technologically feasible instantaneous net investment which maximize instantaneous

NNP (*given* capital stocks k and prices Q). This assumption asserts, roughly speaking, that if prices Q of capital goods outputs are sufficiently high ($\| Q - Q^* \| \geqslant \gamma$) and corresponding capital stocks are *not* too high ($(k - k^*) \cdot (Q - Q^*) \leqslant 0$), then NNP will be maximized by choosing positive investment levels. Thus, the assumption entails that certain capital stock levels can support positive net investment and is in the same spirit as [3, (T4)].

(E5) BOUNDED RATE OF DEPRECIATION.   *There exists* $\lambda > 0$ *such that for* $Q \geqslant 0$ *and* $k \geqslant 0$,

$$\partial H(Q, k)/\partial Q \geqslant -\lambda k.$$

Since $\partial H(Q, k)/\partial Q$ represents an instantaneous net investment z, this is implied by [3, (T7)].

(E6) FREE DISPOSAL IN ALLOCATION.   *For the same* $\lambda > 0$ *as in* (E5), $Q \geqslant 0$ *and* $k \geqslant 0$,

$$-(\partial H(Q, k)/\partial k) \leqslant \lambda Q.$$

This can be shown to be a consequence of the definition of $H(Q, k)$ and the free disposal assumption (T8) of Cass and Shell [3].

3. CONSEQUENCES OF THE EXISTENCE CONDITIONS: A PRIORI BOUNDS

We begin by stating some regularity results.

LEMMA 1.   *Under assumption* (E1) *the mapping*

$$T : (Q, k) \mapsto (\partial H(Q, k)/\partial k, - (\partial H(Q, k)/\partial Q) + \rho Q)$$

(i)   *nonempty, convex, compact-valued;*

(ii) *upper semi-continuous.*

Proof.   This is essentially a result of Rockafellar [7, Lemma 2, p. 415].

LEMMA 2.   *Under assumption* (E1), *if* $(Q(t), k(t))$ *is a pair of absolutely continuous functions on* $[a, b]$ *such that*

$$\dot{k}(t) \in \partial H(Q(t), k(t))/\partial Q, \text{ a.e. on } [a, b],$$

$$\dot{Q}(t) \in - (\partial H(Q(t), k(t))/\partial k) + \rho Q(t), \text{ a.e. on } [a, b],$$

then $H(Q(t), k(t))$ is absolutely continuous on $[a, b]$ and

$$d[H(Q(t), k(t))]/dt = \rho Q(t) \cdot \dot{k}(t) \text{ a.e. on } [a, b].$$

Proof. This can be obtained by slightly modifying another proof of Rockafellar [7, Theorem 3, p.421].

Note that Lemma 2 has an immediate economic interpretation since $H(Q(t), k(t))$ represents NNP along the path $(Q(t), k(t))$ and $\dot{k}(t)$ is instantaneous net investment.

Our mathematical strategy will be to consider first the following problem on the finite time interval $[0, T]$:

$$
\begin{aligned}
&\dot{k} \in (\partial H(Q, k)/\partial Q), \\
&\dot{Q} \in -(\partial H(Q, k)/\partial k) + \rho Q, \\
&k(0) = \bar{k} \geqslant 0, \\
&Q(T) = Q^*.
\end{aligned}
\tag{2.T}
$$

We will then obtain a solution to (1') by considering sequences of solutions to (2.T) with $T \to +\infty$.

The following Lemmas yield a priori information concerning the location of solution trajectories for (2.T). The first lemma is a modification of an argument of Cass and Shell (see [3]).

LEMMA 3. *Under assumptions* (E1) *and* (E2), *if* $(Q(t), k(t))$ *is a solution to* (2.T), *then*

$$(k(t) - k^*)(Q(t) - Q^*) \leqslant 0, \qquad t \in [0, T].$$

Proof. (For simplicity we will often write a·b as ab.) Let
$$V(t) = (k(t) - k^*)(Q(t) - Q^*).$$

We have from (2.T) and (E1) that

$$
\begin{aligned}
\frac{d[e^{-\rho t} V(t)]}{dt} &= e^{-\rho t}[\dot{V}(t) - \rho V(t)] \\
&= e^{-\rho t}[\dot{k}(Q - Q^*) + (k - k^*)\dot{Q} - \rho(k - k^*)(Q - Q^*)] \\
&\in e^{-\rho t}\left[\frac{\partial H(Q, k)}{\partial Q}(Q - Q^*) + (k - k^*)\left(-\frac{\partial H(Q, k)}{\partial k} + \rho Q\right)\right. \\
&\qquad\qquad\qquad\qquad\qquad\qquad\qquad \left. - \rho(k - k^*)(Q - Q^*)\right] \\
&\geqslant e^{-\rho t}[H(Q, k) - H(Q^*, k) + H(Q, k^*) - H(Q, k) \\
&\qquad + \rho(k - k^*)Q^*] \\
&\geqslant e^{-\rho t}[H(Q, k^*) - H(Q^*, k) + \rho(k - k^*)Q^*]
\end{aligned}
$$

where all the relationships hold almost everywhere on $[0, T]$. Since (Q^*, k^*) is a stationary point, we have from (E1) and (E2) that

$$0 \in (Q - Q^*) \frac{\partial H(Q^*, k^*)}{\partial Q} \leqslant H(Q, k^*) - H(Q^*, k^*),$$

$$0 \in \left[\rho Q^* - \frac{\partial H(Q^*, k^*)}{\partial Q} \right] (k - k^*) \leqslant \rho Q^*(k - k^*) + H(Q^*, k^*)$$
$$- H(Q^*, k).$$

But then

$$H(Q^*, k) - \rho Q^* k \leqslant H(Q^*, k^*) - \rho Q^* k^* \leqslant H(Q, k^*) - \rho Q^* k^*.$$

Thus

$$d[e^{-\rho t} V(t)]/dt \geqslant 0.$$

Since $V(T) = (k(T) - k^*)(Q^* - Q^*) = 0$, we have $e^{-\rho t} V(t) \leqslant 0$ on $[0, T]$.

LEMMA 4.   *Under assumptions* (E5) *and* (E6), *if* $(Q(t), k(t))$ *is a solution to* (2.T), *then*

$$k(t) \geqslant \bar{k} e^{-\lambda t} \, ;$$

and

$$Q(t) \geqslant Q^* e^{-(\lambda + \rho)(T-t)}$$

on $[0, T]$.

Proof.   We have that $k(t)$ is absolutely continuous on $[0, T]$ and

$$\dot{k}(t) \in \partial H(Q(t), k(t))/\partial Q \geqslant -\lambda k(t)$$

almost everywhere on $[0, T]$. But then

$$\dot{k}(t) \, e^{\lambda t} + \lambda \underline{k}(t) \, e^{\lambda t} \geqslant 0 \qquad \text{a.e. on } [0, T].$$

Thus

$$d[e^{\lambda t} k(t)]/dt \geqslant 0, \qquad \text{a.e. on } [0, T],$$

and we have

$$e^{\lambda t} k(t) - \bar{k} \geqslant 0$$

or

$$k(t) \geqslant \bar{k} e^{-\lambda t} \qquad \text{a.e. on } [0, T].$$

LEMMA 5.   *Under assumptions* (E1)–(E3), (E5), *and* (E6), *if* $(Q(t), k(t))$ *is a solution to* (2.T), *then*

$$\| k(t) \| \leqslant \max \, [\| \bar{k} \|, K] \equiv K_0 \, .$$

Proof. Suppose

$$\max_{[0,T]} \|k(t)\| = \| k(t_0)\| > K_0 .$$

Then $t_0 \neq 0$, since $k(0) = \bar{k}$. Since $\| k(t_0)\| > K$, there exists an interval $[t_0 - \varDelta, t_0] \subset [0, T]$ such that

$$\| k(t)\| > K$$

on $[t_0 - \varDelta, t_0]$. Moreover, by Lemmas 3 and 4

$$(k(t) - k^*)(Q(t) - Q^*) \leqslant 0,$$

and

$$k(t) \geqslant 0, \, Q(t) \geqslant 0$$

on $[t_0 - \varDelta, t_0]$. Thus, by (2.T) and (E3),

$$d[\| k(t)\|^2]/dt = 2k(t) \cdot \dot{k}(t) \in 2k(t) \cdot (\partial H(Q(t), k(t))/\partial Q) < 0$$

a.e. on $[t_0 - \varDelta, t_0]$. But then

$$\| k(t)\| > \| k(t_0)\|$$

on $[t_0 - \varDelta, t_0)$, which contradicts our choice of t_0.

Before we obtain a similar bound on $\| Q(t)\|$ we need the following technical lemma.

LEMMA 6.   *Under assumptions* (E1)–(E6), *if* $k \geqslant 0, Q \geqslant 0$, $\| Q - Q^* \| \geqslant \gamma, \| k \| \leqslant K_0$, *and* $(k - k^*)(Q - Q^*) \leqslant 0$, *then*

$$H(Q, k) \geqslant h_0 + ((\| Q - Q^* \|/\gamma) - 1) \, \mu$$

where

$$C_0 = \{(Q', k) \colon \| Q' - Q^* \| = \gamma, \| k \| \leqslant K_0 , (k - k^*)(Q' - Q^*) \leqslant 0\},$$
$$h_0 = \min\{H(Q', k) \colon (Q', k) \in C_0\},$$
$$\mu = \min\{(\partial H(Q', k)/\partial Q)(Q' - Q^*) \colon (Q', k) \in C_0\} > 0.$$

Proof. By Lemma 1, $(\partial H(Q, k)/\partial Q) Q$ is upper semicontinuous. Hence, the set appearing in the definition of μ is compact. Thus from (E4), $\mu > 0$.

Let (Q, k) satisfy the hypothesis of the lemma and let

$$Q' = (\gamma/\| Q - Q^* \|)(Q - Q^*) + Q^*.$$

Then
$$\| Q' - Q^* \| = \gamma,$$

and
$$(k - k^*)(Q' - Q^*) = (\gamma/\| Q - Q^* \|)(Q - Q^*)(k - k^*) \leqslant 0.$$

From (E1)
$$H(Q, k) \geqslant H(Q', k) + (Q - Q')\,(\partial H(Q', k)/\partial Q).$$

We have
$$Q - Q' = [(\| Q - Q^* \|/\gamma) - 1](Q' - Q^*),$$

thus
$$H(Q, k) \geqslant h_0 + [(\| Q - Q^* \|/\gamma) - 1]\,\mu.$$

LEMMA 7. *Under assumptions* (E1) *through* (E6), *if* $(Q(t), k(t))$ *is a solution to* (2.T), *then*

$$\| Q(t) \| \leqslant Q_0 \equiv \| Q^* \| + \gamma\{(1/\mu)[H_0 + 2\rho \| Q^* \| K_0 - h_0] + 1\}$$

where μ *and* h_0 *are as in Lemma* 6 *and*

$$H_0 = \max\{H(Q, k)\colon \| Q - Q^* \| \leqslant \gamma, \| k \| \leqslant K_0, (k - k^*)(Q - Q^*) \leqslant 0,$$
$$k \geqslant 0, Q \geqslant 0\}.$$

Proof. We first show that
$$H(Q(t), k(t)) - \rho Q^* k(t) \leqslant H_0 + \rho \| Q^* \| K_0.$$

Suppose not; i.e., suppose
$$\max_{[0, T]} [H(Q(t), k(t)) - \rho Q^* k(t)]$$
$$= H(Q(t_0), k(t_0)) - \rho Q^* k(t_0) > H_0 + \rho \| Q^* \| K_0.$$

By Lemmas 3, 4, and 5 we have
$$\| k(t) \| \leqslant K_0,$$
$$(k(t) - k^*)(Q(t) - Q^*) \leqslant 0,$$

and
$$k(t) \geqslant 0, Q(t) \geqslant 0.$$

Thus we must have, from the definition of H_0,
$$\| Q(t_0) - Q^* \| > \gamma.$$

Moreover, by definition of H_0, since $Q(T) = Q^*$, we must have $t_0 < T$. Thus, there exists an interval $[t_0, t_0 + \Delta]$ on which

$$H(Q(t), k(t)) - \rho Q^* k(t) > H_0 + \rho \| Q^* \| K_0$$

and

$$\| Q(t) - Q^* \| > \gamma.$$

From Lemma 2 and (E4) we have

$$\frac{d[H(Q(t), k(t)) - \rho Q^* k(t)]}{dt}$$
$$= \rho Q(t) \dot{k}(t) - \rho Q^* \dot{k}(t) \in \rho(Q(t) - Q^*) \frac{\partial H(Q(t), k(t))}{\partial Q} > 0$$

a.e. on $[t_0, t_0 + \Delta]$. This contradicts our choice of t_0. By Lemma 6, if $\| Q(t) - Q^* \| \geqslant \gamma$, then

$$H_0 + \rho \| Q^* \| K_0 \geqslant H(Q(t), k(t)) - \rho Q^* k(t)$$
$$\geqslant h_0 + ((\| Q(t) - Q^* \|/\gamma) - 1) \mu - \rho \| Q^* \| K_0.$$

Thus,

$$\| Q(t) - Q^* \| \leqslant \gamma \{ (1/\mu)[H_0 + 2\rho \| Q^* \| K_0 - h_0] + 1 \}$$

and the desired inequality follows.

4. EXISTENCE PROOF

Our preliminary existence theorem dealing with problem (2.T) is based on the following principle.

CONTINUATION PRINCIPLE. *Suppose* (E1) *is satisfied. Suppose there exist* $K_0 > 0$ *and* $Q_0 > 0$ *such that any solution to*

$$\dot{k} \in \sigma \frac{\partial H(Q, k)}{\partial Q},$$

$$\dot{Q} \in -\sigma \frac{\partial H(Q, k)}{\partial k} + \sigma \rho Q, \qquad\qquad (2.T.\sigma)$$

$$k(0) = \bar{k} \geqslant 0,$$

$$Q(T) = Q^*$$

for $\sigma \in (0, 1)$ *satisfies* $\| k(t) \| \leqslant K_0$, $\| Q(t) \| \leqslant Q_0$ *for* $t \in [0, T]$. *Then* (2.T) *has at least one solution* $(k(t), Q(t))$ *satisfying* $\| k(t) \| \leqslant K_0$ *and* $\| Q(t) \| \leqslant Q_0$ *for* $t \in [0, T]$.

This principle is an adaptation to our problem of Leray–Schauder degree theory extended to multifunctions. We outline the proof in an appendix.

As a consequence of Section 3 and the continuation principle we have

THEOREM 1. *Under assumptions* (E1)–(E6), *problem* (2.T) *has at least one solution* $(Q(t), k(t))$ *satisfying* $\| k(t)\| \leqslant K_0$, $\| Q(t)\| \leqslant Q_0$, $k(t) \geqslant 0$, *and* $Q(t) \geqslant 0$.

Proof. We need only observe that (2.T.σ) is a dynamical system corresponding to the Hamiltonian function

$$H_\sigma(Q, k) = \sigma H(Q, k).$$

This new Hamiltonian satisfies hypotheses (E1) through (E6) with the new discount $\sigma\rho$ and new depreciation rate $\sigma\lambda$ and with the same (Q^*, k^*) and the same K and γ.

We may apply Lemma 5 to problem (2.T.σ) obtaining the same bound K_0 for all σ. In Lemmas 6 and 7 the constants μ, h_0, and H_0 must be replaced by

$$\sigma\mu, \; \sigma h_0, \; \sigma H_0.$$

Since ρ is replaced by $\sigma\rho$, Lemma 7 yields the same Q_0 for all values of σ. Thus the continuation principle yields the existence of at least one solution.

We now are in a position to prove the central theorem of this paper.

THEOREM 2. *Under assumptions* (E1)–(E6), *problem* (1)' *has at least one solution satisfying* $\| Q(t)\| \leqslant Q_0$, $\| k(t)\| \leqslant K_0$, $k(t) \geqslant 0$, *and* $Q(t) \geqslant 0$ *on* $[0, +\infty)$.

Proof. Let $\{T_n\} \to +\infty$ and let $(Q(t; T_n), k(t; T_n))$ be a solution to (2.T$_n$). Define

$$k(t; T_n) \equiv k(T_n; T_n), \qquad t > T_n,$$
$$Q(t; T_n) \equiv Q(T_n; T_n) = Q^*, \qquad t > T_n. \tag{3}$$

Since $\| k(t; T_n)\| \leqslant K_0$ and $\| Q(t; T_n)\| \leqslant Q_0$ on $[0, T_n]$, upper semi-continuity (Lemma 1) implies that there exist $\dot{K}_0$, $\dot{Q}_0$ (independent of $k(t; T_n)$ and $Q(t; T_n)$) such that

$$\| \dot{k}(t; T_n)\| \in \left\| \frac{\partial H(Q(t; T_n), k(t; T_n))}{\partial Q} \right\| \leqslant \dot{K}_0,$$
$$\| \dot{Q}(t; T_n)\| \in \left\| -\frac{\partial H(Q(t; T_n), k(t; T_n))}{\partial k} + \rho Q(t; T_n) \right\| \leqslant \dot{Q}_0 \tag{4}$$

almost everywhere on $[0, T_n]$. Since the extended functions defined by (3) are constant for $t \geqslant T_n$, the inequalities (4) hold on $[0, \infty)$ almost everywhere.

We have by absolute continuity [10, p. 107],

$$\| k(t; T_n) - k(s; T_n)\| = \left\| \int_s^t \dot{k}(\tau; T_n)\, d\tau \right\|$$

$$\leqslant \left| \int_s^t \| \dot{k}(\tau; T_n)\|\, d\tau \right|$$

$$\leqslant | t - s | \dot{K}_0 .$$

Similarly,

$$\| Q(t; T_n) - Q(s; T_n)\| \leqslant | t - s | \dot{Q}_0 .$$

Thus, the sequence $\{(Q(t; T_n), k(t; T_n))\}$ is uniformly bounded and equicontinuous on $[0, +\infty)$. By the Ascoli–Arzela theorem [10, p. 179] there exists a subsequence, call it $\{(Q(t; T_k), k(t; T_k))\}$ for simplicity, which converges uniformly on compact subintervals of $[0, +\infty)$ to some $(Q_0(t), k_0(t))$.

It is a consequence of a theorem of Zaremba [13, Theorem II.6] (or also of the Bebernes–Shuur–Kamke theorem [1, p. 275]) that the limit function $(Q_0(t), k_0(t))$ is a solution to the differential correspondence in $(1')$ on $[0, \infty)$; i.e.,

$$\dot{k}_0(t) \in (\partial H(Q_0(t), k_0(t))/\partial Q \qquad \text{a.e. on } [0, +\infty),$$

$$\dot{Q}_0(t) \in -(\partial H(Q_0(t), k_0(t))/\partial k) + \rho Q_0(t) \qquad \text{a.e. on } [0, +\infty).$$

Moreover, it is immediate that $k_0(0) = \bar{k}, \| Q_0(t)\| \leqslant Q_0$ on $[0, \infty)$, $\| k_0(t)\| \leqslant K_0$ on $[0, \infty)$, $k_0(t) \geqslant 0$ on $[0, \infty)$, and $Q_0(t) \geqslant 0$ on $[0, \infty)$. It follows that

$$\lim_{t \to +\infty} Q_0(t)\, e^{-\rho t} k_0(t) = 0.$$

APPENDIX. THE CONTINUATION PRINCIPLE

In this appendix we outline the mathematical justification for the continuation principle stated at the beginning of Section 4. Our first step in this direction is to rewrite problem (2.T) as a fixed point problem in a function space setting. Let

$$C[0, T] = \{(x(t), y(t)): x(t) \text{ and } y(t) \text{ are continuous functions from}$$
$$[0, T] \text{ into } R^n\}$$

with the accompanying norm

$$\|(x, y)\| = \max_{[0,T]} \| x(t)\| + \max_{[0,T]} \| y(t)\| .$$

For $(x, y) \in C[0, T]$ we may consider the problem

$$\begin{aligned}
\dot{k}(t) &\in \partial H(x(t), y(t))/\partial Q, \\
\dot{Q}(t) &\in -(\partial H(x(t), y(t))/\partial k) + \rho x(t), \\
k(0) &= \bar{k}, \\
Q(T) &= Q^*.
\end{aligned} \tag{A1}$$

We define a mapping $\mathcal{H} : C[0, T] \to 2^{C[0,T]}$ (the subsets of $C[0, T]$), by

$$\mathcal{H}(x, y) = \{(Q, k): (Q, k) \text{ is a solution to (A1)}\}.$$

(Note that the functions in $\mathcal{H}(x, y)$ are actually absolutely continuous on $[0, T]$). The mapping $\mathcal{H}(x, y)$ may be given a somewhat more explicit description.

LEMMA A1. *For any $(x, y) \in C[0, T]$,*

$$\mathcal{H}(x, y) = \left\{ \left(\bar{k} + \int_0^t z(s)\, ds, \; Q^* - \int_t^T r(s)\, ds\right): (z(t), r(t)) \in N_0(x, y) \right\}$$

where $N_0(x, y)$ is the set of pairs $(z(t), r(t))$ which are Lebesgue-integrable on $[0, T]$ and such that

$$\begin{aligned}
z(t) &\in \frac{\partial H(x(t), y(t))}{\partial Q} \qquad \text{a.e. in } [0, T] \\
r(t) &\in -\frac{\partial H(x(t), y(t))}{\partial k} + \rho x(t) \qquad \text{a.e. in } [0, T].
\end{aligned} \tag{A2}$$

Proof. If $(Q(t), k(t)) \in \mathcal{H}(x, y)$ then $(Q(t), k(t))$ is a solution to (A1) and $Q(t)$ and $k(t)$ are absolutely continuous on $[0, T]$. Thus $\dot{k}(t)$ and $\dot{Q}(t)$ are Lebesgue-integrable [10, p. 107] and $(\dot{k}(t), \dot{Q}(t)) \in N_0(x, y)$. Moreover,

$$k(t) = k(0) + \int_0^t \dot{k}(s)\, ds = \bar{k} + \int_0^t \dot{k}(s)\, ds,$$

$$Q(t) = Q(T) - \int_t^T \dot{Q}(s)\, ds = Q^* - \int_t^T \dot{Q}(s)\, ds.$$

Conversely, if

$$k(t) = \bar{k} + \int_0^t z(s)\, ds,$$

$$Q(t) = Q^* - \int_t^T r(s)\, ds,$$

where $(z(s), r(s)) \in N_0(x, y)$, then since $(z(s), r(s))$ are Lebesgue-integrable

$$k(t) = z(t) \in \partial H(x(t), y(t))/\partial Q \qquad \text{a.e. on } [0, T],$$
$$\dot{Q}(t) = r(t) \in -(\partial H(x(t), y(t))/\partial k) + \rho x(t) \qquad \text{a.e. on } [0, T],$$
$$k(0) = \bar{k},$$
$$Q(T) = Q^*.$$

The importance of the mapping $\mathcal{H}$ is expressed in the following lemma which follows immediately from the definition of $\mathcal{H}$ and the form of (2.T).

LEMMA A2.   *A pair $(Q(t), k(t))$ is a solution to (2.T) if and only if*

$$(Q, k) \in \mathcal{H}(Q, k). \tag{A3}$$

In order to establish that (A3) has at least one solution we apply Leray–Schauder degree theory for multifunctions as developed by Webb [12]. A complete discussion of this theory is beyond the scope of this appendix. For a concise introduction to degree theory the reader is referred to Rouche and Mawhin [9, pp. 173–185]. In particular, we will employ the following two fundamental properties.

1.   *Existence. Let X be a Banach space and $\Omega \subset X$ be an open bounded subset of X. Suppose $\mathcal{T}: \bar{\Omega} \to 2^X$ is such that:*

(a) $\mathcal{T}(x)$ *is convex, compact and nonempty for each $x \in \bar{\Omega}$;*

(b) $\mathcal{T}$ *is upper-semicontinuous on $\bar{\Omega}$;*

(c) $\overline{\mathcal{T}(\bar{\Omega})}$ *is compact;*

(d) $x \notin \mathcal{T}(x)$ *for $x \in \partial\Omega$ (the boundary of Ω);*

(e) $d[I - \mathcal{T}, \Omega, 0] \neq 0$ *(the Leray–Schauder degree is nonzero).*

Then there exists $x \in \bar{\Omega}$ such that $x \in \mathcal{T}(x)$.

2. *Invariance under Homotopy.   Let X be a Banach space and $\Omega \subset X$ be an open bounded subset of X. Suppose $\mathcal{T}(x, \sigma): \Omega \times [0, 1] \to 2^X$ is such that:*

(a) $\mathcal{T}(x, \sigma)$ *is convex, compact and nonempty for $(x, \sigma) \in \Omega \times [0, 1]$;*

(b) $\mathcal{T}(x, \sigma)$ *is upper semicontinuous on $\bar{\Omega} \times [0, 1]$;*

(c) $\overline{\mathcal{T}(\bar{\Omega}, \sigma)}$ *is compact for each $\sigma \in [0, 1]$;*

(d) $x \notin \mathcal{T}(x, \sigma)$ *for $(x, \sigma) \in \partial\Omega \times [0, 1]$.*

Then

$$d[I - \mathcal{T}(x, 0), \Omega, 0] = d[I - \mathcal{T}(x, 1), \Omega, 0].$$

In order to apply these results in our context we need the following technical lemma.

LEMMA A3.   *Under assumption* (E1) *for any* $\bar{k}$ *and* Q^*:

(a) $\mathscr{H}(x, y)$ *is convex, nonempty, and compact for each* $(x, y) \in C[0, 1]$;

(b) $\mathscr{H}$ *is upper semicontinuous on* $C[0, 1]$;

(c) $\overline{\mathscr{H}(\bar{\bar{\Omega}})}$ *is compact for any open bounded set* Ω.

Proof.   These properties have been established for a general class of mappings containing our map $\mathscr{H}$ by Lasota and Opial [5] (see also the paper of Grandolfi [4]). We will not include the details here. We observe only in passing that it is the properties stated in Lemma 1 which are crucial to the proof of Lemma A3.

Proof of the Continuation Principle.   We define

$$\Omega = \{(Q, k) \in C[0, 1]: \max_{[0,T]} \| k(t) \| < K_0 + \epsilon, \max_{[0,T]} \| Q(t) \| < Q_0 + \epsilon\}$$

where $\epsilon > 0$ is an arbitrary positive number. Then Ω is an open bounded subset of $C[0, T]$. Define

$$\mathscr{T}(x, y, \sigma) = \{(Q, k): (Q, k) \text{ is a solution to (A4)}\}$$

where

$$\begin{aligned}
\dot{k} &= \sigma(\partial H(x(t), y(t))/\partial Q), \\
\dot{Q} &= -\sigma(\partial H(x(t), y(t))/\partial k) + \sigma p x(t), \\
k(0) &= \bar{k}, \\
Q(T) &= Q^*.
\end{aligned} \tag{A4}$$

Note that

$$\mathscr{T}(x, y, 1) = \mathscr{H}(x, y),$$
$$\mathscr{T}(x, y, 0) = (\bar{k}, Q^*)(\text{the constant mapping}).$$

Moreover,

$$\mathscr{T}(x, y, \sigma) = (\bar{k}, Q^*) + \sigma \mathscr{H}_0(x, y) \tag{A5}$$

where $\mathscr{H}_0(x, y)$ is the mapping defined as in Lemma A1 with $\bar{K} = Q^* = 0$.

We first apply the invariance under homotopy property. That hypotheses (a), (b), (c) of Property 2 are satisfied is a consequence of Lemma A3 applied to $\mathscr{H}_0$ and the representation (A5). The inclusion

$$(x, y) \in \mathscr{T}(x, y, \sigma)$$

is equivalent to (2.T.σ). In the statement of the continuation principle we require that solutions to (2.T.σ) satisfy $\| k(t) \| \leqslant K_0$ and $\| Q(t) \| \leqslant Q_0$. Thus, $(Q, k) \notin \partial\Omega$ and hypothesis (d) of Property 2 is satisfied. Thus, we may conclude that

$$d[I - \mathscr{H}, \Omega, 0] = d[I - \mathscr{T}(x, y, 0), \Omega, 0] = d[I - (\bar{k}, Q^*), \Omega, 0] \neq 0,$$

the nonzero degree of the last mapping following from standard arguments of degree theory.

By Property 1 the proof is complete.

ACKNOWLEDGMENTS

The author gratefully acknowledges indispensable guidance obtained from discussions with D. Cass and K. Shell. The mathematical techniques benefitted from several discussions with J. Mawhin. Several revisions were made on the basis of helpful suggestions by participants in the MSSB summer seminar on "The Structure of Dynamical Systems Arising in Economics -and the Social Sciences," Minary Center, Squam Lake, New Hampshire, June 19–27, 1975.

REFERENCES

1. J. BEBERNES AND J. SCHUUR, The Wazewski topological method for contingent equations, *Ann. Mat. Pura. Appl.* **87** (1970), 271–280.
2. D. CASS, Duality: a symmetric approach from the economist's vantage point, *J. Econ. Theory* **7** (1974), 272–295.
3. D. CASS AND K. SHELL, The structure and stability of competitive dynamical systems, *J. Econ. Theory,* **12** (1976), 31–70. Reprinted as Essay III in this volume.
4. M. GRANDOLFI, Problemi ai limiti per le equazioni differenziali multivoche, *Accad. Naz. dei Lincei* **42** (1967), 355–360.
5. A. LASOTA AND Z. OPIAL, An application of the Kakutany–Ky Fan theorem in the theory of ordinary differential equations, *Bull. Acad. Polon. Sci.* **13** (1965), 781–786.
6. E. LEE AND L. MARKUS, "Foundations of Optimal Control," Wiley, New York, 1967.
7. R. T. ROCKAFELLAR, Generalized Hamiltonian equations for convex problems of Lagrange, *Pacific J. Math.* **33** (1970), 411–427.
8. R. T. ROCKAFELLAR, Saddle points of Hamiltonian systems in convex Lagrange problems having a positive discount rate, *J. Econ. Theory,* **12** (1976), 71–113. Reprinted as Essay IV in this volume.
9. N. ROUCHE AND J. MAWHIN, "Equations Différentielles Ordinaires," Tome 2, Stabilité et Solutions Périodiques, Masson, Paris, 1973.
10. H. ROYDEN, "Real Analysis, second ed., Macmillan, London, 1968.

11. K. SHELL, Applications of Pontryagin's maximum principle to economics, *in* "Mathematical Systems Theory and Economics I" (H. Kuhn and G. Szego, Eds.), pp. 241–292, Springer–Verlag, Berlin, 1969.
12. J. WEBB, On degree theory for multivalued mappings and applications, *Bo. Un. Mat. Ital.* **9** (1974), 137–158.
13. S. ZAREMBA, Sur les équations au paratingent, *Bull. Sci. Math.* **60** (1936), 139–160.

ESSAY VI

A Characterization of the Normalized Restricted
Profit Function*

LAWRENCE J. LAU

A duality theorem between production functions and normalized restricted profit functions is derived under the assumptions of joint biconvexity and independence of the production possibilities sets. Biconvexity is a natural generalization of the concept of convexity to the case of overall increasing returns which maintains at the same time the conventional property of diminishing marginal rates of transformation (substitution) amongst certain subsets of commodities.

Specializing to the twice differentiable, locally strongly convex case, certain identities linking the Hessians of the production function and the normalized restricted profit function are derived. Using these identities, Le Chatelier's principle is demonstrated.

1. INTRODUCTION

The purpose of this paper is to provide a complete characterization of the normalized restricted profit function via the conjugate duality approach and under conditions more general than those customarily assumed in the literature.[1] A normalized restricted profit function is defined as the maximized value of the normalized profits given the values of the normalized prices of the variable commodities and the quantities of the fixed commodities. It may be identified with the Hamiltonian function employed by

* This paper is a revision of Technical Report No. 134 of The Economic Series of the Institute for Mathematical Studies in the Social Sciences, Stanford University.

[1] The term "restricted profit function" is due to McFadden [26]. Other terminology includes "gross profit function" [12], "partial profit function" [19], and "variable profit function" [6]. The concept of a normalized profit function is traceable to Hotelling [13], the terminology is due to Jorgenson and Lau [17]. "Normalized restricted profit function" seems a more appropriate terminology because the concept of a normalized restricted profit function also applies to cases in which some commodities are restricted to vary within a closed convex set in addition to the case in which some commodities are restricted to be fixed.

131

Cass [3] and Cass and Shell [4] in the analysis of competitive dynamical systems if the variable commodities are interpreted as the outputs and the fixed commodities are interpreted as the input stocks.

Restricted profit functions have been analyzed and characterized by Samuelson [31], who is an early pioneer of the concept, and by Gorman [12], McFadden [26], and Diewert [6, 7]. Jacobsen [14, 15], McFadden [26], Rosse [28], and Shephard [33] have also examined the properties of multiple-output cost and multiple-input revenue functions, which may be regarded as special cases of the restricted profit function. None of the above treatments is based on the conjugacy correspondence of closed, proper, convex functions.[2] And while Jorgenson and Lau [16, 17] have developed a theory of production with six alternative but equivalent characterizations of the technology (production possibilities set, production function, marginal productivity correspondence, normalized supply correspondence, normalized profit function, and normalized price and profits possibilities set) based on the conjugacy correspondence, they have not analyzed the normalized restricted profit function explicitly.

In this paper, we analyze the properties of the normalized restricted profit function within the framework of conjugacy correspondence. In addition, technological assumptions are relaxed in various directions. First, all commodities (except one) are treated symmetrically. There is no artificial distinction between commodities that are net outputs and commodities that are net inputs. The theory of the normalized restricted profit function thus developed will not only accommodate normalized cost functions (all net outputs fixed) and normalized revenue functions (all net inputs fixed) as special cases, but also all the mixed cases in between (some net outputs and some net inputs fixed; for example, when a firm has long-term fixed output delivery as well as material supply contracts). An analytically simple and unified treatment is hence available for all these related concepts. Second, there is no assumption of free disposal except for the numeraire commodity. The assumption of free disposal in all commodities is unduly restrictive because it rules out the possibility that some of the jointly produced net outputs may be undesirable, that is, may have negative normalized prices. Air pollution is an obvious example. From a practical point of view, allowing the existence of nonfree disposal may be important in many situations. For example, a firm may have to maximize profits subject to a government restriction that its pollution is less than or equal to a given level. Third, the assumption that the production possibilities set is a convex cone is relaxed. It does not need to be a

---

[2] The conjugacy correspondence was first discovered by Fenchel [9, 10]. A modern development with many extensions can be found in Rockafellar [27].

convex cone, or in fact, even convex. Instead, a new assumption of biconvexity, which is weaker than convexity, is introduced. Biconvexity allows the existence of overall increasing returns while preserving the properties of diminishing marginal rates of transformation (substitution) amongst certain subsets of commodities. Fourth, reversibility in production is allowed in a limited sense, not all production plans are reversible, but some production plans may be reversible. In the short run, reversibility in the variable commodities for some subset of production plans is not an unrealistic possibility. Finally, the normalized prices of the commodities are allowed to be either positive, zero, or negative. Only the price of the numeraire commodity is required to be positive.

Normalized restricted profit functions have applications in the analysis of competitive dynamical systems as Hamiltonian functions, as demonstrated by Cass [3] and Cass and Shell [4]. They also have applications in the analysis of production behavior under circumstances in which some commodities are variable and other commodities are fixed over the period of production. Econometric applications of the normalized restricted profit function have been made by Lau and Yotopoulos and their collaborators in their extensive studies of agricultural production.[3] Econometric applications of the cost function are much more numerous. One may refer to Diewert's [7] excellent survey article.

In Section 2, duality theorems relating the production function and the normalized restricted profit functions under alternative assumptions on the technology are given. A proof of the generalized Hotelling's [13] or Shephard's [32] lemma is also included. In Section 3, the results derived in Section 2 are applied to the case of twice differentiable, locally strongly convex technologies, leading to certain identities linking the Hessians of the production function, the normalized restricted profit function, and the normalized (unrestricted) profit function. These identities enable us to deduce the supply elasticities of normalized prices and/or fixed commodities under one environment from a knowledge of their values under another environment. In particular, they allow us to compute the long-run supply elasticities given the short-run elasticities and vice versa. They also allow the direct translation of conditions on the Hessian matrix of the production function into conditions on the Hessian matrix of the normalized restricted profit function (or alternatively the Hamiltonian function) or into conditions on the Hessian matrix of the normalized (unrestricted) profit function, or vice versa. Thus, for instance, the sufficient conditions on the Hamiltonian function for global asymptotic stability of the optimal control systems obtained by Brock and Scheinkman

---

[3] See, for example [22, 23, 21, 24, 35, 36].

[1] may be directly interpreted as conditions on the production function. Finally, based on the identities, an alternative demonstration of Le Chatelier's principle, first introduced into economics by Samuelson [29], is given.[4]

A brief summary and conclusion is given in Section 4.

2. DUALITY THEOREMS

2.1. Conventions and Definitions

A commodity can be either a net output or a net input. Each commodity is measured as if it were a net output. Thus, if the quantity of a commodity is positive, it is a net output; if the quantity is negative, it is a net input; if the quantity is zero, it is neither a net output nor a net input.

It is assumed that there are $(n + 1 + m)$ commodities. The quantities of the first $(n + 1)$ commodities, denoted y_1, y_2,..., y_{n+1}, are assumed to be variable, and the quantities of the last m commodities, denoted K_1, K_2,..., K_m, are assumed to be fixed. They are collectively referred to as vectors $[y'y_{n+1}]'$ and K, respectively.[5] The n-dimensional vector formed by the quantities of the first n commodities is referred to as y.

All prices are measured relative to the price of the $(n + 1)$st commodity. The price of the $(n + 1)$st commodity is always one. Thus the price system is referred to as the normalized price system, and the prices as the normalized prices. Except for the price of the numeraire commodity, the prices, and hence, the normalized prices, of the commodities can be either positive, zero, or negative. Thus the normalized price system is not restricted to the nonnegative orthant. A tax on a commodity such as pollution may be treated as a negative price. The normalized prices of the variable commodities are denoted y_1^*, y_2^*,..., y_n^*; the normalized prices of the fixed commodities are denoted K_1^*, K_2^*,..., K_m^*.

The production possibilities set is the set of all feasible production plans. The production function is defined by the supremum of the quantity of the $(n + 1)$st commodity given the quantities of all the other commodities, such that the production plan is contained in the production possibilities set. The set of production plans $[y'y_{n+1}K']'$ contained in the

---

[4] Samuelson [29] first enunciated this principle and indicated its application in equilibrium systems in economics. See also [30]. This version of the principle is referred to as the "strong" Le Chatelier–Samuelson principle by Eichhorn and Oettli [8].

[5] A prime signifies the transposition operation. Whenever a prime follows a square bracket, it implies the transpose of the row vector enclosed within the square brackets.

production possibilities set for given y and K may be empty. We adhere to the convention that the supremum of an empty set is equal to $-\infty$;

$$\sup\{\varnothing\} = -\infty,$$

a convention which we shall appeal to repeatedly.

The vector $[y'y_{n+1}K']'$ is referred to as a producrion plan. The vector $[y'y_{n+1}]'$ for given K is referred to as a short-run production plan, or where no ambiguity arises, simply as a production plan. The vector y alone is sometimes used to refer to the short-run production plan $[y'y_{n+1}]'$ where y_{n+1} is the maximum value of y_{n+1} such that $[y'y_{n+1}K']'$ is contained in the production possibilities set. If there does not exist any value for y_{n+1} such that $[y'y_{n+1}K']'$ is contained in the production possibilities set, then y refers to the nonfeasible production plan $[y' -\infty]'$.

2.2. Convex Production Functions

With these conventions, we may proceed to define the production possibilities set formally. The production possibilities set is referred to as T. It is a subset of R^{n+1+m} and is assumed to have the following properties.

  T.1. *Origin.* $0 \in T$.

  T.2. *Closure.* T is closed.

  T.3. *Convexity.* T is convex.

  T.4. *Monotonicity.* If $[y'y_{n+1}K']' \in T$, then $[y'y_{n+1}^{\#}K']' \in T$, $\forall y_{n+1}^{\#}$ $\leqslant y_{n+1}$.

  T.5. *Nonproducibility.* If $[y'y_{n+1}K']' \in T$, $y_{n+1} \leqslant 0$.

T.1 through T.3 are standard assumptions and require no discussion. T.4 requires only that one variable commodity be freely disposable. This represents a substantial weakening of the conventional monotonicity assumption and opens up the possibility of analyzing many production processes in which part of the joint output may be considered undesirable, that is, negatively priced. In most production processes, one can usually find a commodity, for example, unskilled labor, that may be considered freely dispoable if found in excess of technical requirements.[6] T.5 implies that there is at least one variable and freely disposable commodity which can only be a net input to the production process, that is, it is a primary

---

[6] Strictly speaking, such an assumption is not necessary. It is introduced for technical convenience. Monotonicity assures that there is a one-to-one correspondence between the production possibilities set and the production function, to be defined below. Otherwise, two production functions may be necessary to characterize one production possibilities set completely. See the example given by Jorgenson and Lau [17].

factor of production.[7] Unskilled labor is an obvious example of a commodity satisfying T.5, because it is not generally considered a producible commodity. Note that nonproducibility is a much weaker assumption than essentiallity, which implies that none of the elements of $[y'y_{n+1}]'$ and K can be positive unless y_{n+1} is negative. T.5 also implies that if a feasible production plan uses any positive quantity of the $(n + 1)$ st commodity as a net input, the production plan with all quantities reversed in sign is not feasible, that is, the production plan is not reversible. However, feasible production plans with y_{n+1} equal to zero may be reversible. Finally, T.5 replaces the conventional boundedness assumption on the production possibilities set.

Corresponding to such a production possibilities set T, Jorgenson and Lau [16, 17][8] have shown that there exists an extended-real-valued production function $F(y, K)$ defined on R^n given by

$$F(y, K) = -\sup\{y_{n+1} \,|\, [y'y_{n+1}K']' \in T\}^9$$

with the convention that $\sup\{\varnothing\}$ where $\{\varnothing\}$ is the empty set is $-\infty$, that is, the negative of the maximum of y_{n+1}, given y and K, such that $[y'y_{n+1}K']'$ is a feasible production plan.[10] The production function has the following properties.

F.1. *Domain.* The effective domain (that is, the set of $[y'K']'$ such that $F(y, K)$ is finite) of $F(y, K)$ is a convex set containing the origin. $F(0, 0) = 0$.

F.2. *Closure.* $F(y, K)$ is closed in $\{y, K\}$.

F.3. *Convexity.* $F(y, K)$ is convex in $\{y, K\}$.

F.4. *Nonnegativity.* $F(y, K)$ is nonnegative.

These assumptions on the production function are again standard, with the possible exception of nonnegativity. We note that the fact the

---

[7] Again, this assumption may also be relaxed. However, the resulting technical complications, especially on the specification of the properties of the marginal productivity correspondences and normalized supply correspondences, are quite substantial. See [17] for a treatment of the duality between production and normalized profit functions without this assumption. A second, and less substantial, reason for this assumption is that it preserves the formal symmetry between the production function and the normalized profit function.

[8] Actually, Jorgenson and Lau [16, 17] do not treat the case considered here explicitly. However, the results used here may be obtained as a convex combination of the results contained in their two papers.

[9] This is the negative of the conventional definition. With this sign convention, the production function is convex rather than concave.

[10] Because of closure of the production possibilities set, the supremum and maximum may actually be used interchangeably here.

production function takes the value zero at the origin together with nonnegativity imply that the production function achieves its minimum at the origin.

Given the production function $F(y, K)$, the production possibilities set may be reconstructed as

$$T^* = \{[y'y_{n+1}K']' \,|\, [y'K']' \in R^{n+m}, \quad y_{n+1} \in R \text{ and } y_{n+1} \leqslant -F(y, K)\}.$$

Under the assumptions T.1 through T.5 on the production possibilities set and F.1 through F.4 on the production function there is a one-to-one correspondence between T and $F(y, K)$, so that T^* is actually equal to T, the original production possibilities set from which $F(y, K)$ is derived in the first place.[11]

The purpose of productive activity is assumed to be maximization of short-run profits, or equivalently, normalized restricted profits, defined as the sum of the values of the net outputs in terms of the numeraire commodity. The producer maximizes

$$P = \langle y^*, y \rangle + y_{n+1}$$

where $\langle \, , \, \rangle$ denotes the inner product operation,[12] with respect to y for given K. Since $y_{n+1} = -F(y, K)$, one may write the maximand equivalently as $P = \langle y^*, y \rangle - F(y, K)$. The maximized value of P, for given y^* and K, considered a function of y^* and K, is precisely the normalized restricted profit function, which will be denoted $H(y^*, K)$. It may be written as

$$H(y^*, K) = \sup_{y} \{\langle y^*, y \rangle - F(y, K)\}.[13]$$

Similarly, the normalized (unrestricted) profit function is given by

$$F^*(y^*, K^*) = \sup_{y, K} \{\langle y^*, y \rangle + \langle K^*, K \rangle - F(y, K)\}$$

where K^* is the normalized price of K. We note that this maximization may be decomposed into two stages, that is,

$$F^*(y^*, K^*) = \sup_{K} \sup_{y} \{\langle y^*, y \rangle + \langle K^*, K \rangle - F(y, K)\}$$
$$= \sup_{K} \{\langle K^*, K \rangle + H(y^*, K)\}.$$

---

[11] Diewert [6] first derived the one-to-one correspondence between the production possibilities set and the production function. His assumptions are different from the ones used here.

[12]
$$\langle x, y \rangle \equiv \sum_{i} x_i y_i .$$

[13] Supremum is used rather than maximum because there may be an upper bound to normalized restricted profits which is not attainable by any finite production plan.

The duality relations between $F(y, K)$ and $F^*(y^*, K^*)$ are well known.[14] We shall concentrate on the duality relations among $F(y, K)$, $H(y^*, K)$, and $F^*(y^*, K^*)$.[15]

The normalized restricted profit function $H(y^*, K)$ is an extended-real-valued function with the following properties.

H.1. *Domain.* The effective domain of $H(y^*, K)$ is a convex set containing the origin. $H(0, 0) = 0$.

H.2. *Closure.* $H(y^*, K)$ is lower-closed.[16]

H.3. *Convexity–concavity.* $H(y^*, K)$ is convex in y^* for every K and concave in K for every y^*.[17]

H.4. *Nonnegativity–nonpositivity.* $H(y^*, 0)$ is nonnegative; $H(0, K)$ is nonpositive.

By conjugate duality, one has

$$H^*(y, K) = \sup_y \{\langle y^*, y \rangle - H(y^*, K)\}$$
$$\equiv F(y, K).$$

We now state the first duality theorem.

THEOREM 1. *There is a one-to-one correspondence between the set of production functions $F(y, K)$ satisfying properties F.1 through F.4 and the set of normalized restricted profit functions $H(y^*, K)$ satisfying properties H.1 through H.4.*

This theorem is based on Rockafellar [27].[18] A proof is attached in the Appendix.

Thus H.1 through H.4 are the properties that a normalized restricted profit function must satisfy if it is to be generated from a production function satisfying F.1 through F.4 above, or equivalently, from a production possibilities set T satisfying T.1 through T.5 above. Gorman [12] and

---

[14] See, for instance [25, 26, 19, 6, 16, 17].

[15] One can also consider the symmetric case of $H(y, K^*)$, but the results will be identical to the case of $H(y^*, K)$ with y and K interchanged.

[16] $H(y^*, K)$ is lower-closed if $cl_{y^*} cl_K H(y^*, K) = H(y^*, K)$ where cl_x denotes the closure operation with respect to the set of variables x. See [27, p. 357]. If it is assumed that $H(y^*, K)$ is finite on R^{n+m}; this assumption may be strengthened to $H(y^*, K)$ is closed.

[17] Convex–concave functions are sometimes known as *saddle functions*. See [27, pp. 350–358].

[18] See [27, pp. 357–358, Theorem 3].

Diewert [6] have proved the duality between T and $H(y^*, K)$ directly, using different methods and employing somewhat different assumptions than the ones used here.[19]

Note that essentially the same theorem goes through if there is a third set of commodities (or factors), denoted t, over which no convexity assumptions are made, so that $F(y, K, t)$ is convex in $\{y, K\}$ for all t. In this case $H(y^*, K, t)$ is convex–concave in $\{y^*, K\}$ for all t. Examples of possible t variables include time, locational variables, and entrepreneurial ability, among others. Note also that because of the definition of $H(y^*, K)$ as a supremum, it is always convex and closed in y^* independently of the properties of $F(y, K)$.[20]

In fact, because $H(y^*, K)$ is a lower-closed, convex–concave function, it is endowed with some exceptional continuity properties. Rockafellar [27] has shown that every finite convex–concave function is jointly continuous in both of its arguments on any product set $C \times D$, where $C \subseteq R^n$, $D \subseteq R^m$ are relatively open convex sets, contained in its effective domain.[21] Moreover, if in addition there is a third set of arguments, say t, $t \in R^l$, and $H(y^*, K, t)$ is a convex–concave function for all t, and continuous in t for all y^* and K, then $H(y^*, K, t)$ is jointly continuous in y^*, K and t on $C \times D \times R^l$.[22]

To specialize to the case of the normalized (unrestricted) profit function, we assume that there are no fixed commodities. To specialize to the case of the negative of the normalized cost function we replace T.5 by T.5'.

T.5'. *Input–output nonswitchability.* $[y' y_{n+1} K']' \in T$ implies that $[y' y_{n+1}]' \leqslant 0$ and $K \geqslant 0$, or equivalently, F.1 by F.1'.

F.1'. *Domain.* The effective domain of $F(y, K)$ is a convex set containing the origin. It is contained in $R_\ominus^n \times R_\oplus^m$ where $R_\ominus^n$ and

---

[19] See Gorman [12, pp. 152–153]. His proof is not based on the conjugacy correspondence between the production function and the normalized restricted profit function as is the proof here. See also [6].

[20] This is a well-known fact. Let y_1, y_2, y_λ be profit maximizing plans at normalized prices $y_1^* y_2^*$ and y_λ^* respectively, where y_λ^* is a convex combination of y_1^* and y_2^*, that is, $y_\lambda^* = (1 - \lambda)y_1^* + \lambda y_2^*$, $0 \leqslant \lambda \leqslant 1$. Consider

$$(1-\lambda)H(y_1^*, K)+\lambda H(y_2^*, K) \geqslant (1-\lambda)[\langle y_1^*, y_\lambda \rangle - F(y_\lambda, K)]+\lambda[\langle y_2^*, y_\lambda \rangle - F(y_\lambda, K)]$$
$$\geqslant \langle y_\lambda^*, y_\lambda \rangle - F(y_\lambda, K)$$
$$\geqslant H(y_\lambda^*, K).$$

Closure follows from the fact that the epigraph of $H(y^*, K)$ for every K contains all its boundary points.

[21] See [27, p. 370, Theorem 35.1].

[22] See [27, p. 371, Theorem 35.3].

$R_{\oplus}{}^m$ are the *nonpositive* orthant and *nonnegative* orthant of R^n and R^m respectively. $F(0, 0) = 0$. Or equivalently, H.1 by H.1' and H.5'.

H.1'. *Domain.* The effective domain of $H(y^*, K)$ is a convex set containing the origin. It is contained in $R^n \times R_{\oplus}{}^m$. $H(0, 0) = 0$.

H.5'. *Monotonicity.* $H(y^*, K)$ is nonincreasing in y^* for all K.

The cost function is thus given by

$$C(p, K) = -p_{n+1}H\left(\frac{p_1}{p_{n+1}}, ..., \frac{p_n}{p_{n+1}} ; K\right)$$

where p is the vector of money prices of the variable commodities and K is the vector of net outputs.

To specialize to the case of normalized revenue function, we replace T.5 by T.5" and add assumption T.6".

T.5". *Input–output nonswitchability.* $[y'y_{n+1}K']' \in T$ implies that $[y'y_{n+1}]' \geqslant 0$ and $K \leqslant 0$.

T.6". *Boundedness.* For at least one variable commodity which is freely disposable and always a net output, say y_{n+1}, if a production plan is feasible, the level of net output of that commodity corresponding to finite levels of net outputs of all other commodities is bounded above.

Or, equivalently we replace F.1 by F.1", F.4 by F.4", and add assumption F.5".

F.1". *Domain.* The effective domain of $F(y, K)$ is a convex set containing the origin. It is contained in $R_{\oplus}{}^n \times R_{\ominus}{}^m$ where $R_{\oplus}{}^n$ and $R_{\ominus}{}^m$ are the nonnegative orthant and nonpositive orthant of R^n and R^m respectively.

F.4". *Nonpositivity.* $F(y, K)$ is nonpositive.

F.5". *Boundedness.* $F(y, K)$ is bounded below. (It nowhere takes the value minus infinity.)

Or equivalently we may replace H.1 by H.1" and add assumptions H.5" and H.6".

H.1". *Domain.* The effective domain of $H(y^*, K)$ is a nonempty convex set containing the origin. It is contained in $R^n \times R_{\ominus}{}^m$.

H.5". *Monotonicity.* $H(y^*, K)$ is nondecreasing in y^* for all K.

H.6". *Boundedness.* $H(0, 0)$ is bounded above.

The revenue function is thus given by

$$R(p, K) = p_{n+1} H \left(\frac{p_1}{p_{n+1}}, \frac{p_2}{p_{n+1}} \cdots \frac{p_n}{p_{n+1}} ; K \right)$$

where p is the vector of money prices of the variable commodities and K is the vector of net inputs.

A convex function is differentiable almost everywhere in the relative interior of its effective domain. Where it is not differentiable a "generalized" derivative always exists, called a *subgradient*. A vector y^* is said to be a *subgradient* of the convex function $F(y)$ at y if

$$F(z) \geqslant F(y) + \langle y^*, z - y \rangle$$

for all z. For a convex function $F(y)$ which is finite at y, the linear function

$$G(z) = F(y) + \langle y^*, z - y \rangle$$

is a nonvertical supporting hyperplane to the epigraph of $F(y)$ (the set of production possibilities) at the point $(y, F(y))$. Corresponding to each y, the subgradient need not be unique. The set of all subgradients y^* at y is said to be the *subdifferential* of $F(y)$ at y. The correspondence which associates with each y, the subdifferential of $F(y)$ at y, is known as the subdifferential of the function $F(y)$, and is denoted $\partial F(y)$.[23]

A concave function is the negative of a convex function. Thus a "generalized" derivative also exists for a concave function in the relative interior of its effective domain. Thus, if $F(y)$ is a concave function, $-F(y)$ is convex, and, hence, in the relative interior of its effective domain there exists $-y^*$, a subgradient of the convex function $-F(y)$, such that

$$-F(z) \geqslant -F(y) + \langle -y^*, z - y \rangle$$

for all z. We note, therefore, y^* satisfies, for all z, the inequality

$$F(z) \leqslant F(y) + \langle y^*, z - y \rangle.[24]$$

We refer to y^* as the supergradient of the concave function $F(y)$ at y. The set of all supergradients y^* at y is said to be the *superdifferential* of the

---

[23] Thus a subdifferential is a generalization of the concept of a gradient to a point where a function is not differentiable. McFadden [26] first employed the concept of a subdifferential in the theory of production.

[24] Note that this is precisely the subgradient inequality with the sense of the inequality reversed. Diewert [6, 7] refers to such a vector also as a subgradient. In order to avoid confusion, we use the term supergradient, it being the coefficients of the supporting hyperplane of $F(y)$ at y that lies completely *above* $F(y)$.

concave function $F(y)$ at y. The correspondence which associates with each y the superdifferential of $F(y)$ at y is known as the superdifferential of the function $F(y)$, and denoted $\partial F(y)$.[25] Wherever the supergradient is unique, that is, the superdifferential is single-valued, it coincides with the ordinary gradient of the function $F(y)$.

It is well known that the subdifferential of $H(y^*, K)$ with respect to y^* at $[y^{*\prime}K^\prime]^\prime$ contains the set of profit maximizing production plans at $[y^{*\prime}K^\prime]^\prime$. This is true, again, independently of the properties of $F(y, K)$, as long as a profit-maximizing production plan exists. Under the additional assumptions of F.1 through F.4, the subdifferential actually coincides with the set of profit-maximizing plans. In the case of differentiable normalized restricted profit functions, this fact is variously referred to as either Hotelling's [13] lemma or Shephard's [32] lemma. Also, in the case of differentiable functions, the gradient of $H(y^*, K)$ at $[y^{*\prime}K^\prime]^\prime$ with respect to K is known to coincide with minus the gradient of $F(y, K)$ with respect to K at $[y^\prime K^\prime]^\prime$ where y is set equal to the profit-maximizing production plan at $[y^{*\prime}K^\prime]^\prime$. There is an appropriate generalization of this fact to the general nondifferentiable case. However, there does not appear to be a generally available proof in the literature of these two propositions. We shall refer to them collectively as the Generalized Hotelling's lemma and give a simple proof in the Appendix.

GENERALIZED HOTELLING'S LEMMA.   *Under the assumptions* F.1 *through* F.4, *the subdifferential of* $H(y^*, K)$ *at* $[y^{*\prime}K^\prime]^\prime$ *with respect to* y^* *coincides with the set of profit-maximizing production plans; the superdifferential of* $H(y^*, K)$ *with respect to* K *at* $[y^{*\prime}K^\prime]^\prime$ *coincides with the negative of the last m components of the subdifferential of* $F(y, K)$ *at* $[y^\prime K^\prime]^\prime$ *where* y *is a profit-maximizing production plan at* $[y^{*\prime}K^\prime]^\prime$.

From the Generalized Hotelling's lemma, one deduces immediately that $F(y, K)$ is nondecreasing (nonincreasing) in K if and only if $H(y^*, K)$ is nonincreasing (nondecreasing) in K.

The supergradient of $H(y^*, K)$ has the interpretation of the set of normalized shadow prices or normalized rental prices of the fixed commodities. It measures the effect on the normalized restricted profit function of a marginal increase in the net output of the fixed commodities. If $K \geqslant 0$, then the supergradient gives the negative of the normalized marginal cost. If $K \leqslant 0$, then the supergradient gives the negative of the normalized shadow prices or normalized rental prices of the net inputs.

---

[25] One can always tell from the context whether that refers to a subdifferential or a superdifferential.

2.3. *Convex–Quasi–convex and Order-Independent Production Functions*

It is sometimes desirable to drop the assumption of convexity of the production function. This is necessary, for instance, if one wants to allow the existence of increasing returns to scale in the overall technology. However, one often wishes to maintain the assumption of a diminishing marginal rate of transformation, at least among some subset of commodities. In the one-output, multiple-input case, the traditional solution is to assume that

$$K = f(y, y_{n+1})$$

is a quasiconcave function where K is identified as the output and $[y'y_{n+1}]'$ the vector of inputs. This is equivalent to, in our notation, the specification that

$$-y_{n+1} = F(y, K)$$

where F is convex in y for all K. In addition, if $F(y, K)$ is nondecreasing in K, as will be the case if $f(y, y_{n+1})$ is nondecreasing in y_{n+1}, $F(y, K)$ is also quasiconvex in K for all y. We note also that given this monotonicity assumption on K, from the point of view of the production possibilities set, the sets $T^K = \{[y'y_{n+1}]' \,|\, [y'y_{n+1}K']' \in T\}$ and $T^{[y'y_{n+1}]'} = \{K \,|\, [y'y_{n+1}K']' \in T\}$ are all convex. Thus, a natural generalization to the case of many fixed commodities is the concept of biconvexity.

A production possibilities set is *disjointly biconvex* if the set T^K is convex for all K and the set $T^{[y'y_{n+1}]'}$ is convex for all $[y'y_{n+1}]'$, where the sets of commodities $[y'y_{n+1}]'$ and K are disjoint. We thus replace the assumptions on the production possibilities set by the following.

T.1A. *Origin.* $0 \in T$.

T.2A. *Closure.* T is closed.

T.3A. *Disjoint biconvexity.* The sets $T^K = \{[y'y_{n+1}]' \,|\, [y'y_{n+1}K']' \in T\}$ are convex for every K; the sets $T^{[y'y_{n+1}]'} = \{K \,|\, [y'y_{n+1}K']' \in T\}$ are convex for every $[y'y_{n+1}]'$.

T.4A. *Monotonicity.* If $[y'y_{n+1}K']' \in T$, then $[y'y_{n+1}^\#K']' \in T$, $\forall y_{n+1}^\# \leqslant y_{n+1}$.

T.5A. *Nonproducibility.* If $[y'y_{n+1}K']' \in T$, $y_{n+1} \leqslant 0$.

For such a production possibilities set T, it can be shown that there exists a production function $F(y, K)$ defined as before, with the following properties.

F.1A. *Origin.* $F(0, 0) = 0$.

F.2A. *Closure.* $F(y, K)$ is closed.

F.3A. *Convexity-quasiconvexity.* $F(y, K)$ is convex in y for every K, and quasiconvex in K for every y.[26]

F.4A. *Nonnegativity.* $F(y, K) \geqslant 0$.

Note that no monotonicity assumption is made concerning the production function, just as before. Thus, y and K can be either net outputs or net inputs, or combinations of both. Formally, we state Theorem 2.

THEOREM 2. *There is a one-to-one correspondence between the set of production possibilities sets T satisfying properties* T.1A *through* T.5A *and the set of production functions $F(y, K)$ satisfying properties* F.1A *through* F.4A.

A proof is sketched in the Appendix.

We note that convexity of T implies disjoint biconvexity of T but not vice versa.[27] Similarly, convexity of $F(y, K)$ in $\{y, K\}$ implies convexity of $F(y, K)$ in y for every K and quasiconvexity of $F(y, K)$ in K for every y, but not vice versa. Economically, biconvexity means there is not necessarily overall generalized dimininishing returns. But each subset of commodities taken by themselves show generalized diminishing returns. Biconvex production possibilities sets may be useful in other areas of economic analysis such as externalities, public goods, and regulation.

A natural question which arises is: What are the properties of a normalized restricted profit function $H(y^*, K)$ which corresponds to a convex–quasiconvex production function, or more specifically, to a production function satisfying properties F.1A through F.4A? It turns out that these properties are rather complicated, although it can be shown in a straightforward manner that a normalized restricted profit function $H(y^*, K)$ is quasiconcave in K for every y^* only if the production function $F(y, K)$ is quasiconvex in K for every y. The converse, unfortunately, is not true. However, under an additional assumption of independence on the production possibilities set, it is possible to establish a one-to-one correspondence between the set of convex–quasiconvex production functions satisfying an independence assumption and the set of convex–

---

[26] Let $y_\lambda = (1 - \lambda)y_1 + \lambda y_2$. A function $F(y)$ is quasiconvex if

$$\max\{F(y_1), F(y_2)\} \geqslant F(y_\lambda), \qquad \forall \lambda, 0 \leqslant \lambda \leqslant 1.$$

It is quasiconcave if

$$\min\{F(y_1), F(y_2)\} \leqslant F(y_\lambda), \qquad \forall \lambda, 0 \leqslant \lambda \leqslant 1.$$

[27] In fact, convexity of T is necessary and sufficient for the disjoint biconvexity of T in all possible partitions of the set of commodities.

quasiconcave normalized restricted profit functions satisfying an independence assumption.

First, we give a symmetric definition of the concept of independence which follows Jorgenson and Lau [18]. A production possibilities set T is said to be *independent* in the $[y'y_{n+1}]' - K$ partition if

$$[y'y_{n+1}K_1']' \in T \qquad \text{and} \qquad [y'y_{n+1}K_2']' \notin T$$

for some y, y_{n+1}, K_1, K_2 imply that

$$T^{K_2} \equiv \{[y'y_{n+1}]' \mid [y'y_{n+1}K_2']' \in T\}$$
$$\subset T^{K_1} \equiv \{[y'y_{n+1}]' \mid [y'y_{n+1}K_1']' \in T\}.$$

It has been shown by Jorgenson and Lau [18] that this definition is symmetric with respect to the two groups of commodities $[y'y_{n+1}]'$ and K.[28]

If we add the independence assumption on the production possibilities set as T.6A,

   T.6A. *Independence.*   If $[y'y_{n+1}K_1']' \in T$ and $[y'y_{n+1}K_2']' \in T$ for some y, y_{n+1}, K_1, K_2, then

$$T^{K_2} \equiv \{[y'y_{n+1}]' \mid [y_{n+1}K_2']' \in T\}$$
$$\subset T^{K_1} \equiv \{[y'y_{n+1}]' \mid [y'y_{n+1}K_1']' \in T\},$$

it induces a corresponding independence assumption on the production function.

A production function $F(y, K)$ is said to be *order-independent* in K if

$$F(y, K_1) > F(y, K_2)$$

for some y, K_1, K_2 implies that

$$F(y^{\neq}, K_1) \geqslant F(y^{\neq}, K_2) \qquad \forall y^{\neq}.$$

We therefore add the order-independence assumption on the production function as F.5A.

   F.5A. *Order-independence.*   If $F(y, K_1) > F(y, K_2)$ for some y, K_1, K_2, then $F(y^{\neq}, K_1) \geqslant F(y^{\neq}, K_2), \forall y^{\neq}$.

Corresponding to a production possibilities set T satisfying T.1A through T.6A, there exists a production function $F(y, K)$ satisfying F.1A through F.5A, and vice versa. Formally, we state Theorem 3.

---

[28] See [18].

THEOREM 3. *There is a one-to-one correspondence between the set of production possibilities sets T satisfying properties* T.1A *through* T.6A *and the set of production functions satisfying properties* F.1A *through* F.5A.

A proof is sketched in the Appendix.

Corresponding to a production function satisfying F.1A through F.5A above, there exist a normalized restricted profit function with the following properties.

H.1A. *Domain.* The effective domain of $H(y^*, K)$ is a convex set containing the origin. $H(0, 0) = 0$.

H.2A. *Closure.* $H(y^*, K)$ is lower-closed.

H.3A. *Convexity–quasiconcavity.* $H(y^*, K)$ is convex in y^* for every K and quasiconcave in K for every y^*.

H.4A. *Nonnegativity–nonpositivity.* $H(y^*, 0)$ is nonnegative; $H(0, K)$ is nonpositive.

H.5A. *Order-independence.* If $H(y^*, K_1) > H(y^*, K_2)$ for some y^*, K_1, K_2, then $F(y^{*\#}, K_1) \geqslant F(y^{*\#}, K_2), \forall y^{*\#}$.

By conjugate duality, one has

$$F^{**}(y, K) = \sup_{y^*} \{\langle y^*, y \rangle - H(y^*, K)\}$$
$$= F(y, K).$$

We now state our second duality theorem between production functions and normalized restricted profit functions.

THEOREM 4. *There is a one-to-one correspondence between the set of production functions satisfying properties* F.1A *through* F.5A *above and the set of normalized restricted profit functions satisfying* H.1A *through* H.5A *above.*

This theorem does not appear to have been proved elsewhere. A simple proof is given in the Appendix.

We note that the same theorem goes through if there is a third set of commodities (or factors), denoted t, over which no convexity assumptions are made, so that $F(y, K, t)$ is convex in y for all $\{K, t\}$ and quasiconvex in K for all $\{y, t\}$. In this case $H(y^*, K, t)$ is convex in y^* for all $\{K, t\}$ and quasiconcave in K for all $\{y^*, t\}$. Examples of possible t variables include time, locational variables, and entrepreneurial ability, among others.

We note, in passing, that order-independence of $F(y, K)$ in K implies and is implied by order-independence of $H(y^*, K)$ in K. This is true independently of any assumption on the convexity properties of $F(y, K)$ or $H(y^*, K)$ with respect to K. Moreover, strict monotonicity of $F(y, K)$ in K implies and is implied by strict monotonicity of $H(y^*, K)$ in K. This is true, again, independently of any assumption on the convexity properties of $F(y, K)$ or $H(y^*, K)$ with respect to K.

If we assume, in addition to F.1A through F.5A, that $F(y, K)$ is continuous in $[y'K']'$ and strictly monotonic in K, then it can be shown that $F(y, K)$ has the form $F(y, G(K))$ where $F(y, G)$ is continuous in $[y'G]'$ and strictly monotonic in G, and G is a continuous and strictly monotonic real-valued function of K. The corresponding normalized restricted profit function has the form $H(y^*, K) = H(y^*, G(K))$ with the same $G(K)$ function. In this form, the property of order-independence is also referred to as *separability*.

An example of an order-independent convex–quasiconvex production function is the following.

$$-y_{n+1} = F(y, G(K))$$

where $K \geqslant 0$, and $G(K)$, net output aggregate, is convex in K. The normalized restricted profit function is given by

$$H(y^*, G(K)),$$

and is quasiconcave in K (and, hence, the cost function is quasiconvex in K).

The concept of disjoint biconvexity may be generalized to that of disjoint multiconvexity in an obvious manner. Theorem 2 will apply to these cases with minimum modifications. It may be generalized in another direction to that of joint biconvexity, that is, the subsets of commodities $[y'y_{n+1}]'$ and K contain an overlapping subset of commodities. More specifically, a production possibilities set T is jointly biconvex if the set of $[y'y_{n+1}]'$ contained in T is convex for all K and the set of $[y_{n+1}K']'$ contained in T is convex for all y. Note that y_{n+1} overlaps in the two partitions. It can be shown that such a production possibilities set always generates a production function $F(y, K)$ that is convex in y for every K and convex in K for every y and vice versa. We refer to such a function as a convex–convex function.[29]

---

[29] We can call this a biconvex function, but that will be confusing because a biconvex function is not equivalent to biconvexity of T.

3. Hessian Matrix Identities

3.1. Hessian Identities

In this section we strengthen our assumptions on T so that both $F(y, K)$ and $F^*(y^*, K^*)$, the normalized unrestricted profit function are twice differentiable everywhere. This implies that both $F(y, K)$ and $F^*(y^*, K^*)$ are *locally strongly convex* everywhere, and that $H(y^*, K)$ is twice differentiable in $\{y^*, K\}$, locally strongly convex everywhere in y^* for every K, and locally strongly concave everywhere in K for every y^*.[30] A twice differentiable function defined on an open convex set contained in R^n is said to be *locally strongly convex* everywhere if its Hessian matrix is positive definite everywhere. It is said to be *strongly convex* if there exists a positive constant α such that the matrix formed by subtracting α times the identity matrix from the Hessian matrix is a positive semidefinite matrix everywhere. A twice differentiable strongly convex function is locally strongly convex everywhere; however, the converse is not true. Under the assumptions of twice differentiability and local strong convexity, the relationships among the Hessian matrices of the production function, the normalized restricted profit function (or Hamiltonian function), and the normalized (unrestricted) profit function may be derived. The purpose of establishing the relationship between the various Hessians is to enable us to derive the comparative statics results in one environment given the comparative statics result in another environment. For example, if we know the supply elasticities (with respect to both normalized prices and quantities of fixed commodities) of a commodity, we should be able to deduce the supply elasticities when some fixed commodities become variable. The Hessian matrix is a first step in the computation of the supply elasticities. Given the Hessian matrix, the supply elasticities can be obtained directly and vice versa. These Hessian matrix identities also enable us to translate conditions on the production function into conditions on the normalized restricted profit function (or Hamiltonian function) and vice versa.

The relationship between the Hessians of $F(y, K)$ and $F^*(y^*, K^*)$ is well known. They are related by

$$
\begin{bmatrix}
\dfrac{\partial^2 F^*}{\partial y^{*2}} & \dfrac{\partial^2 F^*}{\partial y^* \, \partial K^*} \\[2ex]
\dfrac{\partial^2 F^*}{\partial K^* \, \partial y^*} & \dfrac{\partial^2 F^*}{\partial K^{*2}}
\end{bmatrix}
=
\begin{bmatrix}
\dfrac{\partial^2 F}{\partial y^2} & \dfrac{\partial^2 F}{\partial y \, \partial K} \\[2ex]
\dfrac{\partial^2 F}{\partial K \, \partial y} & \dfrac{\partial^2 F}{\partial K^2}
\end{bmatrix}^{-1}
.[31]
$$

[30] See [16] for a discussion.
[31] See, for instance [19].

We consider the relationship between the Hessians of $F(y, K)$ and $H(y^*, K)$. The first-order conditions of restricted profit maximization are

$$y^* - \frac{\partial F}{\partial y}(y, K) = 0; \tag{1}$$

$$\frac{\partial H(y^*, K)}{\partial y^*} = y, \tag{2}$$

and

$$\frac{\partial H(y^*, K)}{\partial K} = \frac{-\partial F(y, K)}{\partial K}. \tag{3}$$

By differentiating Eq (1) with respect to y^*, we obtain

$$I - \left[\frac{\partial^2 F}{\partial y^2}\right]\frac{\partial y}{\partial y^*} = 0. \tag{4}$$

By differentiating Eqs. (2) and (3) with respect to y^* and K, we obtain

$$\left[\frac{\partial^2 H}{\partial y^{*2}}\right] = \frac{\partial y}{\partial y^*}, \tag{5}$$

$$\left[\frac{\partial^2 H}{\partial K\,\partial y^*}\right] = \frac{\partial y}{\partial K}, \tag{6}$$

$$\left[\frac{\partial^2 H}{\partial y^*\,\partial K}\right] = -\left[\frac{\partial y}{\partial y^*}\right]'\left[\frac{\partial^2 F}{\partial y\,\partial K}\right], \tag{7}$$

$$\left[\frac{\partial^2 H}{\partial K^2}\right] = -\left[\frac{\partial^2 F}{\partial K^2}\right] - \left[\frac{\partial y}{\partial K}\right]'\left[\frac{\partial^2 F}{\partial y\,\partial K}\right]. \tag{8}$$

Solving these equations, we have

$$\left[\frac{\partial^2 H}{\partial y^{*2}}\right] = \left[\frac{\partial^2 F}{\partial y^2}\right]^{-1}, \tag{9}$$

$$\left[\frac{\partial^2 H}{\partial y^*\,\partial K}\right] = -\left[\frac{\partial^2 F}{\partial y^2}\right]^{-1}\left[\frac{\partial^2 F}{\partial y\,\partial K}\right], \tag{10}$$

$$\left[\frac{\partial^2 H}{\partial K^2}\right] = -\left[\frac{\partial^2 F}{\partial K^2}\right] - \left[\frac{\partial^2 F}{\partial K\,\partial y}\right]\left[\frac{\partial^2 F}{\partial y^2}\right]^{-1}\left[\frac{\partial^2 F}{\partial y\,\partial K}\right]. \tag{11}$$

We note that Eqs. (9) through (11) are true even if $F(y, K)$ is only convex in y rather than convex in $[y'K']'$.

Next, we derive a similar relationship between $[H_{ij}]$ and $[F_{ij}^*]$. The point of departure is the fact that

$$F^*(y^*, K^*) = \sup_K \{\langle K^*, K\rangle + H\langle y^*, K\rangle\}.$$

Under the assumptions of differentiability, one has immediately at the profit-maximizing equilibrium,

$$K^* + \frac{\partial H(y^*, K)}{\partial K} = 0, \tag{12}$$

$$\frac{\partial F^*(y^*, K^*)}{\partial K^*} = K, \tag{13}$$

$$\frac{\partial F^*(y^*, K^*)}{\partial y^*} = \frac{\partial H(y^*, K)}{\partial y^*}. \tag{14}$$

By differentiating Eq (12) with respect to K^*, we obtain

$$I + \left[\frac{\partial^2 H(y^*, K)}{\partial K^2}\right]\frac{\partial K}{\partial K^*} = 0,$$

$$\therefore, \qquad \qquad \frac{\partial K}{\partial K^*} = -\left[\frac{\partial^2 H}{\partial K^2}\right]^{-1}.$$

By differentiating Eqs. (13) and (14) with respect to y^* and K^*, we obtain

$$\left[\frac{\partial^2 F^*(y^*, K^*)}{\partial y^* \partial K^*}\right] = \frac{\partial K}{\partial y^*}, \tag{15}$$

$$\left[\frac{\partial^2 F^*(y^*, K^*)}{\partial K^{*2}}\right] = \frac{\partial K}{\partial K^*}, \tag{16}$$

$$\left[\frac{\partial^2 F^*(y^*, K^*)}{\partial y^{*2}}\right] = \left[\frac{\partial^2 H(y^*, K)}{\partial y^{*2}}\right] + \left[\frac{\partial K}{\partial y^*}\right]'\left[\frac{\partial^2 H(y^*, K)}{\partial K \partial y^*}\right], \tag{17}$$

$$\left[\frac{\partial^2 F^*(y^*, K^*)}{\partial K^* \partial y^*}\right] = \left[\frac{\partial K}{\partial K^*}\right]'\left[\frac{\partial^2 H(y^*, K)}{\partial K \partial y^*}\right]. \tag{18}$$

Solving these equations, we obtain

$$\left[\frac{\partial^2 H}{\partial K^2}\right] = -\left[\frac{\partial^2 F^*}{\partial K^{*2}}\right]^{-1}, \tag{19}$$

$$\left[\frac{\partial^2 H}{\partial y^* \partial K}\right] = \left[\frac{\partial^2 F^*}{\partial y^* \partial K^*}\right]\left[\frac{\partial^2 F^*}{\partial K^{*2}}\right]^{-1}, \tag{20}$$

$$\left[\frac{\partial^2 H}{\partial y^{*2}}\right] = \left[\frac{\partial^2 F^*}{\partial y^{*2}}\right] - \left[\frac{\partial^2 F^*}{\partial y^* \partial K^*}\right]\left[\frac{\partial^2 F^*}{\partial K^{*2}}\right]^{-1}\left[\frac{\partial^2 F^*}{\partial K^* \partial y^*}\right]. \tag{21}$$

Of course, all these identities hold only when K is actually equal to the last m components of the long-run profit-maximizing production plan at normalized prices $[y^{*\prime}K^{*\prime}]'$. Thus, given the values of one Hessian matrix, we can evaluate the other Hessian matrices in the neighborhood of the long-run equilibrium.

We know that $[\partial^2 H/\partial y^{*2}]$ must be positive semidefinite because $H(y^*, K)$ is convex in y^* for all K. One can reach the same conclusion by using the fact that the matrix $(A_{22} - A'_{12}A_{11}^{-1}A_{12})$ is always positive semidefinite whenever $\begin{bmatrix} A_{11}A_{12} \\ A'_{12}A_{22} \end{bmatrix}$ is positive semidefinite, and that $[F^*_{ij}]$ is positive semidefinite.[32] Similarly, we know that $[\partial^2 H/\partial K^2]$ must be negative semidefinite.

3.2. Le Chatelier's Principle Revisited

Samuelson [29] first enunciated Le Chatelier's principle for the behavior of equilibrium economic systems. Basically, Le Chatelier's principle may be stated as follows. Let $y_1 = g_1(y^*)$ be the values of y for which the function $G(y, y^*) = \langle y^*, y \rangle - F(y)$ is at a maximum with respect to y for given values of y^*. Let $y_2 = g_2(y^*)$ be the values of y for which the function $G(y, y^*)$ is at a maximum with respect to y for given values of y^*, where y is subject to additional constraints. If $g_1(y^*)$ and $g_2(y^*)$ are both differentiable, then

$$0 \leqslant \frac{\partial g^*_{2i}(y^*)}{\partial y_i^*} \leqslant \frac{\partial g^*_{1i}(y^*)}{\partial y_i^*}, \qquad \forall i.$$

In other words, the effect on the maximizing y_i of an increase in y_i^* is larger for all i when y is unconstrained than when y is subject to constraints. Diewert [7] derived a local version of this principle using the restricted profit function.

We shall demonstrate the principle, using the Hessian matrix identities we have developed and without resorting to determinants. We note first of all from Eq. (21) that the matrix

$$\left[\frac{\partial^2 H}{\partial y^{*2}}\right] = \left[\frac{\partial^2 F^*}{\partial y^{*2}}\right] - \left[\frac{\partial^2 F^*}{\partial y^* \partial K^*}\right]\left[\frac{\partial^2 F^*}{\partial K^{*2}}\right]\left[\frac{\partial^2 F^*}{\partial K^* \partial y^*}\right]$$

[32] Consider the quadratic form

$$\begin{bmatrix} x_1 \\ x_2 \end{bmatrix}'\begin{bmatrix} A_{11}A_{12} \\ A'_{12}A_{22} \end{bmatrix}\begin{bmatrix} x_1 \\ x_2 \end{bmatrix} = x_1'A_{11}x_1 + 2x_1'A_{12}x_2 + x_2'A_{22}x_2 \geqslant 0, \qquad \forall \begin{bmatrix} x_1 \\ x_2 \end{bmatrix}.$$

By letting

$$x_1 = -A_{11}^{-1}A_{12}x_2$$

$$= x_2'A'_{12}A_{11}^{-1}A_{11}A_{11}^{-1}A_{12}x_2 - 2x_2'A'_{12}A_{11}^{-1}A_{12}x_2 + x_2'A_{22}x_2$$

$$= x_2'(A_{22} - A'_{12}A_{11}^{-1}A_{12})x_2 \geqslant 0, \qquad \forall x_2.$$

is the difference between two positive semidefinite matrices. Thus, we conclude immediately that

$$\frac{\partial^2 H}{\partial y_i^{*2}} \leqslant \frac{\partial^2 F^*}{\partial y_i^{*2}},$$

or, equivalently,

$$\frac{\partial x_i^K}{\partial y_i^*} \leqslant \frac{\partial x_i^*}{\partial y_i^*};$$

that is, the own price effect with all commodities variable is greater than the own price effect with some commodities fixed.

Next, we investigate the effect of fixing one more commodity. We refer to the vector of $(n-1)$ normalized prices of variable commodities as y_-^* and the additional fixed commodity as y_n. By substituting H^{K+} for H and H for F^* in Eq (21) where K^+ denotes the fact that one more commodity is fixed, we obtain

$$\left[\frac{\partial^2 H^{K+}}{\partial y_-^{*2}}\right] = \left[\frac{\partial^2 H}{\partial y_-^{*2}}\right] - \left[\frac{\partial^2 H}{\partial y_-^* \, \partial y_n^*}\right]\left[\frac{\partial^2 H}{\partial y_n^{*2}}\right]^{-1}\left[\frac{\partial^2 H}{\partial y_n^* \, \partial y_-^*}\right];$$

we conclude again that

$$0 \leqslant \frac{\partial x_i^{K+}}{\partial y_i^*} \leqslant \frac{\partial x_i^K}{\partial y_i^*} \leqslant \frac{\partial x_i^*}{\partial y_i^*}. \tag{22}$$

Thus, we have Samuelson's result that the own price effect of the remaining variable commodities decreases monotonically as the quantities of additional commodities are fixed. And as Samuelson has pointed out, these results are completely independent of whether the commodities are complements or substitutes. These inequalities become equalities if and only if the normalized restricted profit function is additive in the commodities. Similarly, we obtain from Eq. (19),

$$\frac{\partial^2 H^{K+}}{\partial y_n^{\,2}} = -\left[\frac{\partial^2 H}{\partial y_n^{*2}}\right]^{-1}.$$

Now suppose we perform the reverse experiment, that is, we allow y_n to become variable again. We have

$$H(y^*, K) = \sup_{y_n} \{\langle y_n^*, y_n \rangle + H^{K+}(y_-^*, y_n, K)\}.$$

By substituting H^{K+} for F in Eq. (11), we obtain

$$\left[\frac{\partial^2 H}{\partial K^2}\right] = \left[\frac{\partial^2 H^{K+}}{\partial K^2}\right] - \left[\frac{\partial^2 H^{K+}}{\partial K \, \partial y_n}\right]\left[\frac{\partial^2 H^{K+}}{\partial y_n^{\,2}}\right]^{-1}\left[\frac{\partial^2 H^{K+}}{\partial y_n \, \partial K}\right].$$

Since

$$\left[\frac{\partial^2 H}{\partial K^2}\right], \left[\frac{\partial^2 H^{K+}}{\partial K^2}\right] \quad \text{and} \quad \left[\frac{\partial^2 H^{K+}}{\partial K\,\partial y_n}\right]\left[\frac{\partial^2 H^{K+}}{\partial y_n{}^2}\right]^{-1}\left[\frac{\partial^2 H^{K+}}{\partial y_n\,\partial K}\right]$$

are all negative semidefinite matrices, by an argument similar to the one used earlier we conclude that the own effect of changes in the quantities of the fixed commodities on their implicit normalized shadow prices decreases monotonically as the quantities of an additional number of commodities are fixed; that is,

$$0 \geqslant \frac{\partial(\partial H/\partial K_i)}{\partial K_i} \geqslant \frac{\partial(\partial H^{K+}/\partial K_i)}{\partial K_i}. \tag{23}$$

Again, these inequalities become equalities if and only if the normalized restricted profit function is additive in the commodities.

4. Concluding Remarks

We have shown that there is a one-to-one correspondence between production functions and normalized restricted profit functions under alternative sets of conditions. Thus, for the purposes of economic analysis, theoretical or empirical, one may just as well start with the appropriate normalized restricted profit function. In many short-run situations, the normalized restricted profit function is often the most suitable concept for analysis and interpretation. Given a normalized profit function, we can always recover the original production function by the conjugacy operation.

More duality results linking the production function and the normalized restricted profit function can be found in Lau [19].

We have provided formulae for the computation of the Hessian matrices of the normalized restricted profit functions under alternative specifications of the environment given knowledge of one environment. Thus, one can deduce long-run behavior from short-run behavior or vice versa. From these Hessians, the matrix of supply elasticities can be easily calculated.

For econometric purposes, various functional forms are available. Diewert [7] has proposed several, including the generalized linear and transcendental logarithmic functions. In view of the formulae linking the Hessian matrices, however, the quadratic functional form seems to have special appeal, the Hessian matrices of all the normalized profit functions corresponding to the same production possibilities set are constant matrices.[33] Hence, given the parameters for one, the parameters of the others can be computed directly using our Hessian matrix identities. For the other functional forms, the computation is likely to be involved.

APPENDIX

1. Proof of Theorem 1

We note that the closure assumptions assure that the dual of the dual of a convex function is the primal function itself. We shall not repeat Rockafellar's [27] proof here. We shall, however, show equivalence of the other properties.

A. *Domain.* By definition,

$$H(0, 0) = \sup_{y} \{\langle 0, y \rangle - F(y, 0)\}$$
$$= 0,$$

since $F(y, K) = 0$. Conversely,

$$F(0, 0) = \sup_{y^*} \{\langle y^*, 0 \rangle - H(y^*, 0)\}$$
$$= 0,$$

since $H(y^*, 0) \geqslant 0$.

B. *Convexity–Concavity.* Convexity of $H(y^*, K)$ in y^* is well known and will not be repeated here. It remains to be shown that $H(y^*, K)$ is concave in K. Let y_1, y_2 be the profit-maximizing production plans at $[y^{*\prime} K_1']'$ and $[y^{*\prime} K_2']'$, respectively. Let

$$y_\lambda \equiv (1 - \lambda) y_1 + \lambda y_2 ;$$
$$K_\lambda \equiv (1 - \lambda) K_1 + \lambda K_2 , \qquad 0 < \lambda < 1.$$

Then,

$$
\begin{aligned}
H(y^*, K_\lambda) &\geqslant \langle y^*, y_\lambda \rangle - F(y_\lambda, K_\lambda) \\
&\geqslant \langle y^*, (1 - \lambda) y_1 + \lambda y_2 \rangle - [(1 - \lambda) F(y_1, K_1) + \lambda F(y_2, K_2)] \\
&\qquad \text{by convexity of } F(y, K) \\
&\geqslant (1 - \lambda)[\langle y^*, y_1 \rangle - F(y_1, K_1)] + \lambda[\langle y^*, y_2 \rangle - F(y_2, K_2)] \\
&\geqslant (1 - \lambda) H(y^*, K_1) + \lambda H(y^*, K_2).
\end{aligned}
$$

Thus, $H(y^*, K)$ is concave in K.

---

[33] Lau [20] first proposed the use of the quadratic function as a normalized profit function and production function.

Conversely, if $H(y^*, K)$ is a convex–concave function, we shall show that

$$F(y, K) = \sup_{y^*} \{\langle y^*, y \rangle - H(y^*, K)\}$$

is convex. Let y_λ^* by the production function maximizing prices at $[y_\lambda' K_\lambda']'$. Consider

$$\begin{aligned}
(1 - \lambda) F(y_1, K_1) + \lambda F(y_2, K_2) &\geqslant (1 - \lambda)[\langle y_\lambda^*, y_1 \rangle - H(y_\lambda^*, K_1)] \\
&\quad + \lambda[\langle y_\lambda^*, y_2 \rangle - H(y_\lambda^*, K_2)] \\
&\geqslant \langle y_\lambda^*, y_\lambda \rangle - H(y_\lambda^*, K_\lambda), \\
&\qquad \text{by concavity of } H(y^*, K) \text{ in } K \\
&\geqslant F(y_\lambda, K_\lambda).
\end{aligned}$$

Thus, $F(y, K)$ is convex.

D. *Nonnegativity*

$$\begin{aligned}
H(y^*, 0) &= \sup_y \{\langle y^*, y \rangle - F(y, 0)\} \\
&= 0
\end{aligned}$$

since $F(0, 0) = 0$.

$$\begin{aligned}
H(0, K) &= \sup_y \{-F(y, K)\} \\
&\leqslant 0
\end{aligned}$$

since $F(y, K) \geqslant 0$. Conversely,

$$\begin{aligned}
F(y, K) &= \sup_{y^*} \{\langle y^*, y \rangle - H(y^*, K)\} \\
&\geqslant 0,
\end{aligned}$$

since $H(0, K) \leqslant 0$.   Q.E.D.

2. *Proof of Generalized Hotelling's Lemma*

First, we show that a profit-maximizing production plan at $[y^{*\prime} K']'$ must be a subgradient of $H(y^*, K)$ with respect to y^* at $[y^{*\prime} K']'$. Let y be the profit-maximizing production plan at $[y^{*\prime} K']'$. Thus, $H(y^*, K) = \langle y^*, y \rangle - F(y, K)$. By definition, $H(y^{*\#}, K) \geqslant \langle y^{*\#}, y \rangle - F(y, K), \forall y^{*\#}$. Thus, $H(y^{*\#}, K) \geqslant H(y^*, K) + \langle y, y^{*\#} - y^* \rangle, \forall y^{*\#}$.

Conversely, if y is a subgradient of $H(y^*, K)$ at $[y^{*\prime} K']$ with respect to y^*, one has, by the subgradient inequality,

$$H(y^{*\#}, K) \geqslant H(y^*, K) + \langle y, y^{*\#} - y^* \rangle, \qquad \forall y^{*\#},$$

which may be rewritten as

$$\langle y^*, y \rangle - H(y^*, K) \geqslant \langle y^{**}, y \rangle - H(y^{**}, K), \qquad \forall y^{**}$$
$$\geqslant \sup_{y^{**}} \{ \langle y^{**}, y \rangle - H(y^{**}, K) \}$$
$$\geqslant F(y, K).^{34}$$

On the other hand,

$$F(y, K) = \sup_{y^*} \{ \langle y^*, y \rangle - H(y^*, K) \}$$
$$\geqslant \langle y^*, y \rangle - H(y^*, K).$$

Hence, one has

$$F(y, K) \geqslant \langle y^*, y \rangle - H(y^*, K) \geqslant F(y, K),$$

which implies $H(y^*, K) = \langle y^*, y \rangle - F(y, K)$. Hence, y is indeed a profit-maximizing production plan at $[y^{*\prime}K']'$.

Second, if K^* is a supergradient of $H(y^*, K)$ with respect to K, one needs to show that $[y^{*\prime}K^{*\prime}]'$ is a subgradient of $F(y, K)$ at $[y'K']'$, where y is a profit-maximizing plan at $[y^{*\prime}K']'$. From the supergradient inequality one has

$$H(y^*, K^{\#}) \leqslant H(y^*, K) + \langle K^*, K^{\#} - K \rangle, \qquad \forall K^{\#}.$$

y is a profit-maximizing production plan implies

$$H(y^*, K) = \langle y^*, y \rangle - F(y, K).$$

Adding the second equation to the first inequality and rearranging the terms, one has

$$H(y^*, K^{\#}) \leqslant \langle y^*, y \rangle - F(y, K) + \langle K^*, K^{\#} - K \rangle, \qquad \forall K^{\#}.$$

But $H(y^*, K^{\#}) \geqslant \langle y^*, y^{\#} \rangle - F(y^{\#}, K^{\#}), \forall y^{\#}$. Hence, $\langle y^*, y^{\#} \rangle - F(y^{\#}, K^{\#})$ $\leqslant \langle y^*, y \rangle - F(y, K) + \langle K^*, K^{\#} - K \rangle, \forall K^{\#}$, which finally yields

$$F(y^{\#}, K^{\#}) \geqslant F(y, K) + \langle [y^{*\prime} - K^{*\prime}]', [y^{\#\prime}K^{\#\prime}]' - [y'K']' \rangle, \forall [y^{*\prime}K^{\#\prime}]',$$

where $-K^{*\prime}$ is indeed the last m component of a subgradient of $F(y, K)$.

---

[34] Note that $\sup_{y^{**}} \{ \langle y^{*\#}, y \rangle - H(y^{*\#}, K) \} = F(y, K)$ if and only if $F(y, K)$ is convex and closed in $\{y\}$. That is why assumptions F. 1 through F. 4 have to be satisfied for the coincidence of the subdifferential and the set of profit-maximizing production plans.

Conversely, if $[y^{*\prime} - K^{*\prime}]'$ is a subgradient of $F(y, K)$ where y is a profit-maximizing production plan at $[y^{*\prime}K']'$, one has, by the subgradient inequality,

$$F(y^{\#}, K^{\#}) \geqslant F(y, K) + \langle [y^{*\prime} - K^{*\prime}]', [y^{\#\prime}K^{\#\prime}]' - [y'K']' \rangle, \quad \forall [y^{\#\prime}K^{\#\prime}]',$$

$$H(y^*, K) = \langle y^*, y \rangle - F(y, K).$$

By adding the second equation to the first inequality and rearranging terms, one has

$$F(y^{\#}, K^{\#}) + H(y^*, K) \geqslant \langle y^*, y \rangle + \langle y^*, y^{\#} - y \rangle - \langle K^*, K^{\#} - K \rangle,$$
$$\forall y^{\#}, K^{\#},$$

or

$$H(y^*, K) + \langle K^*, K^{\#} - K \rangle \geqslant \langle y^*, y^{\#} \rangle - F(y^{\#}, K^{\#}), \quad \forall y^{\#}, K^{\#},$$
$$\geqslant H(y^*, K^{\#}), \quad \forall K^{\#}.$$

Hence, K^* is a supergradient of $H(y^*, K)$ with respect to K at $[y^{*\prime}K']'$.
Q.E.D.

3. Proof of Theorem 2

We need only show that T.3A is equivalent to F.3A. Convexity of T^K for all K immediately implies that $F(y, K)$ is convex in y for all K. It remains to be shown that $F(y, K)$ is quasiconvex in K for all y. Let

$$y_{n+1}^{K_1} \equiv -F(y, K_1); \qquad y_{n+1}^{K_2} \equiv -F(y, K_2).$$

Then by monotonicity,

$$\begin{bmatrix} y \\ \min\{y_{n+1}^{K_1}, y_{n+1}^{K_2}\} \\ K_1 \end{bmatrix} \in T \quad \text{and} \quad \begin{bmatrix} y \\ \min\{y_{n+1}^{K_1}, y_{n+1}^{K_2}\} \\ K_2 \end{bmatrix} \in T.$$

By convexity,

$$\begin{bmatrix} y \\ \min\{y_{n+1}^{K_1}, y_{n+1}^{K_2}\} \\ K_\lambda \end{bmatrix} \in T,$$

where

$$K_\lambda = (1 - \lambda) K_1 + \lambda K_2, \qquad 0 < \lambda < 1.$$

Then

$$-F(y, K_\lambda) = \sup\{y_{n+1} \mid [y'y_{n+1}K_\lambda']' \in T\}$$
$$\geqslant \min\{y_{n+1}^{K_1}, y_{n+1}^{K_2}\}$$
$$\geqslant - \max\{F(y, K_1), F(y, K_2)\}.$$

Reversing the signs, we have

$$\max\{F(y, K_1), F(y, K_2)\} \geqslant F(y, K_\lambda), \qquad 0 < \lambda < 1.$$

Conversely, if $F(y, K)$ is convex–quasiconvex, we need to show that the production possibilities set T^* defined by

$$T^* - \{[y'y_{n+1}K']' \mid y_{n+1} \leqslant -F(y, K)\}$$

is convex in $[y'y_{n+1}]'$ for every K, and convex in K for every $[y'y_{n+1}]'$. Let $[y_1'y_{n+1,1}K']'$ and $[y_2'y_{n+1,2}K']' \in T^*$. Let $y_\lambda = (1 - \lambda) y_1 + \lambda y_2$; $y_{n+1,\lambda} = (1 - \lambda) y_{n+1,1} + \lambda y_{n+1,2}$; $\forall y, 0 < \lambda < 1$. Consider

$$-F(y_\lambda, K) \geqslant (1 - \lambda)[-F(y_1, K)] + \lambda[-F(y_2, K)],$$
$$\text{by concavity of } -F(y, K),$$
$$\geqslant (1 - \lambda) y_{n+1,1} + \lambda y_{n+1,2}$$
$$\geqslant y_{n+1,\lambda}, \qquad \forall \lambda, \quad 0 < \lambda < 1. \cdot$$

Thus, $[y_\lambda' y_{n+1,\lambda}K']' \in T^*$. Now let $[y'y_{n+1}K_1']'$ and $[y'y_{n+1}K_2']' \in T^*$. Let $K_\lambda = (1 - \lambda) K_1 + \lambda K_2$; $\forall \lambda, \quad 0 < \lambda < 1$. By quasiconcavity of $-F(y, K)$,

$$-F(y, K_\lambda) \geqslant \min\{-F(y, K_1), -F(y, K_2)\}$$
$$\geqslant y_{n+1}, \qquad \text{by the definition of } -F(y, K).$$

Thus, $[y'y_{n+1}K_\lambda']' \in T^*$.   Q.E.D.

4. Proof of Theorem 3

It only needs to be shown that independence of the production possibilities set T in the $[y'y_{n+1}]' - K$ partition implies and is implied by order-independence of the production function $F(y, K)$.

Suppose T is independent. Let $F(y, K_1) > F(y, K_2)$ for some y, K_1, K_2 ; then, by the definition of the production function and monotonicity of the production possibilities set,

$$\begin{bmatrix} y \\ -F(y, K_2) \\ K_2 \end{bmatrix} \in T \qquad \text{and} \qquad \begin{bmatrix} y \\ -F(y, K_2) \\ K_1 \end{bmatrix} \notin T.$$

Thus, independence of T implies that $T^{K_1} \subset T^{K_2}$. Hence, if $[y^{*'}y_{n+1}^{\#}K_1']' \in T$, $[y^{*'}y_{n+1}^{\#}K_2']' \in T$, $\forall[y^{*'}y_{n+1}^{\#}]'$. Therefore,

$$F(y^\#, K_1) \equiv -\sup\{y_{n+1}^\# \mid [y^{*'}y_{n+1}^\#K_1']' \in T\}$$
$$\geqslant F(y^\#, K_2) \equiv -\sup\{y_{n+1}^\# \mid [y^{*'}y_{n+1}^\#K_2']' \in T\}, \qquad \forall y^\#.$$

Now suppose $F(y, K)$ is order-independent. Let $[y'y_{n+1}K_1']' \in T$ and $[y'y_{n+1}K_2']' \notin T$, then $F(y, K_2) > F(y, K_1)$ by monotonicity of the production possibilities set. Hence, $F(y^{\#}, K_2) \geqslant F(y^{\#}, K_1) \forall y^{\#}$. This implies that $[y^{\#'}y_{n+1}^{\#}K_2']' \in T$ implies that $[y^{\#'}y_{n+1}^{\#}K_1']' \in T$ or $T^{K_2} \subset T^{K_1}$. Hence, T is independent in the $[y'y_{n+1}]' - K$ partition.   Q.E.D.

5. *Proof of Theorem* 4

We first show that F.5A is equivalent to H.5A. Suppose $F(y, K)$ is order-independent. Let $H(y^*, K_1) > H(y^*, K_2)$ for some y^*, K_1, K_2. By the definition of $H(y^*, K)$, the inequality implies that there is y such that

$$
\begin{aligned}
H(y^*, K_1) &= \langle y^*, y \rangle - F(y, K_1) \\
&> H(y^*, K_2) \\
&\geqslant \langle y^*, y \rangle - F(y, K_2),
\end{aligned}
$$

and, thus, $F(y, K_2) > F(y, K_1)$. It then follows from order-independence of $F(y, K)$ in K that

$$
F(y^{\#}, K_2) \geqslant F(y^{\#}, K_1), \qquad \forall y^{\#}.
$$

Consider now for any y^{**},

$$
\begin{aligned}
H(y^{**}, K_1) &\geqslant \langle y^{**}, y^{\#} \rangle - F(y^{\#}, K_1), \qquad \forall y^{\#} \\
&\geqslant (y^{**}, y^{\#}) - F(y^{\#}, K_2), \qquad \forall y^{\#}, \\
&\quad \text{since} \quad F(y^{\#}, K_2) \geqslant F(y^{\#}, K_1) \qquad \forall y^{\#}, \\
&\geqslant \sup_{y^{\#}} \{\langle y^{**}, y^{\#} \rangle - F(y^{\#}, K_2)\} \\
&= H(y^{**}, K_2).
\end{aligned}
$$

Thus $H(y^*, K)$ is order-independent in K.

Conversely, suppose $H(y^*, K)$ is order-independent. Let $F(y, K_1) > F(y, K_2)$ for some y, K_1, and K_2. By the fact that the dual of the dual is the primal function itself, there is y^* such that

$$
\begin{aligned}
F(y, K_1) &= \langle y^*, y \rangle - H(y^*, K_1) \\
&> F(y, K_2) \\
&\geqslant \langle y^*, y \rangle - H(y^*, K_2),
\end{aligned}
$$

and, thus, $H(y^*, K_2) > H(y^*, K_1)$. It then follows from order-independence of $H(y^*, K)$ in K that

$$
H(y^{**}, K_2) \geqslant H(y^{**}, K_1), \qquad \forall y^{**}.
$$

Consider now for any $y^{\#}$,

$$F(y^{\#}, K_1) \geq \langle y^{*\#}, y^{\#} \rangle - H(y^{*\#}, K_1), \qquad \forall y^*$$

$$\geq \langle y^{*\#}, y^{\#} \rangle - H(y^{*\#}, K_2), \qquad \forall y^{*\#},$$

$$\text{since} \quad H(y^{*\#}, K_2) \geq H(y^{*\#}, K_1), \qquad \forall y^{*\#}$$

$$\geq \sup_{y^{*\#}} \{\langle y^{*\#}, y^{\#} \rangle - H(y^{*\#}, K_2)\}$$

$$= F(y^{\#}, K_2).$$

Thus, $F(y, K)$ is order-independent in K.

It remains to be shown that under the assumptions of F.1A through F.5A, the corresponding $H(y^*, K)$ is quasiconcave in K for every y^*, and that similarly, under the assumptions of H.1A through H.5A, the corresponding $F(y, K)$ is quasiconcave in K for every y.

Consider y_1, y_2 which are optimal at some y^* and K_1, K_2, respectively. Let y_λ and K_λ be any convex combination of y_1, y_2 and K_1, K_2, respectively. Then

$$H(y^*, K_\lambda) \geq \langle y^*, y \rangle - F(y, K_\lambda), \qquad \forall y$$

$$\geq \langle y^*, y \rangle - \max[F(y, K_1), F(y, K_2)], \qquad \forall y$$
by quasiconvexity of $F(y, K)$ in K

$$\geq - \max[F(y, K_1) - \langle y^*, y \rangle, F(y, K_2) - \langle y^*, y \rangle], \qquad \forall y$$
by subtraction of an identical quantity from both arguments of the max function

$$\geq \min[\langle y^*, y \rangle - F(y, K_1), \langle y^*, y \rangle - F(y, K_2)], \qquad \forall y$$

$$\geq \sup_{y} \{\min[\langle y^*, y \rangle - F(y, K_1), \langle y^*, y \rangle - F(y, K_2)]\}.$$

But by order-independence, if $\langle y^*, y \rangle - F(y, K_1) > \langle y^*, y \rangle - F(y, K_2)$ for some y (or vice versa), the sense of the inequality is not reversed for all y. Thus, one may interchange the order of $\sup_y$ and min so that

$$H(y^*, K_\lambda) \geq \min[\sup_{y} \{\langle y^*, y \rangle - F(y, K_1)\}, \sup_{y} \{\langle y^*, y \rangle - F(y, K_2)\}]$$

$$\geq \min[H(y^*, K_1), H(y^*, K_2)].$$

This is true for all λ and all y^*, K_1, K_2. Thus, $H(y^*, K)$ is quasiconcave in K.

Conversely, if $H(y^*, K)$ is quasiconcave and order-independent in K, then consider

$$\max[F(y, K_1), F(y, K_2)]$$

$$= \max[\sup_{y^*} \{\langle y^*, y \rangle - H(y^*, K_1)\}, \sup_{y^*} \{\langle y^*, y \rangle - H(y^*, K_2)\}]$$

$$= \sup_{y^*}\{\max[\langle y^*, y \rangle - H(y^*, K_1), \langle y^*, y \rangle - H(y^*, K_2)]\}$$

because $\max_{K_1, K_2} \sup_{y^*} = \sup_{y^*} \max_{K_1, K_2}$

$$\geq \sup_{y^*} \{\langle y^*, y \rangle - H(y^*, K_\lambda)\}$$

by quasiconvexity of $\langle y^*, y \rangle - H(y^*, K)$ in K

$$\geq F(y, K_\lambda).$$

Thus $F(y, K)$ is quasiconvex in K.

We conclude therefore order-independence and quasiconvexity in K of $F(y, K)$ implies order-independence and quasiconcavity in K of $H(y^*, K)$ and vice versa.   Q.E.D.

Note that in the proof of quasiconvexity of $F(y, K)$ in K, we do not need to use the order-independence property. Thus, in general, quasiconcavity of $H(y^*, K)$ in K implies quasiconvexity of $F(y, K)$. But the converse is not true.

ACKNOWLEDGMENTS

The author wishes to thank Erwin Diewert and Dale Jorgenson for useful discussions and David Cass for very helpful comments on an earlier draft of this paper. This research was supported in part by National Science Foundation Grant GS-40104. Financial assistance from the John Simon Guggenheim Foundation is also gratefully acknowledged. This work was completed during the author's tenure as a Visiting Scholar at the Department of Economics, Massachusetts Institute of Technology. Responsibility of errors rests entirely with the author.

REFERENCES

1. W. A. BROCK AND J. A. SCHEINKMAN, Global asymptotic stability of optimal control systems with applications to the theory of economic growth, *J. Econ. Theory*, **12** (1976), 164–190. Reprinted as Essay VII in this volume.
2. D. CASS, Duality: a symmetric approach from the economist's vantage point, *J. Econ. Theory* **7** (1974), 272–295.

3. D. CASS, The Hamiltonian representation of static competitive or efficient allocation, *in*   "Essays in Modern Capital Theory"   (M. Brown, K. Sato and
   P. Zarembka, Eds.), pp. 159-178, North-Holland, Amsterdam, 1976.

4. D. CASS AND K. SHELL, The structure and stability of competitive dynamical systems,
   J. Econ. Theory, **12** (1976), 31-70. Reprinted as Essay III in this volume. 31-70.

5. W. E. DIEWERT, An application of the Shephard duality theorem: a generalized
   Leontief production function, *J. Polit. Econ.* **79** (1971), 481-507.

6. W. E. DIEWERT, Functional forms for profit and transformation functions, *J.
   Econ. Theory* **6** (1973), 284-316.

7. W. E. DIEWERT, Applications of duality theory, *in* "Frontiers of Quantitative
   Economics" (D. A. Kendrick and M. D. Intriligator, Eds.), Vol. II, pp. 106-171,
   North-Holland, Amsterdam, 1974.

8. W. EICHHORN AND W. OETTLI, A general formulation of the Le Chatelier–Samuelson
   principle, *Econometrica* **40** (1972), 711-717.

9. W. FENCHEL, On conjugate convex functions, *Can. J. Math.* **1** (1949), 73-77.

10. W. FENCHEL, "Convex Cones, Sets and Functions," Department of Mathematics,
    Princeton University, Princeton, N.J., mimeographed, 1953.

11. J. W. FRIEDMAN, Duality principles in the theory of cost and production revisited,
    Int. Econ. Rev. **13** (1972), 167-170.

12. W. M. GORMAN, Measuring the quantities of fixed factors, *in* "Value, Capital
    and Growth: Papers in Honour of Sir John Hicks" (J. N. Wolfe, Ed.), pp. 141-172,
    Aldine, Chicago, 1968.

13. H. HOTELLING, Edgeworth's taxation paradox and the nature of demand and
    supply functions, *J. Polit. Econ.* **40** (1932), 577-616.

14. S. E. JACOBSEN, Production correspondences, *Econometrica* **38** (1970), 754-770.

15. S. E. JACOBSEN, On Shephard's duality theorem, *J. Econ. Theory* **4** (1972), 458-464.

16. D. W. JORGENSON AND L. J. LAU, Duality and differentiability in production,
    J. Econ. **9** (1974a), 23-42.

17. D. W. JORGENSON AND L. J. LAU, Duality of technology and economic behaviour,
    Rev. Econ. Stud. **41** (1974b), 181-200.

18. D. W. JORGENSON AND L. J. LAU, "Duality in the Theory of Production," North-
    Holland, Amsterdam, to appear.

19. L. J. LAU, "Some Applications of Profit Functions," Memorandum No. 86A and
    B, Center for Research in Economic Growth, Stanford University, Stanford,
    California, mimeographed, 1969.

20. L. J. LAU, Applications of duality theory: a comment, *in* "Frontiers in Quantitative
    Economics" (M. D. Intriligator and D. A. Kendricks, Eds.), Vol. II, pp. 176-199,
    North-Holland, Amsterdam, 1974.

21. L. J. LAU AND P. LERTTAMRAB, "Production Behavior of Thai Agricultural House-
    holds with and without the Liquidity Constraint: An Application of the Quadratic
    Normalized Restricted Profit Function," Working Paper, Department of Econom-
    ics, Stanford University, mimeographed, 1975.

22. L. J. LAU AND P. A. YOTOPOULOS, A test for relative efficiency and an application
    to Indian agriculture, *Amer. Econ. Rev.* **61** (1971), 94-109.

23. L. J. LAU AND P. A. YOTOPOULOS, Profit, supply, and factor demand functions,
    Amer. J. Agric. Econ. **54** (1972), 11-18.

24. W. LIN, L. J. LAU, AND P. A. YOTOPOULOS, "The Transcendental Logarithmic
    Normalized Restricted Profit Function: An Application to the Agriculture of
    Taiwan," Working Paper, Department of Economics, Stanford University, mimeo-
    graphed, 1975.

25. D. L. McFADDEN, "Cost, Revenue, and Profit Functions: A Cursory Review," Working Paper No. 86, Institute for Business and Economic Research, University of California, Berkeley, mimeographed, 1966.

26. D. L. McFADDEN, "Cost, Revenue, and Profit Functions," Department of Economics, University of California, Berkeley, mimeographed, 1970.

27. R. T. ROCKAFELLAR, "Convex Analysis," Princeton Univ. Press, Princeton, N.J., 1970.

28. J. N. ROSSE, "Equivalent Structures of Production, Cost, and Input Demand with Multiple Inputs and Outputs," Memorandum No. 101 and 101A, Center for Research in Economic Growth, Stanford University, mimeographed, 1970.

29. P. A. SAMUELSON, "Foundations of Economic Analysis," Harvard Univ. Press, Cambridge, Mass., 1947.

30. P. A. SAMUELSON, The Le Chatelier principle in linear programming, Rand Corporation, Santa Monica, California, *reprinted in* "The Collected Scientific Papers of Paul A. Samuelson" (J. E. Stiglitz, Ed.), Vol. 1, pp. 638–650, The Massachusetts Institute of Technology Press, Cambridge, Mass., 1949.

31. P. A. SAMUELSON, Prices of factors and goods in general equilibrium, *Rev. Econ. Stud.* **21** (1953–1954), 1–20.

32. R. W. SHEPHARD, "Cost and Production Functions," Princeton Univ. Press. Princeton, N.J., 1953.

33. R. W. SHEPHARD, "Theory of Cost and Production Functions," Princeton Univ. Press, Princeton, N.J., 1970.

34. H. UZAWA, Duality principles in the theory of cost and production, *Int. Econ. Rev.* **5** (1964), 216–220.

35. P. A. YOTOPOULOS AND L. J. LAU, A test for relative efficiency: some further results, *Amer. Econ. Rev.* **63** (1973), 214–223.

36. P. A. YOTOPOULOS, L. J. LAU, AND W. LIN, "Microeconomic Output Supply and Factor Demand Functions in the Agriculture of the Province of Taiwan," Memorandum No. 193, Center for Research in Economic Growth, Stanford University, mimeographed, 1975.

ESSAY VII

Global Asymptotic Stability of Optimal Control Systems with Applications to the Theory of Economic Growth*

WILLIAM A. BROCK

AND

JOSÉ A. SCHEINKMAN

1

The qualitative study of optimal economic growth has attracted the attention of economic theorists for some number of years. One major focus of this research has been to find sufficient conditions on models of economic growth for the convergence of growth paths to a steady state. In this symposium volume of the *Journal of Economic Theory*, Cass and Shell [16] present the Hamiltonian formulation of competitive dynamical systems that arise in capital theory. In this paper, we present a set of sufficient conditions on the Hamiltonian for such dynamical systems to converge to a steady state as time tends to infinity.

We refer the reader to the Cass–Shell paper for an introduction to competitive dynamical systems, and a complete survey of the literature. Only a very brief survey, that is useful for leading the reader into our approach, will be given here.

* The research reported here was initiated while the authors were attending the M.S.S.B. Workshop on Monetary Theory in the summer of 1973, at the University of California at Berkeley. We would like to thank J. Aitken, S. Bernfeld, D. Cass, J. Haddock, P. Hartman, E. Keeler, A. Mas-Colell, L. McKenzie, L. Markus, R. C. Robinson, and K. Shell with whom we had enlightening discussions. Thanks are due especially to David Cass, Karl Shell, and Lionel McKenzie. Part of this research was conducted while William Brock was Visiting Professor of Economics at the University of Rochester, Rochester, New York. Financial support of the National Science Foundation is gratefully acknowledged.

164

A general formulation of capital theory or optimal growth problems is

$$\text{Max} \int_0^\infty e^{-\rho t} u[k(t), \dot{k}(t)]\, dt$$

subject to

$$k(0) = k_0 .$$

Here $u: B \subset \mathring{R}_+^n \times R^n \to R$ is usually assumed C^2 and concave. Here $\mathring{R}_+^n = \{x \in R^n / x_i > 0;\ i = 1,..., n\}$, and B is convex with nonempty interior.

$$R(k_0) = \text{Max} \int_0^\infty e^{-\rho t} u[k(t), \dot{k}(t)]\, dt$$

is called the value of the initial stock k_0 .

A capital theory model generates a capital–price differential equation by using the Hesteness–Pontriagin [22, 35] maximal principle to write down necessary conditions for an optimal solution. This process generates a type of differential equation system that we will call a "modified Hamiltonian dynamical system." The adjective "modified" appears because it is a certain type of perturbation peculiar to economics of the standard Hamiltonian system.

Since the standard Hamiltonian case will be a special case of our problem, our results will be of independent interest to mathematicians working in the field of Hamiltonian dynamical systems.

In order to discuss our approach, we need a definition. A modified Hamiltonian dynamical system (call it an MDHS for short) is a differential equation system of the form

$$\dot{q}_j = \rho q_j - \frac{\partial H}{\partial k_j}(q, k), \qquad H(q, k) \equiv \underset{k;(k,\dot{k})\in B}{\text{maximum}} \{u(k, \dot{k}) + q\dot{k}\},$$

$$\dot{k}_j = \frac{\partial H}{\partial q_j}(q, k), \qquad j = 1, 2,..., n. \tag{1.1}$$

Here $H: \mathring{R}_+^n \times \mathring{R}_+^n \to R$, and $\rho \in R_+$. In economics, k_j is stock of capital good j and q_j is the price of capital good j. The function H is called a Hamiltonian, and it is well defined on $\mathring{R}_+^n \times \mathring{R}_+^n$ for many economic problems. However, what follows only depends on H being defined on an open convex subset of R^{2n}, provided the obvious changes are made. H turns out to be the current value of national income evaluated at prices q. The number ρ is a discount factor on future welfare arising from the structure of social preferences. See Cass and Shell for a complete interpretation of (1.1).

Clearly not all solutions of (1.1) which satisfy $k(0) = k_0$ will, in general, be optimal. We will call a solution $[q(t), k(t)]$ of (1.1) optimal if $k(t)$ is the optimal solution of the optimal growth problem when $k(0) = k_0$.

The problem that we shall address in this paper may now be defined.

PROBLEM 1.   Find sufficient conditions on optimal solutions ϕ_t of (1.1) such that $\phi_t \to (\bar{q}, \bar{k})$, $t \to \infty$. Also find sufficient conditions such that the steady state $(\bar{q}, \bar{k})$ is independent of the initial condition (q_0, k_0).

The literature on Problem 1 has two main branches: (1) analysis of the local behavior of (1.1) in a neighborhood of a steady state, and (2) analysis of global behavior of solutions of (1.1).

The first branch of the literature is fairly complete. It studies the linear approximation of (1.1) in a neighborhood of a rest point. Eigenvalues have a well-known symmetric structure that determines the local behavior. Since we have nothing new to contribute to this branch of study, we, therefore, cite some representative references and move on [27, 41, 28]. To the global problem we now turn.

The literature on Problem 1 is very large yet there are no general results on global stability. Representative literature on existing global stability results for optimal paths follows. The case $n = 1$ (the one good optimal growth model) is well understood. See [11, 14, 25, 27]. Ryder and Heal [39] analyze a case of (1.1) for $n = 2$. They generate a variety of examples of different qualitative behavior of optimal paths. Burmeister and Graham [12] present an analysis of a model where there is a set S containing the steady state capital $\bar{k}$ such that for $k \in S$, the value of q along an optimal path is independent of k. See [12, Theorem 2, p. 149].

The case $\rho = 0$ is the famous Ramsey problem, studied first by Ramsey for the one good model, then by Gale [18], McKenzie [33], McFadden [32], and Brock [4] for the n goods model in discrete time and by Rockafellar [36] for continuous time. These results state, roughly speaking, that if $H(q, k)$ is strictly convex in q and strictly concave in k and $\rho = 0$, then all solution paths of (1.1) that are optimal converge to a unique steady state $(\bar{q}, \bar{k})$ as $t \to \infty$ independently of (q_0, k_0).

Scheinkman [42] has recently proved a result that shows that the qualitative behavior for $\rho = 0$ is preserved for small changes in ρ near $\rho = 0$.

Until very recently no general results on the convergence of optimal solutions of (1.1) were available. In fact, little was known about sufficient conditions for the uniqueness of steady states of (1.1). Recently, papers of Brock [5] and Brock and Burmeister [46] gave a fairly general set of sufficient conditions for uniqueness of the steady state. There was nothing done in the Brock paper on convergence, however.

In this paper we will present new results that build on the work of Cass and Shell [16], Rockafellar [38], and Hartman and Olech [21]. We start by discussing the three basic types of results obtained and their relation to the literature.

The following problem has been analyzed extensively in the differential equations literature. Let

$$\dot{x} = f(x), \, x(0) = x_0$$

be a differential equation system. Let $\bar{x}$ satisfy $f(\bar{x}) = 0$. Under what conditions is the solution $x(t) \equiv \bar{x}$ globally asymptotically stable for all x_0?

DEFINITION 1.1.   The solution $x(t) \equiv \bar{x}$ of $\dot{x} = f(x)$ is *globally asymptotically stable* (GAS) if for all x_0 the solution $\phi_t(x_0) \to \bar{x}, \, t \to \infty$.

DEFINITION 1.2.   The solution $x(t) \equiv \bar{x}$ of $\dot{x} = f(x)$ is *locally asymptotically stable* (LAS) if there is $\epsilon > 0$ such that $|x_0 - \bar{x}| < \epsilon$ implies $\phi_t(x_0) \to \bar{x}, \, t \to \infty$.

If f is a modified Hamiltonian, new problems arise. In this case, $x(t) = \bar{x}$ is usually never even locally asymptotically stable in a neighborhood of $\bar{x}$. This is so because if λ is an eigenvalue of the linear approximation so also is $-\lambda + \rho$ (see [27], e.g.). Thus, a natural question to pose is our Problem 1 for MHDS.

DEFINITION 1.3. $\phi_t(q_0, k_0)$ will be called *a bounded solution of* (1.1) if there exists a compact set $K \subseteq \mathring{R}_+^n \times \mathring{R}_+^n$ such that $\phi_t(q_0, k_0) \subseteq K$ for all t.

Note that our definition of bounded solutions requires not only boundedness on the (q, k) space, but also that there exists $\epsilon > 0$ such that

$$q_i(t) \geqslant \epsilon, \qquad k_i(t) \geqslant \epsilon, \qquad i = 1,..., n; \qquad 0 \leqslant t < \infty.$$

In many optimal growth problems, "Inada"-type conditions guarantee that in fact optimal solutions will satisfy our boundedness condition. For this reason, we concentrate on the convergence of bounded solutions.

DEFINITION 1.4.   The steady state solution $(q, k) = (\bar{q}, \bar{k})$ of (1.1) is said to be *globally asymptotically stable* for bounded solutions of (1.1) [i.e., those who satisfy Definition 1.3] if for all (q_0, k_0) such that $\phi_t(q_0, k_0)$ is bounded, we have

$$\phi_t(q_0, k_0) \to (\bar{q}, \bar{k}), \, t \to \infty.$$

DEFINITION 1.5.   The steady state solution $(q, k) = (\bar{q}, \bar{k})$ of (1.1) is said to be *locally asymptotically stable* for bounded solutions of (1.1) if there is $\epsilon > 0$ such that $|(q_0, k_0) - (q, k)| < \epsilon$ implies $\phi_t(q_0, k_0) \to (\bar{q}, \bar{k}), \, t \to \infty$, provided that $\phi_t(q_0, k_0)$ is bounded.

For MHDS, the words "GAS" and "LAS" will always apply to bounded solutions alone in this paper. We will sometimes call MHDS "saddle-point" systems when we want to emphasize their saddle-point structure.

Let us denote by $(\bar{q}, \bar{k})$ some rest point of (1.1); then we can rewrite (1.1) as

$$\dot{z}_1 = F_1(z_1, z_2),$$
$$\dot{z}_2 = F_2(z_1, z_2),$$
(1.2)

where $F_i: A \subseteq R^{2n} \to R^n$ where A is open and convex, by letting

$$q - \bar{q} = z_1, k - \bar{k} = z_2, F_1(z) \equiv -H_2[z + (\bar{q}, \bar{k})] + \rho(z_1 + \bar{q}), F_2(z)$$

$\equiv H_1[z + (\bar{q}, \bar{k})]$. Here again a "bounded" solution will mean a solution which is contained in a compact set $K \subset A$.

Most of our assumptions will refer to the "curvature" matrix

$$Q(z) = \begin{bmatrix} H_{11}(z) & \rho/2\ I_n \\ \rho/2\ I_n & -H_{22}(z) \end{bmatrix}$$

where $H_{11}(z) \equiv (\partial H_1/\partial z_1)(z + (\bar{q}, \bar{k}))$, $H_{22}(z) \equiv (\partial H_2/\partial z_2)(z + (\bar{q}, \bar{k}))$, and I_n is the $n \times n$ identity matrix.

In Section 2, we show that *if $F(z)\ Q(z)\ F(z) > 0$ for all z such that $F(z) \neq 0$, then every bounded trajectory converges to a rest point.* This is the "Hamiltonian version" of the well known result in differential equations which states that if $f: R^n \to R$ and $J(x) = (\partial f(x)/\partial x)$, then $f^T(x)\ J(x)\ f(x) < 0$ for all x with $f(x) \neq 0$ implies that all solutions of $\dot{x} = f(x)$ converge to a rest point. Our result is obtained by using the "Lyapunov" function $F_1^T(z)\ F_2(z)$.

In Section 3, we show that *if $z_1{}^T F_2(z) + z_2{}^T F_1(z) = 0$ implies $z^T Q(z)\ z > 0$ and if $Q(0)$ is positive definite, then all bounded trajectories of (1.2) converge to the origin.* This result is related to a result by Hartman and Olech [21] that states that if $w^T J(x)\ w < 0$ for all w such that $|w| = 1$ and $w^T f(x) = 0$, then every solution to $\dot{x} = f(x)$ converges to the origin provided that 0 is LAS. The proof is inspired by the elegant proof of a Hartman–Olech type of result obtained by Mas–Colell [31]. As a by-product of the proof, we show that the above conditions are sufficient for the function $z_1{}^T z_2$ to be monotonically increasing along trajectories, which is the Cass and Shell hypothesis. Note that the assumptions of Sections 2 and 3 are somewhat complementary.

The method of proof of Section 3 does not, unfortunately, generalize to prove results analogous to Hartman and Olech's [21] most general results. For this reason, in Section 4 we outline the method of proof of a more general theorem. This method is similar to the method used by

Hartman and Olech of constructing an "orthogonal" field of trajectories to the trajectories generated by a system of differential equations $\dot{z} = F(z)$, and placing conditions on the Jacobian matrix of F so that all trajectories of the original field come together monotonically as $t \to \infty$, in the metric induced by the arc length measure along the "orthogonal" field of trajectories. The complete proof is quite messy and the reader is referred to our paper [8].

Furthermore, the results in this section have a nice geometrical interpretation in terms of quasi-convexity and quasi-concavity. In particular, we show that *for the case $\rho = 0$, if the Hamiltonian is quasi-concave in the state variable, then GAS holds* (although in this case "optimality" may not make sense). A notion of α-quasi-convexity is introduced to provide a geometric interpretation for the case where $\rho > 0$.

Curvature Matrix Q: Geometric and Economic Meaning

The curvature matrix Q is a natural economic and geometric quantity. As Cass and Shell [16] point out, the Hamiltonian is convex in q and concave in k for optimal control problems with a concave objective function. Hence H_{11}, $-H_{22}$ are positive semidefinite matrices.

Geometric Content of Q

For the one-dimensional case Q is positive definite provided that

$$(H_{11})(-H_{22}) > \rho^2/4.$$

This suggests that if the smallest eigenvalue α of H_{11} and the smallest eigenvalue β of $-H_{22}$ satisfy

$$\alpha\beta > \rho^2/4, \qquad (R)$$

then Q is positive definite. It is easy to show that (R), which is Rockafellar's [38] basic stability hypothesis, does indeed imply that Q is positive definite.[1]

---

[1] Let the minimum eigenvalue of $H_{11}(q, k)$ be $\alpha(q, k)$ and the minimum eigenvalue of $-H_{22}(q, k)$ be $\beta(q, k)$. Then if $\alpha\beta > \rho^2/4$, it follows that

$$Q(q, k) = \begin{bmatrix} H_{11}(q, k), & \rho/2\, I_n \\ \rho/2\, I_n, & -H_{22}(q, k) \end{bmatrix}$$

is positive definite.

To prove this, examine

$$\begin{aligned} x^T Q x &= x_1^T H_{11} x_1 + x_2^T(-H_{22})x_2 + \rho x_1^T x_2 \\ &\geqslant \alpha x_1^T x_1 + \beta x_2^T x_2 + \rho x_1^T x_2 \\ &\geqslant \alpha x_1^T x_1 + \beta x_2^T x_2 - \rho \mid x_1^T x_2 \mid \\ &\geqslant \alpha \| x_1 \|^2 + \beta \| x_2 \|^2 - \rho \| x_1 \| \| x_2 \| \end{aligned}$$

where $\| z \| \equiv (z^T z)^{1/2}$ for any vector z.

Economic Content of Q

It is well known that the Hamiltonian $H(q, k)$ can be interpreted as "shadow profit" when q is the shadow price of investment, all with utility as numeraire. Cass and Shell [16] develop in detail the economic meaning of the Hamiltonian. They show, in particular,

$$\partial H/\partial q = \text{optimum investment level,}$$

and

$$\partial H/\partial k = \text{marginal value product of } k.$$

Therefore, $\partial H/\partial q$ is an "internal supply curve for investment," and $\partial H/\partial k$ is a "Marshallian" demand curve for capital services. Thus,

$$H_{11} = \partial^2 H/\partial q^2, \quad H_{22} = \partial^2 H/\partial k^2,$$

are generalized slopes of supply and demand curves for investment and capital services. The matrix Q is just a convenient way of tabulating information on supply, demand, and the "interest" rate ρ, that is important for stability analysis.

More specifically, a sufficient condition for stability is that

$$Q = \begin{bmatrix} H_{11} & \rho/2\, I_n \\ \rho/2\, I_n & -H_{22} \end{bmatrix}$$

be positive definite. An intuitive way of putting this is that the slopes of the supply curves for investment and the demand curves for capital services are large relative to the interest rate ρ, and that cross terms are small relative to own terms.

Let us expand upon the economics here. Along an optimum path, $q(t)$

Now,

$$\alpha \| x_1 \|^2 + \beta \| x_2 \|^2 - \rho \| x_1 \| \| x_2 \|$$
$$> \alpha \| x_1 \|^2 + \beta \| x_2 \|^2 - (4\alpha\beta)^{1/2} \| x_1 \| \| x_2 \|.$$

So our problem reduces to showing that

$$\alpha \| x_1 \|^2 + \beta \| x_2 \|^2 - (4\alpha\beta)^{1/2} \| x_1 \| \| x_2 \| \geqslant 0.$$

But this last quantity is just

$$(\alpha^{1/2} \| x_1 \| - \beta^{1/2} \| x_2 \|)^2$$

which is nonnegative. This ends the proof.

is the current value of the demand price for capital goods. Thus, $q(t)$ is a Marshallian demand curve for capital equipment; i.e.,

$$q(t) = \frac{\partial}{\partial k} \left\{ \text{Maximum} \int_t^\infty e^{-\rho(s-t)} u(y, \dot{y}) \, ds, \quad \text{s.t.} \quad y(t) = k(t) \right\}$$

$$= \frac{\partial R[k(t)]}{\partial k} = R'[k(t)]$$

if $\partial R/\partial k$ exists. Like any demand curve, the demand for k should be downward-sloping. For $u(y, \dot{y})$ concave the Hessian of R, $R''(k)$, is a negative semidefinite matrix which exists for almost every k [24, p. 405].

Look at the "reduced form" and its equation of first variation,

$$\dot{k}(t) = H_1(R'[k(t)], k(t)), \tag{1.3}$$

$$\ddot{k} = (H_{11}R'' + H_{12}) k. \tag{1.4}$$

Stabilizing forces are forces that lead to increased negative feedback in (1.3). An "increase" in H_{11} is stabilizing because R'' is negative semidefinite.

It is a little more difficult to explain why an increase in $-H_{22}$ is stabilizing. For an increase in $-H_{22}$ is clearly a destabilizing force for q as can be seen intuitively by examining

$$\dot{q} = \rho q - H_2 .$$

But since along an optimum path, q decreases in k, a destabilizing force for q is stabilizing for k.

It is also intuitively clear that moving ρ closer to 0 is stabilizing. This is so because if $\rho = 0$, the system strives to maximize long-run static profit since the future is worth as much as the present.

Inspection of (1.4) hints that an increase in H_{12} is destabilizing. This source of instability is not exposed by the Q matrix. The quantity H_{12} represents a shift in the internal supply curve of investment when capital stock is increased. Therefore, an *increase* in H_{12} represents a type of increase of nonnormality. I.e., since H_{12} is the derivative of the internal supply curve w.r.t. k, therefore, it is likely that H_{12} will be negative in some sense. For an increase in the number of machines (an increase in k) is likely to lead to a decrease in new machines supplied by the "firm" to itself when q increases, if some sort of diminishing returns to capital services and substitutability between investment goods and capital goods is present.

We would expect an increase in H_{12} to contribute to instability because an increase in k leads to more new machines, which leads to yet larger k.

See [6] for stability results that focus on the role of H_{12}, and that are based on a different class of Lyapunov functions than what is presented here.

2. A First Result on G.A.S.

The work in this section is closely related to work by Cass and Shell [16], a paper by Rockafellar [38], papers by Arrow and Hurwicz [3]; Arrow, Block, and Hurwicz [2]; Hartman [19]; and Markus and Yamabe [30]. Consider the modified Hamiltonian system

$$\dot{q} - \rho q = -H_k(q, k),$$
$$\dot{k} = H_q(q, k), \qquad k(0) = k_0, \qquad q(0) = q_0. \tag{2.1}$$

Let $(\bar{q}, \bar{k})$ be a rest point of (2.1) and let $z_1 = q - \bar{q}, z_2 = k - \bar{k}, F_1(z) = \rho(z_1 + \bar{q}) - H_2(z + (\bar{q}, \bar{k}), F_2(z) = H_1(z + (\bar{q}, \bar{k}))$. Then (2.1) becomes

$$\dot{z}_1 = F_1(z),$$
$$\dot{z}_2 = F_2(z). \tag{2.2}$$

In [30] and in [3], sufficient conditions for global stability of differential equations, $\dot{x} = f(x)$ are given. Let $J(x) \equiv \partial f/\partial x$. Arrow and Hurwicz and Markus and Yamabe prove (roughly speaking) that the negative definiteness of $J^T + J$ is sufficient for global stability of $\dot{x} = f(x)$ by differentiating $(\dot{x})^T \dot{x} = W$ with respect to t and showing, thereby, that $x(t) \to 0$, $t \to \infty$ along trajectories. Here x^T denotes x transposed. We are going to present an analog of this type of result for Hamiltonian systems.

Consider a trajectory $z(t) \equiv \phi_t(q_0, k_0)$ of (2.1) where q_0 is chosen so that $\phi_t(q_0, k_0)$ is bounded. Optimal growth paths will have this boundedness property under reasonable conditions. Cass and Shell [16][2] prove global stability of such a trajectory by differentiating the Lyapunov function $V \equiv z_1^T z_2$ w.r.t. t. It is, therefore, natural to ask what may be obtained by differentiating the closely related Lyapunov function $F_1^T F_2$.

We will make use of the following result, which is basically the result in Hartman's book [20, p. 539].

LEMMA 2.1. *Let $F(z)$ be continuous on an open set $E \subseteq R^m$, and such that solutions of*

$$\dot{z} = F(z) \tag{$*$}$$

---

[2] Cass and Shell are the first to obtain GAS results for (2.1) by use of the Lyapunov function $V \equiv z_1^T z_2$ for the discounted case. Their methods provided inspiration for many of our results. Rockafellar [37] and Samuelson [41] have used the same function to investigate stability for the case $\rho = 0$. Magill [45] used V to obtain GAS results for a discounted linear quadratic problem.

are uniquely determined by initial conditions. Let $W(z)$ be a real-valued function on E with the following properties:

(a) W is C^1 on E,

(b) $0 \leqslant \dot{W}(z)$ [where $\dot{W}(z)$ is the trajectory derivative of $W(z)$ for any $z \in E$].

Let $z(t)$ be a solution of $(*)$ for $t \geqslant 0$. Then the limit points of $z(t)$ for $t \geqslant 0$, in E, if any, are contained in the set $E_0 = \{z \mid \dot{W}(z) = 0\}$.

Proof. Let $t_n < t_{n+1} \to \infty$, $z(t_n) \to z_0$ as $n \to \infty$, and $z_0 \in E$. Then $W[z(t_n)] \to W(z_0)$ as $n \to \infty$, and by (b) $W[z(t)] \leqslant W(z_0)$ for $t \geqslant 0$. Suppose $z_0 \notin E_0$ so that $\dot{W}(z_0) > 0$ by (b). Let $z_0(t)$ be a solution of $(*)$ satisfying $z_0(0) = z_0$. Since W is C^1 and $\dot{W}(z_0) > 0$, there exists by the mean value theorem $\epsilon > 0$ and $\delta > 0$ such that for $0 \leqslant t \leqslant \epsilon$,

$$W[z_0(t)] - W(z_0) > \delta t,$$

and, in particular,

$$W[z_0(\epsilon)] - W(z_0) > \delta\epsilon. \tag{2.3}$$

Since $z(t_n) \to z_0$, and solutions are continuously dependent on initial values, given any $\eta > 0$, there exists $N(\eta)$ such that for $n \geqslant N(\eta)$,

$$\| z(t + t_n) - z_0(t)\| < \eta \qquad \text{for} \quad 0 \leqslant t \leqslant \epsilon.$$

And in particular,

$$\| z(\epsilon + t_n) - z_0(\epsilon)\| < \eta \qquad \text{for} \quad n \geqslant N(\eta).$$

The continuity of W guarantees that for η sufficiently small,

$$| W[z(\epsilon + t_n)] - W[z_0(\epsilon)]| < \delta\epsilon/2. \tag{2.4}$$

Inequalities (2.3) and (2.4) imply that $W[z(\epsilon + t_n)] > W(z_0)$, and this contradicts $W[z(t)] \leqslant W(z_0)$.   Q.E.D.

We can now prove

THEOREM 2.1.   *Let*

$$Q(z) = \begin{bmatrix} H_{11}(z) & \rho/2\, I_n \\ \rho/2\, I_n & -H_{22}(z) \end{bmatrix}$$

where $H_{11} = \partial F_2/\partial z_1$, $H_{22} = -\partial F_1/\partial z_2$, and I_n denotes the $n \times n$ identity matrix. If $F^T(z)\, Q(z)\, F(z) > 0$ for all z with $F(z) \neq 0$, and if the rest points *of* (2.2) *are isolated, then given any* z_0 *such that* $\phi_t(z_0)$ *is bounded, there exists a rest point* $\bar{z}$, *which may depend on* z_0, *such that* $\lim_{t \to \infty} \phi_t(z_0) = \bar{z}$.

Proof. Let $\gamma^+ = \{z \in R^n / z = \phi_t(z_0)$ for some $t \geqslant 0\}$, and $\Omega(\gamma^+) = \{z \in R^n / $ there exists increasing sequence $\{t_n\}_{n=0}^{\infty}$ such that $\lim_{n \to \infty} \phi_{t_n}(z_0) = z\}$.

Since γ^+ has compact closure on the domain of F, $\Omega(\gamma^+)$ is nonempty, compact and connected [20, Theorem 1.1, p. 145].

Let $W(z) = F_1^T(z) F_2(z)$. Then $\dot{W}(z) = \dot{F}_1^T(z) F_2(z) + F_1^T(z) \dot{F}_2(z) = \rho F_1^T(z) F_2(z) + F_1^T(z) H_{11}(z) F_1(z) - F_2^T(z) H_{22}(z) F_2(z) = F^T(z) Q(z) F(z) \geqslant 0$. By the previous lemma, if $\bar{z} \in \Omega(\gamma^+)$, then $F^T(\bar{z}) Q(\bar{z}) F(\bar{z}) = 0$, and, hence, $F(\bar{z}) = 0$; i.e., $\bar{z}$ is a rest point. Since the rest points are isolated and $\Omega(\gamma^+)$ is connected, $\Omega(\gamma^+) = \{\bar{z}\}$. Hence, $\lim_{t \to \infty} \phi_t(z_0) = \bar{z}$.

Remark 1. For MHDS derived from optimal growth problems, it would be useful to replace the condition "$\phi_t(z_0)$ is bounded" by "$\phi_t(z_0)$ is optimal," since it is possible to find models in which optimal paths are not bounded. One can, however, bound the Lyapunov function W by assuming regularity and concavity conditions on the so-called "value function." In fact, consider an optimal growth problem

$$\text{Max} \int_0^{\infty} e^{-\rho t} u[k(t), \dot{k}(t)] \, dt \tag{2.5}$$

given $k(0) = k_0$.

Here $u: R^{2n} \to R$ is usually assumed concave and C^2.

Let $k^*(t, k_0)$ be the optimal solution and $R(k_0) = \int_0^{\infty} e^{-\rho t} u[k^*(t, k_0), \dot{k}^*(t, k_0)] \, dt$; i.e., R is the value of the objective function along the optimal path (the value function).

If we assume that R is C^2, then one can show that $R'(k) = q$ where (q, k) solve the MHDS corresponding to (2.5). Benveniste and Scheinkman [47] provide a general set of conditions on u that imply that R' exists.

Hence, $\dot{q} = (d/dt) R'(k) = R''(k) \dot{k}$. The concavity of u implies that R is concave, and, hence, $R''(k)$ is seminegative definite. If one assumes that in fact $R''(k)$ is negative definite, then $\dot{k}^T \dot{q} = \dot{k}^T R''(k) \dot{k} < 0$ along any optimal path provided $\dot{k} \neq 0$. Thus, $W = \dot{k}^T \dot{q}$ is bounded above on optimal paths.

Remark 2. The Lyapunov function $V \equiv z_1^T z_2 = (q - \bar{q})^T (k - \bar{k})$ amounts to

$$(q - \bar{q})^T (k - \bar{k}) = [R'(k) - R'(\bar{k})]^T (k - \bar{k}) \tag{i}$$

Since the value function $R(\cdot)$ is concave,

$$[R'(k) - R'(\bar{k})](k - \bar{k}) \leqslant 0 \tag{ii}$$

for all k. Inequality (ii) is well known for concave functions. It holds with strict inequality for strictly concave functions. Thus, it is natural to search for sufficient conditions on the Hamiltonian that imply V is increasing on trajectories, and the matrix Q plays an important role in such sufficient conditions.

3

A General Result on Convergence of Bounded Trajectories

In this section, we shall present a general theorem that will generate a result that is closely related to Hartman and Olech's basic theorem [21, p. 157, Theorem 2.3], our result of Theorem 3.1, and many other results, all as simple corollaries. Furthermore, the general theorem will be stated and proved in such a way as to highlight a general Lyapunov method that is especially useful for the stability analysis of optimal paths generated by optimal control problems arising in capital theory.

THEOREM 3.1. *Let* $f: E \subset R^m \to R^m$ *be* C^2, *E open and convex. Consider the differential equation system*

$$\dot{x} = f(x). \tag{3a.1}$$

Assume there is x such that $f(x) = 0$ (W.L.O.G. put $x = 0$) such that there is $V: E \to R$ satisfying:

(a) *for all* $x \neq 0$, $x^T \nabla^2 V(0)[J(0)\, x] < 0$,

(b) $\nabla V(0) = 0$,

(c) *for all* $x \neq 0$, $[\nabla V(x)]^T f(x) = 0$ *implies* $x^T \nabla^2 V(x)\, f(x) = 0$,

(d) *for all* $x \neq 0$, $x^T \nabla^2 V(x)\, f(x) = 0$ *implies* $[\nabla V(x)]^T J(x)\, x < 0$.

Then

(α) $[\nabla V(x)]^T f(x) < 0$ *for all* $x \neq 0$,

(β) *all trajectories that remain "bounded" (i.e., are contained in a compact set $k \subset E$) for $t \geqslant 0$ converge to 0.*

Proof. Let $x \neq 0$, and put

$$g(\lambda) \equiv [\nabla V(\lambda x)]^T f(\lambda x). \tag{3a.2}$$

We shall show that $g(1) < 0$ in order to obtain (α). We do this by showing that $g(0) = 0$, $g'(0) = 0$, $g''(0) < 0$, and $g(\bar{\lambda}) = 0$ implies $g'(\bar{\lambda}) < 0$ for $\bar{\lambda} > 0$. (At this point, the reader will do well to draw a graph of $g(\lambda)$ in

order to convince himself that the above statements imply $g(1) < 0$.)
Calculating, we get

$$g'(\lambda) = x^T \, \nabla^2 V(\lambda x) f(\lambda x) + [\nabla V(\lambda x)]^T \, J(\lambda x) \, x, \qquad (3a.3)$$

$$g''(\lambda) = x^T \left[\frac{d}{d\lambda} \, \nabla^2 V(\lambda x) \right] f(\lambda x) + x^T \nabla^2 V(\lambda x)[J(\lambda x) \, x]$$

$$+ \, x^T \, \nabla^2 V(\lambda x)[J(\lambda x) \, x] + [\nabla V(\lambda x)]^T \left[\frac{d}{d\lambda} \, J(\lambda x) \right] x. \quad (3a.4)$$

Now $\lambda = 0$ implies $f(\lambda x) = 0$, so $g(0) = 0$. Also $g'(0) = 0$
from $f(0) = 0$, and (b). Furthermore, $f(0) = 0$, (b) imply

$$g''(0) = 2x^T \nabla^2 V(0)[J(0) \, x] \qquad (3a.5)$$

But this is negative by (a). By continuity of g'' in λ, it must be true that there
is $\epsilon_0 > 0$ such that $g(\lambda) < 0$ for $\lambda \epsilon [0, \epsilon_0]$. Suppose now that there is $\lambda > 0$
such that $g(\lambda) = 0$. Then there must be a smallest $\bar\lambda > 0$ such that $g(\bar\lambda) = 0$.
Also, $g'(\bar\lambda) \geq 0$. Let us calculate $g'(\bar\lambda)$, show that $g'(\bar\lambda) < 0$, and get an
immediate contradiction. From (3a.3),

$$g'(\bar\lambda) = x^T \nabla^2 V(\bar\lambda x) f(\bar\lambda x) + [\nabla V(\bar\lambda x)]^T \, J(\bar\lambda x) \, x. \qquad (3a.6)$$

Now $g(\bar\lambda) = 0$ implies $[\nabla V(\bar\lambda x)]^T f(\bar\lambda x) = 0$. But this, in turn, implies that
$\bar\lambda x^T \nabla^2 V(\bar\lambda x) \, f(\bar\lambda x) = 0$ by (c). Finally, (d) implies that $[\nabla V(\bar\lambda x)]^T \times$
$J(\bar\lambda x)(\bar\lambda x) < 0$. Thus, $g'(\bar\lambda) < 0$, a contradiction to $g'(\bar\lambda) \geq 0$. Therefore,

$$[\nabla V(x)]^T f(x) < 0 \qquad \text{for all} \quad x \neq 0. \qquad (3a.7)$$

By Lemma 2.1, all the rest points of $\phi_t(x_0)$ satisfy $[\nabla V(x)]^T f(x) = 0$, and,
hence, $x = 0$ is the only candidate. But if $\phi_t(x_0)$ is bounded, $\phi_t(x_0)$ must
have a limit point. Hence, $\lim_{t \to \infty} \phi_t(x_0) = 0$.   Q.E.D.

Note that to get global asymptotic stability results for bounded trajectories, all one needs to do is find a V that is monotone on bounded trajectories and assume that $E_0 = \{x \mid [\nabla V(x)]^T f(x) = 0\} = \{0\}$. This result is
important for global asymptotic stability analysis of optimal paths
generated by control problems arising in capital theory. Also, Hartman–
Olech [21] type results emerge as simple corollaries. Let us demonstrate
the power of the theorem by extracting some corollaries.

COROLLARY 3.1.   *Let $f: R^m \to R^m$. Consider the ordinary differential
equations $\dot x = f(x)$, $f(0) = 0$. If $J(x) + J^T(x)$ is negative definite for each x,
then 0 is globally asymptotically stable.*

Proof. Put $V = x^T x$. Then $\nabla V(x) = 2x$, $\nabla^2 V(x) = 2I$ where I is the $n \times n$ identity matrix. Assumption (a) becomes

$$x^T J(0)\, x < 0 \qquad \text{for all} \quad x \neq 0.$$

But this follows because

$$2x^T J(0)x = x^T[J(0) + J^T(0)]\, x < 0.$$

Assumption (b) trivially holds since $\nabla V(x) = 2x$. Assumption (c) amounts to $2xf(x) = 0$ implies $x^T(2I) f(x) = 0$ which obviously holds. Assumption (d) obviously holds because $2x^T J(x)\, x < 0$ for *all* $x \neq 0$. Thus, all bounded trajectories converge to 0, as $t \to \infty$. It is easy to use $V = x^T x$ decreasing in t in order to show that all trajectories are bounded. This ends the proof.

The following corollary is a stronger result than Hartman and Olech [21] in one way and weaker in another. We will explain the difference in more detail below.

COROLLARY 3.2. (*Mas-Colell* [31]). *Consider* $\dot{x} = f(x)$, $f(0) = 0$. *Assume that* $x^T[J(0) + J^T(0)]\, x < 0$ *for all* $x \neq 0$, *and*

$$x^T f(x) = 0 \text{ implies } x^T[J(x) + J^T(x)]\, x < 0 \qquad \text{for all} \quad x \neq 0. \qquad (3a.8)$$

Then 0 *is globally asymptotically stable.*

Proof. Let $V = x^T x$. We show that

$$\frac{dV}{dt} = 2x^T f(x) < 0 \qquad \text{for} \quad x \neq 0. \qquad (3a.9)$$

Assumptions (a–d) of the theorem are trivially verified.[3] Therefore, $dV/dt < 0$, and the rest of the proof proceeds as in Corollary 3.1.

---

[3] The condition

$$x^T f(x) < 0 \qquad \text{for} \quad x \neq 0 \qquad (i)$$

has a natural geometric interpretation when $\dot{x} = f(x)$ is a "gradient" flow; i.e., there is a "potential" $F: R^n \to R$ such that

$$\nabla F(x) = f(x) \qquad (ii)$$

for all x. A function $F: R^n \to R$ is said to be pseudoconcave at x_0 if

$$F(x_0) > F(x_1) \qquad \text{implies} \quad \nabla F(x_1)^T(x_0 - x_1) > 0. \qquad (iii)$$

But put $x_0 = 0$, assume that F is maximum at $x_0 = 0$, and note that (iii) is just

$$x_1^T f(x_1) < 0.$$

Thus, condition (i) amounts to pseudoconcavity of the potential F.

This type of result is reported in Hartman and Olech [21] and in Hartman's book [20]. In [20] and [21], 0 is assumed to be the only rest point, and it is assumed to be locally asymptotically stable. On the one hand, Mas-Colell puts the stronger assumption: $x[J(0) + J^T(0)] x < 0$ for $x \neq 0$ on the rest point. It is well known that negative real parts of the eigenvalues of $J(0)$ does not imply negative definiteness of $J(0) + J^T(0)$, but negative definiteness of $J(0) + J^T(0)$ does imply negative real parts for $J(0)$.

But on the other hand, Hartman and Olech [21] make the assumption: for all $x \neq 0$, $w^T f(x) = 0$ implies $w^T[J(x) + J^T(x)] w \leq 0$ for all vectors w. Note that Mas-Colell only assumes $x^T f(x) = 0$ implies $x^T[J(x) + J^T(x)] x < 0$. So he places the restriction on a much smaller set of w, but he requires the strong inequality. Furthermore, the proof of the Mas-Colell result is much simpler than that of Hartman and Olech.

It is possible to obtain general results of Hartman and Olech type from the theorem. For example,

COROLLARY 3.3.   *Let G be a positive definite symmetric matrix, and let 0 be the unique rest point of $\dot{x} = f(x)$. Assume that*

$$x^T[GJ(0)] x < 0 \qquad \text{for all} \quad x \neq 0,$$

and

$$x^T G f(x) = 0 \text{ implies } x^T[GJ(x)] x < 0 \qquad \text{for all} \quad x \neq 0.$$

Then $x = 0$ is globally asymptotically stable for bounded trajectories.

Proof.   Let $V(x) = x^T G x$. Then,

$$\nabla V(x) = 2Gx.$$

Also,

$$\nabla^2 V(x) = 2G.$$

The rest of the proof is now routine.

Corollary 3.3 is closely related to Hartman and Olech's [21, Theorem 2.3, p. 157] and to a theorem in Hartman's book [20, Theorem 1.4, p. 549]. Hartman and Olech also treat the case of G depending on x. We have not been able to obtain their result for nonconstant G as a special case of our theorem. Thus, their different methods of proof yield theorems that our methods presented in this section are unable to obtain. This leads us to believe that the original method of proof developed in [8] and outlined above is necessary for developing Hartman and Olech type generalizations for nonconstant G for modified Hamiltonian dynamical systems. We turn now to an application of the general theorem to modified Hamiltonian dynamical systems.

Convergence of Bounded Trajectories of MHDS

In this section, we apply the results obtained in Section 3a to MHDS systems. We will assume that the MHDS has a singularity $(\bar{q}, \bar{k})$, and rewrite it as

$$\dot{z}_1 = \rho(z_1 + \bar{q}) - H_2 z + (\bar{q}, \bar{k}) \equiv F_1(z), \qquad z \equiv (q, k) - (\bar{q}, \bar{k}),$$
$$\dot{z}_2 = H_1(z + (\bar{q}, \bar{k})) \equiv F_2(z). \tag{3b.1}$$

We may now state and prove

THEOREM 3.2. *Let*

$$Q(z) = \begin{bmatrix} H_{11}(z) & \rho/2 \ I \\ \rho/2 \ I & -H_{22}(z) \end{bmatrix} \tag{3b.2}$$

where I is the $n \times n$ identity matrix. Assume

(a) $0 = F(0)$ *is the unique rest point of $\dot{z} = F(z)$,*

(b) *for all $z \neq 0$,*

$$z_1{}^T F_2(z) + z_2{}^T F_1(z) = 0 \qquad \text{implies } z^T Q(z) \ z > 0, \tag{3b.3}$$

(c) *for all $w \neq 0$, $w^T Q(0) \ w > 0$.*

Then all trajectories that are bounded for $t \geqslant 0$ converge to 0 as $t \to \infty$.

Proof. Let $V = z^T A z$ where

$$A = - \begin{bmatrix} 0 & I \\ I & 0 \end{bmatrix}$$

where I is the $n \times n$ identity matrix. Note that $z^T A z = -2z_1{}^T z_2$. Since $\nabla^2 V(0) = A + A^T = 2A$ and $(w^T A)^T (J(0) \ w) = -w^T Q(0) \ w$, we have that (c) implies (a) of Theorem 3.1. Also $[\nabla V(z)]^T = z^T(A + A^T) = 2z^T A$, and, hence, $\nabla V(0) = 0$. Hence, (b) of Theorem 3.1 follows. Now (c) of Theorem 3.1 amounts to $[\nabla V(z)]^T F(z) \equiv 2z^T AF(z) = 0$ implies $z^T \nabla^2 V(z) \ F(z) \equiv 2z^T AF(z) = 0$, which is trivially true. Furthermore, (d) amounts to

$$2z^T AF(z) = 0 \text{ implies } 2(z^T A) \ J(z) \ z > 0. \tag{3b.4}$$

But (3b.4) is identical to (3b.3), as an easy calculation will immediately show. Thus, $\dot{V} < 0$ except at the rest point 0. The rest of the proof is routine by now.   Q.E.D.

The proof of Theorem 3.2 also yields the result that the Lyapunov function $z_1^T z_2 = (q - \bar{q})^T (k - \bar{k})$ is monotonically increasing along trajectories. Theorem 3.2 is a "local" sufficient condition for the hypothesis of the Cass and Shell stability theorem to hold. This is so because Theorem 3.2 gives conditions for the trajectory derivative of $V = z_1^T z_2$ to be positive for all $z \neq 0$, and that is the Cass and Shell[4] hypothesis.

Sufficient conditions (of local form such as our Q condition of Theorem 3.3) for positive trajectory derivative are useful for computations. Applications and economic interpretations of "local" conditions for stability to the adjustment cost literature are discussed in [10], which will be appearing in the Vienna 1974 Conference volume.

There is a neat sufficient condition for the positive definiteness of Q. If H is convexo–concave, the matrix Q is clearly positive semidefinite for $\rho = 0$. Furthermore, if the minimum eigenvalue of H_{11} is larger than α and the maximum eigenvalue of H_{22} is less than $-\beta$ where $\alpha\beta > \rho^2/4$, then Q is positive definite (cf. Footnote 1, Section 1). The hypothesis $\alpha\beta > \rho^2/4$ is the basic curvature assumption in Rockafellar's [38] analysis.

The positive definiteness of Q is also related to the Burmeister and Turnovsky [13] regularity condition.[5] Let $[\bar{q}(\rho), \bar{k}(\rho)]$ be the steady state associated with ρ. It solves

$$0 = \rho q - H_2(q, k)$$
$$0 = H_1(q, k). \tag{i}$$

---

[4] It is worth pointing out here that the hypothesis

$$\dot{V}(z) > 0 \qquad \text{for} \quad z \neq 0 \tag{a}$$

has a geometric interpretation for the case $\rho = 0$. Viz., it implies pseudoconvexity, pseudoconcavity at $(\bar{q}, \bar{k})$ of $H(q, k)$ in q, k respectively. For the special case

$$H(q, k) = f_1(q) + f_2(k),$$

inequality (a) is equivalent to pseudoconcavity at $(\bar{q}, \bar{k})$ of

$$G(q, k) \equiv -f_1(q) + f_2(k).$$

These statements may be easily checked by referring to the definition of pseudoconcavity in Mangasarian [29, p. 147].

[5] We thank Ed Burmeister for this observation.

Differentiate (i) w.r.t. ρ to obtain

$$0 = \bar{q} + \rho\bar{q}' - H_{21}\bar{q}' - H_{22}\bar{k}',$$

$$0 = H_{11}\bar{q}' + H_{12}\bar{k}',$$

where

$$(\bar{q}', \bar{k}') = \left(\frac{d\bar{q}}{d\rho}, \frac{d\bar{k}}{d\rho}\right).$$

Rewrite this as

$$-\begin{pmatrix}\bar{q}\\0\end{pmatrix} = \begin{bmatrix}\rho & -H_{21} & -H_{22}\\ & H_{11} & H_{12}\end{bmatrix}\begin{pmatrix}\bar{q}'\\\bar{k}'\end{pmatrix}.$$

Multiply both sides of this by the row vector $(\bar{k}', \bar{q}')$ to get

$$-\bar{q}^T\bar{k}' = (\bar{k}', \bar{q}')\begin{bmatrix}\rho & -H_{21} & -H_{22}\\ & H_{11} & H_{12}\end{bmatrix}\begin{pmatrix}\bar{q}'\\\bar{k}'\end{pmatrix}$$

$$= (\bar{q}', \bar{k}')^T Q[\bar{q}(\rho), \bar{k}(\rho)](\bar{q}', \bar{k}').$$

But the quantity

$$\Theta = \bar{q}^T\bar{k}'$$

is the Burmeister–Turnovsky [13] "regularity" quantity. Burmeister and Turnovsky use the quantity Θ as an aggregate measure of capital deepening response. Thus, the positive definiteness of Q in the directions $(\bar{q}', \bar{k}')$ as ρ varies is equivalent to capital deepening response in the Burmeister–Turnovsky sense for each value of ρ.

4. A More General Result

In this section, we present a result, Theorem 4.2 below, on convergence of bounded trajectories of MHDS that is related to a theorem of Hartman and Olech [21, p. 549]. We start by presenting a sketch of the proof of a result, Theorem 4.1, that is, in fact, almost contained in Theorem 3.2. The method of proof, however, is the same as the one used in [8] to prove the more general result of Theorem 4.2. The reader is referred to [8] for a complete proof. Furthermore, Corollary 4.1 below gives us a nice geometric interpretation of our hypothesis in terms of quasi-convexity and quasi-concavity of the Hamiltonian function.

A Sketch of the Proof of the Hartman–Olech Type of Result for MHDS

Let us reconsider the system (3b.1),

$$\dot{z}_1 = F_1(z),$$

$$\dot{z}_2 = F_2(z).$$

Put

$$F(z) = [F_1(z), F_2(z)] \tag{4.1}$$

Assume $F(0) = 0$, $F(z) \neq 0$ for $z \neq 0$, $F \in C^1$. Let $\phi_t(z_0)$ be the solution of (4.1) given z_0; let W_s be the stable manifold of (4.1), i.e., $W_s = \{\bar{z}_0 \mid \phi_t(\bar{z}_0) \to 0, t \to \infty\}$; and let Λ be the bounded manifold of (4.1), i.e., $\Lambda = \{\bar{z}_0 \mid$ there is $M > 0$ such that for all $t \geq 0 \, \| \phi_t(\bar{z}_0)\| \leq M\}$. Assume that for each $z_{20} \in R^n$ there is a unique z_{10} such that $(z_{10}, z_{20}) \in \Lambda$. Write

$$z_{10} = g(z_{20}) \tag{4.2}$$

for this functional relation, and assume that g is differentiable.[6] (We can get by with less, but why mess up the picture with generality at this stage?) We are after sufficient conditions to guarantee that $\phi_t[\, g(z_{20}), z_{20}] \to 0$, $t \to \infty$ for all $z_{20} \in R^n$.

We could just apply the Hartman–Olech result to the "reduced form"

$$\dot{z}_2 = F_2[\, g(z_2), z_2], \tag{4.3}$$

but this requires knowledge of $\partial g/\partial z_2$. In most problems, not much is known about g other than its existence and differentiability and other general properties. In some problems g is badly behaved, but we shall ignore those here. Thus, we shall formulate a sufficient condition involving $\partial F/\partial z$, alone.

Let us proceed in a way that uncovers a "natural" set of sufficient conditions for the global asymptotic stability of (4.1) on bounded trajectories. Assume the solution $z_2 = 0_2$ is locally asymptotically stable for (4.3). (Here $F_2[\, g(0_2), 0_2] = 0_2$.) This means that there is an open neighborhood $N_2(0_2) \subseteq R^n$ such that $z_{20} \in N_2$ implies $\phi_t[\, g(z_{20}), z_{20}] \to 0$, $t \to \infty$. Let $A_2(0_2) = \{z_{20} \mid \phi_t[\, g(z_{20}), z_{20}] \to 0, t \to \infty\}$. If $A_2(0_2)$ is the whole of R^n, we have global asymptotic stability. So suppose that z_{20} is in the boundary of $A_2(0_2)$. Let $u_2 \in R^n$ have unit norm. Consider the vector $z_0(p, u_2) \equiv [\, g(z_{20} + pu_2), z_{20} + pu_2], p \in [0, \beta]$. Put $y(t, p) \equiv \phi_t[z_0(p, u_2)]$. Let $y_p(t, p) \equiv \partial \phi_t[z_0(p, u_2)]/\partial p$. Consider the following differential equation (let us drop transpose notation except that needed for clarity).

$$T_p \equiv \frac{dT}{dp} = -\frac{y_{1p}F_2[\, y(T, p)] + y_{2p}F_1[\, y(T, p)]}{2F_1[\, y(T, p)]\, F_2[\, y(T, p)]} \equiv h(T, p),$$
$$T(0, q) = q. \tag{4.4}$$

---

[6] The function g is the derivative of the value function. If the value is concave, then g will be differentiable almost everywhere [24, p. 405].

Let $y[T(p, q), p] \equiv x(q, p)$ be a solution (if a solution exists), and denote $(\partial/\partial p) x(q, p)$ by x_p. Note that

$$x_p = \frac{\partial y}{\partial T} T_p + y_p = F[x(q, p)] T_p + y_p[T(p, q), p]. \qquad (4.5)$$

Also note that

$$x_{1p}F_2[x(q, p)] + x_{2p}F_1[x(q, p)] = 0. \qquad (4.6)$$

The latter follows from

$$(F_1 T_p + y_{1p}) F_2 + (F_2 T_p + y_{2p}) F_1$$
$$= 2T_p F_1 F_2 + y_{1p}F_2 + y_{2p}F_1 = 0. \qquad (4.7)$$

But (4.7) is identical to (4.4).

We will call the system of trajectories satisfying (4.6) *Hamiltonian orthogonal* trajectories. They are not the same kind of orthogonal trajectories as in the original Hartman–Olech result. We shall see, however, that it is natural to construct trajectories of type (4.6) for our type of problem.

Consider

$$w(q, p) \equiv x_{1p}(q, p) \cdot x_{2p}(q, p). \qquad (4.8)$$

The object w is natural to look at in light of our previous results and the Hartman–Olech technique.

$$\frac{\partial w}{\partial q} = T_{pq}[F_1 x_{2p} + F_2 x_{1p}] + T_q x_p Q x_p$$
$$= T_q x_p Q x_p. \qquad (4.9)$$

The last follows from the definition of Hamiltonian orthogonal trajectories, Eq. (4.6). The reader will recall

$$Q(x) \equiv \begin{bmatrix} H_{11}(x) & \rho/2 \, I_n \\ \rho/2 \, I_n & -H_{22}(x) \end{bmatrix}, \qquad x = x(q, p),$$

$$x_q = F(x) T_q, \qquad x_{pq} = T_{pq}F(x) + T_q J(x) x_p, \qquad T_q > 0. \qquad (4.10)$$

Notice here that both the "Lyapunov" function (4.8) and the method of constructing the "transverse" trajectories (4.4) are different from Hartman–Olech. The method of proof is also different.

A theorem may now be stated.

THEOREM 4.1. *Assume that* (a) $F \in C^1$, (b) $F(0) = 0$, $F(z) \neq 0$ *for* $z \neq 0$, (c) $z_2 = 0_2$ *is a locally asymptotically stable solution of*

$\dot{z}_2 = F_2[\,g(z_2), z_2]$, and (d) *for all bounded trajectories* $z(t)$, *for all vectors* $c \in R^{2n}$ *such that* $\| c \| = 1$, $c = (c_1, c_2)$, $c_1 = J_g c_2$ *where* $J_g = g'(z_2)$, $c_1 F_2[z(t)] + c_2 F_1[z(t)] = 0$ *hold, we have*

$$c^T Q[z(t)]\, c > 0. \tag{4.11}$$

Then $z_2 = 0_2$ *is GAS for* $\dot{z}_2 = F_2[\,g(z_2), z_2]$. *I.e., all bounded trajectories of* $\dot{z} = f(z)$ *converge to* 0 *as* $t \to \infty$.

The reader should notice that although in the hypothesis (d) of the theorem we used information on the Jacobian matrix of g, we could have stated the stronger hypothesis that for all $z \in R^{2n}$, for all $c \in R^{2n}$ with $\| c \| = 1$, $c_1^T F_2[z(t)] + c_2^T F_1[z(t)] = 0$ implies $c^T Q[z(t)]\, c > 0$, which does not use any properties of J_g. The reason Theorem 4.1 is stated in the form above is that one can obtain the following corollary.

COROLLARY 4.1. *Given an MHDS like* (3b.1) *under hypotheses* (a)–(c) *of Theorem* 4.1, *suppose* J_g *is symmetric and that the Hamiltonian function satisfies for all* $z = (\,g(z_2), z_2)$

(i) $c_1^T H_{11}(z)\, c_1 > \alpha \mid c_1 \mid^2$ *for all* $c_1 \neq 0$ *such that* $c_1^T H_1(z) = 0$,
(ii) $c_2^T[-H_{22}(z)]\, c_2 > \beta \mid c_2 \mid^2$ *for all* $c_2 \neq 0$ *such that* $c_2^T[H_2(z) - \rho(z_1 + \bar{q})] = 0$ *for some* $(\alpha, \beta) \in R^2$ *with* $\alpha\beta \geqslant \rho^2/4$.

Then global asymptotic stability of bounded trajectories holds.

Proof. Since in Theorem 4.1, $z(t)$ is a bounded trajectory and (4.2) holds, we have $F_1(z) \equiv \rho(z_1 + \bar{q}) - H_2(z + (\bar{q}, \bar{k})) = J_g F_2(z) \equiv J_g H_1(z + (\bar{q}, \bar{k}))$. Since $c_1 = J_g c_2$, $c_1^T F_2[z(t)] + c_2^T F_1[z(t)] = 0$ iff $(J_g c_2)^T F_2 + c_2^T J_g F_2 = 0$. Hence, (d) of Theorem 4.1 holds iff $c_2^T F_1 = c_1^T F_2 = 0$. By (i) and (ii), $c^T Q[z(t)]\, c > 0$ for all c satisfying (d) of Theorem 4.1. Hence, GAS must hold.

Remark 3.   In Corollary 4.1, only the fact that J_g is symmetric was used. As in Remark 1 of Section 2, if a value function R exists and is C^2, $J_g = R''$, and, hence, symmetric.

Remark 4.   For $\rho = 0$, (i) and (ii) can be interpreted as quasiconcavity of the Hamiltonian function H. (The Hamiltonian is in fact, always a convex function of q.) Therefore, the equivalent bordered matrix conditions so beloved by economists may be written down in place of (i) and (ii). This generalizes the result of Rockafellar [36] on the GAS of convexo-concave Hamiltonians to the quasi-convex-quasi-concave case.

Remark 5.   Given a function $F: R^n \to R$ we will say that F is α-quasi-convex at x if for any $c \neq 0$, $c^T Df(x) = 0$ implies $c^T D^2 f(x)\, c > \alpha \mid c \mid^2$. Define α-quasi-concavity in the obvious way. Inequality (i) of Corollary 4.1

simply says that the Hamiltonian is α-quasi-convex in z_1. Let $\tilde{H}(z) = H(z + (\bar{q}, \bar{k})) - \rho(z_1 + \bar{q})^T z_2$. Then (ii) says that $\tilde{H}$ is β-quasi-concave in z_2. Note that ρ introduces a "distortion" that vanishes at $\rho = 0$.

The general result of [8] may now be stated. Let $G: R^{2n} \to M[R^{2n}, R^{2n}]$ (the set of all $2n \times 2n$ real matrices) be such that $G(z)$ is positive definite for all z. In what follows, $G(z)$ will be assumed to be continuously differentiable. Let

$$j \equiv \begin{bmatrix} 0 & I_n \\ I_n & 0 \end{bmatrix}$$

where I_n is the $n \times n$ identity matrix. Put $\alpha(z) \equiv jG + (jG)^T$. Let $D(z) \equiv [(\alpha(z) J(z))^T + (\alpha(z) J(z)] + \alpha'(z)$ where $\alpha'(z) \equiv \sum_{r=1}^{2n} (\partial\alpha/\partial z_r) F_r$, the "trajectory" derivative of the matrix $\alpha(z)$. Now consider the system

$$\dot{z} = F(z). \tag{4.12}$$

We may now state the following theorem.

THEOREM 4.2. *Suppose that (4.12) obeys assumptions*

(a)   0 *is the unique rest point of* (4.12),

(b)   0 *is LAS in the sense that the linearization of* $\dot{z}_2 = F_2[g(z_2), z_2]$ *at* $z_2 = 0$ *has all eigenvalues with negative real parts,*

(c)   *Let K be a compact subset of the bounded manifold. Then,* $\bigcup_{z \in K} \bigcup_{t \geqslant 0} \phi_t(z)$ *is bounded, and, furthermore, the following basic property holds.*

ASSUMPTION 1.   *For all $w \in R^{2n}$, $w \neq 0$ for all $z \neq 0$, we have*

$$w^T \alpha(z) F(z) = 0 \tag{4.13}$$

implies

$$w^T D(z) w > 0. \tag{4.14}$$

Then all trajectories in the bounded manifold converge to 0 as $t \to \infty$.

The proof of this theorem is long and involved, and is done in a sequence of lemmas. See [8] for the proof.

Hartman and Olech's basic result [21, Theorem 14.1] is closely related to our theorem. To see this, put $\alpha(z) = -2G(z)$. Assumption 1 then becomes Hartman and Olech's (H–0) assumption.

Our theorem would not be interesting if all it did was restate Hartman and Olech. It's interest lies in applicability to systems where the stable manifold $W(W \equiv \{z_0 \mid \phi_t(z_0) \to 0, t \to \infty\})$ *is not all of* R^{2n}. In particular, the important special case of MHDS that we are interested in generates systems where W is n-dimensional.

For example, let $G(z) \equiv I_{2n}$, the $2n \times 2n$ identity matrix. Assumption 1 becomes

$$w^T j F(z) = 0 \text{ implies } w^T[jJ(z) + j^T(z)j] w > 0. \qquad (4.15)$$

Note that

$$w^T[jJ(z) + J^T(z)j] w = 2w^T Q(z) w \qquad (4.16)$$

where

$$Q(z) = \begin{bmatrix} H_{11}(z) & \rho/2\, I_n \\ \rho/2\, I_n & -H_{22}(z) \end{bmatrix}. \qquad (4.17)$$

5. Suggestions For Future Research

We have made in this paper only small progress toward providing a comprehensive analysis of GAS of optimal controls generated by MHDS's. Several topics for future research follow.

1.   A more general notion of long-run behavior needs to be formulated. There is really no economic reason to rule out limit cycles, for example. It is, therefore, necessary to build a theory that allows more general limit sets than rest points, and find sufficient conditions on preferences and technology for a "minimal" limit set to be stable in some sense.

2.   Both our results and the CSR results are "small ρ" theorems. I.e., the sufficient conditions for GAS are most likely to hold when ρ is small. But the Cass–Koopmans' one good model is GAS independently of the size of ρ. Intuition suggests that if we perturb such an economy slightly that it will still be GAS. This suggests development of a notion of block dominant diagonal for MHDS's to parallel the development of dominant diagonal notions in the study of the Walrasian tâtonnement [34]. An initial rather unsuccessful attempt to do this is reported in [9]. Perhaps a more fruitful approach will build on Pearce's notion of block dominance.

3.   It is natural to extend our results and the CSR results to uncertainty. Some results in this area are reported in [7], but much more remains to be done. There is nothing done in the area of extending this work to continuous time stochastic processes,[7] in the nonlinear case.

---

[7] Magill [45], of Indiana University's Department of Economics, has obtained results for linear quadratic stochastic optimal control problems.

4. One of the original motivations for introducing positive definite matrices, $G(x)$, into the Hartman–Olech framework was that this is needed to obtain their result. Consider the differential equations

$$\dot{x} = f(x), f(0) = 0.$$

Let

$$\Gamma(x) = \underset{1 \leqslant i < j \leqslant n}{\text{maximum}} \{\lambda_i(x) + \lambda_j(x)\}$$

where $\lambda_r(x)$ is an eigenvalue of the symmetric matrix $(J^T(x) + J(x))/2$.

THEOREM (Hartman and Olech [21, p. 549]).   *If $\Gamma(x) \leqslant 0$ for all $x \neq 0$ and 0 is LAS, then 0 is GAS.*

See page 549 of Hartman [20] in order to be convinced that matrices of the form $G(x) = p(x) I_n$, $p(x) > 0$ for all x, $p: R^n \to R$ must be introduced into the basic Hartman and Olech method in order to obtain the above theorem. The above theorem is important because Γ is an easy quantity to interpret.

Some analog of the above theorem may exist for MHDS, but we have been unable to obtain it.

5. Burmeister and Graham [12] have exhibited a class of models where GAS obtains under conditions not sensitive to the size of ρ. Furthermore, their GAS models do not satisfy either the CSR hypotheses or our hypotheses. Therefore, a general stability hypothesis that covers the one good model, the Burmeister–Graham models and the CSR–Brock–Scheinkman models, remains to be developed. Further evidence to support this proposition is the Ryder–Heal [39] experience. Some of their GAS results are not dependent on the size of ρ. Recent results reported in [6] on adjustment cost models (see [10] for references to the adjustment cost literature) indicate the existence of a large class of models where the CSR–Brock–Scheinkman "small ρ" conditions do not hold, but GAS does hold. This class is basically the class where the Lyapunov function $V = k^T H_{qq}^{-1} k$ together with the concavity of the value function yields $\dot{V} < 0$. The reader is referred to [6] for details.

6. Araujo and Scheinkman [1] obtain conditions for GAS for discrete time models that are independent of the discount rate, except around the steady state.

These results seem to indicate that there exist many other interesting stability theorems to be developed.

REFERENCES

1. A. ARAUJO AND J. SCHEINKMAN, Smoothness, Comparative Dynamics and the Turnpike Property, unpublished manuscript, February 1975.
2. K. ARROW, D. BLOCK, AND L. HURWICZ, On the stability of the competitive equilibrium, II, *Econometrica* **27** (1959), 82–109.
3. K. ARROW AND L. HURWICZ, On the stability of the competitive equilibrium, I, *Econometrica* **26** (1958), 522–552.
4. W. A. BROCK, On existence of weakly maximal programmes in a multisector economy, *Rev. Econ. Stud.* **37** (1970).
5. W. A. BROCK, Some results on the uniqueness of steady states in multisector models of optimum growth when future utilities are discounted, *Int. Econ. Rev.* **14** (1973).
6. W. A. BROCK AND J. SCHEINKMAN, "The Global Asymptotic Stability of Optimal Control with Applications to Dynamic Economic Theory," University of Chicago, May 1975.
7. W. BROCK AND M. MAJUMDAR, "Asymptotic Stability Results for Multisector Models of Optimal Growth When Future Utilities are Discounted," Cornell University, Department of Economics, Discussion Paper; University of Chicago, Working Paper, February, 1975.
8. W. BROCK AND J. SCHEINKMAN, "Some Results on Global Asymptotic Stability of Control Systems," Report 7422, Center for Mathematical Studies in Business and Economics, University of Chicago, May, 1974.
9. W. BROCK AND J. SCHEINKMAN, "Global Asymptotic Stability of Optimal Control Systems with Applications to the Theory of Economic Growth," Report 7426, Center for Mathematical Studies in Business and Economics, University of Chicago, May 1974.
10. W. BROCK AND J. SCHEINKMAN, "On The Long Run Behavior of a Competitive Firm," to appear in the 1974 Vienna Conference volume on equilibrium and disequilibrium in economic theory.
11. E. BURMEISTER AND R. DOBELL, "Mathematical Theories of Economic Growth" Macmillan, New York, 1970.
12. E. BURMEISTER AND D. GRAHAM, "Price Expectations and Stability in Descriptive and Optimally Controlled Macro-Economic Models," J.E.E. Conference Publication No. 101, Institute of Electrical Engineers, London, England, 1973.
13. E. BURMEISTER AND S. TURNOVSKY, Capital deepening response in an economy with heterogeneous capital goods, *Amer. Econ. Rev.* **62** (1972), 842–853.
14. D. CASS, Optimum growth in an aggregative model of capital accumulation, *Rev. Econ. Stud.* **32** (1965), 233–240.
15. D. CASS, Duality: a symmetric approach from the economist's vantage point, *J. Econ. Theory* **7**, 272–295.
16. D. CASS AND K. SHELL, The structure and stability of competitive dynamical systems, *J. Econ. Theory* **12** (1976), 31–70.   Reprinted as Essay III in this volume.
17. E. CODDINGTON AND N. LEVINSON, "Theory of Ordinary Differential Equations," McGraw Hill, New York, 1955.
18. D. GALE, On optimal development in a multisector economy, *Rev. Econ. Stud.* **34** (1967), 1–18.
19. P. HARTMAN, On stability in the large for systems of ordinary differential equations, *Can. J. Math.* **13** (1961), 480–492.

20. P. HARTMAN, "Ordinary Differential Equations," John Wiley and Sons, New York, 1964.

21. P. HARTMAN AND C. OLECH, On global asymptotic stability of solutions of ordinary differential equations, *Trans. Amer. Math. Soc.* **104** (1962), 154–178.

22. M. HESTENES, "Calculus of Variations and Optimal Control Theory," John Wiley and Sons, New York, 1966.

23. M. HIRSH AND C. PUGH, Stable manifolds and hyperbolic sets, *in* "Global Analysis" (S. Chern and S. Smale, Eds.), Proceedings of Symposia in Pure Mathematica, Vol. XIV, Amer, Math. Soc., Providence, Rhode Island, 1970.

24. S. KARLIN, "Mathematical Methods and Theory in Games, Programming and Economics," Vol. 1, Addison Wesley, Reading, Mass., 1959.

25. T. KOOPMANS, On the concept of optimal economic growth, *Pontiface Academiae Scientiarum Scripta Varia*, 225–300.

26. M. KURZ, Optimal economic growth and wealth effects, *Int. Econ. Rev.* **9** (1968).

27. M. KURZ, The general instability of a class of competitive growth processes, *Rev. Econ. Stud.* **35** (1968), 155–174.

28. D. LEVHARI AND N. LEVIATAN, On stability in the saddle point sense, *J. Econ. Theory* **4** (1972).

29. O. MANGASARIAN, "Non-Linear Programming," McGraw Hill, New York, 1969.

30. L. MARKUS AND H. YAMABE, Global stability criteria for differential systems, *Osaka Math. J.* **12** (1960), 305–317.

31. A. MAS-COLELL, private communication, winter, 1974.

32. D. McFADDEN, The evaluation of development programs, *Rev. Econ. Stud.* **34** (1967), 25–50.

33. L. W. McKENZIE, Accumulation programs of maximal utility and the von Neumann facet, *in* "Value Capital and Growth, Papers in Honor of Sir John Hicks" (Wolfe, Ed.), Edinburgh Univ. Press, Edinburgh, 1968.

34. L. W. McKENZIE, Matrices with dominant diagonal and economic theory, *in* "Mathematical Methods in the Social Sciences, (Arrow, Karlin, and Suppes, Eds.), Stanford Univ. Press, Stanford, Calif., 1959.

35. L. S. PONTRIAGIN *et al.*, "The Mathematical Theory of Optimal Processes," Interscience, New York, 1962.

36. T. ROCKAFELLAR, Generalized Hamiltonian equations for convex problems of Lagrange, *Pacific J. Math.* **33** (1970), 411–427.

37. T. ROCKAFELLAR, Saddle points of Hamiltonian systems in convex problems of Lagrange, *J. Optimization Theory Appl.* **12**, No. 4 (1973).

38. T. ROCKAFELLAR, Saddle points of Hamiltonian systems in convex Lagrange problems having a nonzero discount rate, *J. Econ. Theory* **12** (1976), 71–113. Reprinted as Essay IV in this volume.

39. H. RYDER AND G. HEAL, Optimal growth with intertemporally dependent preferences, *Rev. Econ. Stud.* **40**, 1–31.

40. P. SAMUELSON, "Foundations of Economic Analysis," Harvard Univ. Press, Cambridge, Mass., 1947.

41. P. SAMUELSON, The general saddle point property of optimal control motions, *J. Econ. Theory* **5** (1972).

42. J. A. SCHEINKMAN, "On Optimal Steady States of *n*-Sector Growth Models When Utility is Discounted," *J. Econ. Theory* **12** (1976), 11–30. Reprinted as Essay II in this volume.

43. H. UZAWA, Optimal growth in a two-sector model of capital accumulation, *Rev. Econ. Stud.* **31** (1964), 1–24.

44. WILLIAMSON, "Lebesque Integration," Holt, Rinehard, and Winston, New York, 1962.
45. M. J. P. MAGILL, A local analysis of n-sector capital accumulation under uncertainty, presented at European Meeting of the Econometric Society, Grenoble, France, September 3–6, 1974.
46. W. BROCK AND E. BURMEISTER, Regular economies and conditions for uniqueness of steady states in optimal multi-sector economic models, *Internat. Econ. Rev.* (February 1976).
47. L. BENVENISTE AND J. SCHEINKMAN, "Differentiable Value Functions in Concave Dynamic Optimization Problems," Report 7549, Center for Mathematical Studies in Business and Economics, The University of Chicago, November 1975.

ESSAY VIII

A Growth Property in Concave–Convex Hamiltonian Systems

R. T. ROCKAFELLAR*

The analysis of the stability of Hamiltonian dynamical systems in various economic models depends on the "curvature" of the Hamiltonian function at a rest point of the system, or equivalently, on growth properties involving gradients or subgradients. The purpose of this note is to establish a general property pointing in particular to a simplification of conditions assumed by Cass and Shell [1].

In this context, a Hamiltonian $H: R^n \times R^n \to [-\infty, +\infty]$ is an extended-real-valued function such that $H(k, Q)$ is concave in k and convex in Q. The dynamical system of interest in the case of a constant discount rate ρ is

$$\dot{k} \in \partial_Q H(k, Q), \quad -\dot{Q} + \rho \dot{Q} \in \partial_k H(k, Q) \tag{1}$$

where $\partial_Q H$ and $\partial_k H$ are the subdifferentials [2] with respect to Q and k (or if differentiability is present, the gradients), and a rest point is a pair, (k^*, Q^*) satisfying

$$0 \in \partial_Q H(k^*, Q^*), \quad \rho Q^* \in \partial_k H(k^*, Q^*). \tag{2}$$

Particular attention is directed to determining the existence of solutions to (1) satisfying

$$k(0) = \bar{k} \quad \text{and} \quad \lim_{t \to \infty} e^{-\rho t}(k(t) - k^*) \cdot (Q(t) - Q^*) = 0, \tag{3}$$

and whether such a solution is stable in the sense of converging to (k^*, Q^*) as $t \to +\infty$.

The author in [3] and [4] developed results on existence and stability on the basis of assuming H was strictly or strongly convex–concave in a neighborhood of (2). Cass and Shell [1] showed under different assumptions, to be considered below, that (1) and (3) imply convergence of

* This research was supported in part by the Air Force Office of Scientific Research, Air Force Systems Command, USAF, under AFOSR grant number 72-2269 at the University of Washington.

191

$k(t)$ to k^*. Brock and Scheinkman [5] obtained convergence of $(k(t), Q(t))$ to (k^*, Q^*) under more differentiability but less convexity. Gaines [6] proved the existence of solutions to (1), (3), using a different approach and different growth assumptions on H than the author.

In the paper of Cass and Shell, a certain global growth property of H is implicit in the conditions they impose on the underlying technology. For instance, it is a consequence of their model that solutions to (1) satisfy a universal bound $\| k(t) \| \leq B$. We wish to discuss not this aspect of their work, but their conditions involving the function

$$\Phi(k, Q) = \inf\{-R \cdot (k - k^*) + z \cdot (Q - Q^*) + \rho Q^* \cdot (k - k^*) |$$
$$\times \ R \in \partial_k H(k, Q), z \in \partial_Q H(k, 0)\}. \tag{4}$$

(where inf $\varnothing = +\infty$). Clearly $\Phi(k^*, Q^*) = 0$. It is known that Φ is everywhere nonnegative by virtue of the concavity–convexity of H (see below).

The crucial condition invoked by Cass and Shell can be stated as follows:

(S) For every $\epsilon > 0$ there exists $\delta > 0$ such that

$$\| k - k^* \| > \epsilon \Rightarrow \Phi(k, Q) + \rho(k - k^*) \cdot (Q - Q^*) > \delta.$$

We shall establish that (S) can be expressed equivalently in the apparently weaker forms in Theorem 1 below. For this we need the harmless technical assumption that H is *closed* in the sense of [2, Section 34]. (This is always true for H arising from an economic model. A direct *sufficient* condition is that $H < +\infty$ everywhere and $H(k, Q)$ is upper semicontinuous in k.)

·THEOREM 1. *Suppose H is finite on a neighborhood of (k^*, Q^*) and closed.*

(a) *If $\rho = 0$, (S) holds if merely $\Phi(k, Q) > 0$ for all (k, Q) $\neq (k^*, Q^*)$.*

(b) *If $\rho \neq 0$, (S) holds if for every (k', Q') with $k' \cdot Q' \leq 0$ the function*

$$\varphi(t) = \Phi(k^* + tk', Q^* + tQ') + \rho t^2 k' \cdot Q'$$

satisfies $\varphi(t) > 0$ for all $t > 0$ and

$$\liminf_{t \to \infty} \varphi(t) > 0.$$

Theorem 1 will be derived from a more general result. Consider an arbitrary multifunction $A: R^N \to R^N$ and any pair x^*, y^* such that $y^* \in A(x^*)$. Define

$$\Phi(x) = \inf\{(x - x^*) \cdot (y - y^*) | \ y \in A(x)\}. \tag{5}$$

The case above corresponds to $x = (k, Q) \in R^n \times R^n$,

$$A(k, Q) = \{(-R, z) \mid R \in \partial_k H(k, Q), z \in \partial_Q H(k, Q)\}, \tag{6}$$

$$x^* = (k^*, Q^*), \quad y^* = (\rho Q^*, 0). \tag{7}$$

One says in general that A is *monotone* if

$$y_i \in A(x_i) \quad \text{for } i = 0, 1, \text{ implies } (x_1 - x_0) \cdot (y_1 - y_0) \geqslant 0. \tag{8}$$

It is *maximal monotone* if it is monotone and its graph

$$G(A) = \{(x, y) \in R^N \times R^N \mid y \in A(x)\}$$

is not properly contained in the graph of any other monotone $A' : R^N \to R^N$. The *effective domain* of A is

$$D(A) = \{x \mid A(x) \neq \varnothing\}.$$

The connection with monotonicity and the present context is the following.

THEOREM 2 [7]. *If A is given by (6) for a closed concave–convex function H which is finite on a neighborhood of a point (k^*, Q^*), then A is maximal monotone and $(k^*, Q^*) \in \text{int } D(A)$.*

THEOREM 3. *Let $A : R^N \to R^N$ be an arbitrary maximal monotone multifunction and let Φ be defined by (5) for any x^* and y^* satisfying $x^* \in \text{int } D(A)$ and $y^* \in A(x^*)$. Then the inf in (5) is always attained, and Φ is an everywhere lower semicontinuous function with*

$$\Phi(x) \geqslant \Phi(x^*) = 0 \quad \text{for all } x.$$

Moreover, the expression $\Phi(x^* + sx')/s$ is for any x' nondecreasing as a function of $s > 0$.
In particular, the function

$$\theta(s) = (1/s) \min\{\Phi(x) \mid \|x - x^*\| = s\}, \quad s > 0.$$

is nonnegative, lower semicontinuous, nondecreasing, and

$$\Phi(x) \geqslant \theta(\|x - x^*\|) \|x - x^*\| \quad \text{for all } x \neq x^*. \tag{10}$$

Proof. Consider two values $s_1 > s_2 > 0$ and any $y_i \in A(x^* + s_i x')$, $i = 1, 2$. The monotonicity of A implies

$$0 \leqslant [(x^* + s_1 x') - (x^* + s_2 x')] \cdot (y_1 - y_2)$$
$$= (s_1 - s_2) x' \cdot (y_1 - y_2)$$
$$= (s_1 - s_2)[s_1^{-1}((x^* + s_1 x') - x^*) \cdot (y_1 - y^*)$$
$$\quad - s_2^{-1}((x^* + s_2 x') - x^*) \cdot (y_2 - y^*),$$

and consequently, since the y_i are arbitrary,

$$0 \leqslant (s_1 - s_2)[s_1^{-1}\Phi(x^* + s_1 x') - s_2^{-1}\Phi(x^* + s_2 x')].$$

Thus $s^{-1}\Phi(x^* + sx')$ is nondecreasing in $s > 0$ as claimed.

The maximal monotonicity of A is known [8] to imply that int $D(A)$ is convex and (since int $D(A)$ is nonempty by hypothesis),

$$D(A) \subset \text{cl int } D(A). \tag{11}$$

Furthermore A is compact-valued and upper semicontinuous on int $D(A)$ (cf. [8]). Therefore, Φ is lower semicontinuous on int $D(A)$ and the inf in (5) is attained there.

Consider now a noninterior point $\bar{x}$ of $D(A)$. By (11) and the convexity of int $D(A)$ we have $x^* + s(\bar{x} - x^*) \in \text{int } D(A)$ for $0 \leqslant s < 1$. In view of this and the monotonicity of $\Phi(x^* + sx')/s$ in $s > 0$ for all x', the global lower semicontinuity of Φ will follow if we show that the restriction of Φ to the line

$$L = \{x^* + \lambda(\bar{x} - x^*) | -\infty < \lambda < +\infty\}$$

is lower semicontinuous at $\bar{x}$. Let

$$M = \{u \mid u(\bar{x} - x^*) = 0\},$$

i.e., M is the $N - 1$ dimensional subspace of R^N orthogonal to L. Define

$$
\begin{aligned}
A_0(x) &= M && \text{if } x \in L \\
&= \varnothing && \text{if } x \notin L \\
A_1(x) &= (A + A_0)(x) = A_0(x) + M && \text{if } x \in L \\
&= \varnothing && \text{if } x \notin L.
\end{aligned}
$$

The multifunction A_0 is trivially maximal monotone. Therefore, A_1 is maximal monotone, because $A_1 = A + A_0$ and $D(A_0) \cap \text{int } D(A) \neq \varnothing$ [9]. In particular $A_1(x)$ is closed for each $x \in L$. Note that since M is $N - 1$ dimensional, $A_1(x)$ actually has a very simple structure:

$$A_1(x) = (A(x) \cap L) + M \qquad \text{for } x \in L$$

(equivalent to a *one-dimensional* maximal monotone multifunction). Also $y^* \in A_1(x^*)$, and the function

$$\Phi_1(x) = \inf\{\{x - x^*) \cdot (y - y^*) | y \in A_1(x)\} \tag{12}$$

coincides on L with $\Phi(x)$. One sees easily from the "one-dimensional" nature of A_1 that, relative to L, Φ_1 is lower semicontinuous and the inf in (12) is always attained. Therefore, Φ is lower semicontinuous relative to L and (inasmuch as $x - x^* \perp M$ for $x \in L$) the inf in (5) is attained for all $x \in L$. This finishes the argument that Φ is globally lower semicontinuous.

Proof of Theorem 1. (a) is obvious from (10) and the lower semicontinuity of Φ: if $\Phi(x) > 0$ for all $x \neq x^*$, then $\theta(s) > 0$ for all $s > 0$. For (b), we make use merely of the lower semicontinuity of

$$\Psi(k', Q') = \Phi(k^* + k', Q^* + Q') + \rho k' \cdot Q'.$$

We have $\Psi(k', Q')$ positive by hypothesis except at the origin, where it vanishes. The hypothesis that

$$\lim_{t \to \infty} \inf \Psi(tk', tQ') > 0$$

implies by a simple compactness argument that actually for some $r > 0$ and $\bar{\delta} > 0$

$$\Psi(k', Q') \leqslant \bar{\delta} \Rightarrow \|(k', Q')\| \leqslant r.$$

Therefore, for any $\epsilon > 0$,

$$\inf\{\Psi(k', Q')|\ \|k'\| \geqslant \epsilon\} \geqslant \min\{\bar{\delta}, \delta_\epsilon\} > 0$$

where

$$\delta_\epsilon = \min\{\Psi(k', Q')|\ \|k', Q'\| \leqslant r, \|k'\| \geqslant \epsilon\}.$$

This is the desired conclusion.

References

1. D. Cass and K. Shell, The structure and stability of competitive dynamical systems, *J. Econ. Theory* **12** (1976), 31-70. Reprinted as Essay III in this volume.
2. R. T. Rockafellar, "Convex Analysis," Princeton Univ. Press, Princeton, N.J., 1970.
3. R. T. Rockafellar, Saddlepoints of Hamiltonian systems in convex problems of Lagrange, *J. Optimization Theory Appl.* **12** (1973), 367–390.
4. R. T. Rockafellar, Saddlepoints of Hamiltonian systems in convex Lagrange problems having a positive discount rate, *J. Econ. Theory* **12** (1976), 71-113. Reprinted as Essay IV in this volume.
5. W. Brock and J. Scheinkman, Global asymptotic stability of optimal control systems with applications to the theory of economic growth, *J. Econ. Theory* **12** (1976), 164-190. Reprinted as Essay VII in this volume.
6. R. Gaines, Existence of solutions to Hamiltonian dynamical systems of optimal growth, *J. Econ. Theory* **12** (1976), 114-130. Reprinted as Essay V in this volume.

7. R. T. ROCKAFELLAR, Monotone operators associated with saddle-functions and minimax problems, *in* "Nonlinear Functional Analysis, Part 1," (F. E. Browder (Ed.), pp. 241–250, Proc. of Symposia in Pure Math., Vol. 18, Amer. Math. Soc., Providence, R.I., 1970.

8. R. T. ROCKAFELLAR, Local boundedness of nonlinear monotone operators, *Michigan Math. J.* **16** (1969), 397–407.

9. R. T. ROCKAFELLAR, Maximality of sums of nonlinear monotone operators, *Trans. Amer. Math. Soc.* **149** (1970), 75–88.

Index

Definitional references are indicated by italicized page numbers.

197